T0354760

Invading
the Kingdom
OF
Darkness

INVADING THE KINGDOM

OF

DARKNESS

Rescuing Families and Nations

SAMUEL T. PADMORE

INVADING THE KINGDOM OF DARKNESS

iUniverse books may be ordered through booksellers or by contacting:

iUniverse
1663 Liberty Drive
Bloomington, IN 47403
www.iuniverse.com
1-800-Authors (1-800-288-4677)

ISBN: 978-1-5320-1713-1 (sc)
ISBN: 978-1-5320-2394-1 (hc)
ISBN: 978-1-5320-1712-4 (e)

Library of Congress Control Number: 2017901978

Print information available on the last page.

iUniverse rev. date: 05/16/2017

To my late grandfather, who loved and raised me in the fear of God. He also honored me first and introduced me to the entire community as his pastor while I was still young so that traditional elders would not compel me to buy them drinks or do anything that would defile me. Nene Emmanuel A. Tetteh-Ngua, I cherish you. This dedication is not limited to all the pastors and intercessors in the Kroboland as well as New England, U.S.

CONTENTS

ACKNOWLEDGMENTS

To God be the glory. He is the author and finisher of our faith.

I would like to express my profound gratitude to First Lady & Prophetess Providencia Padmore, who daily shared her thoughts and prayers with me. I wish to say a special thank you to my daughters, Miatta K. who ran my errands during the commencement of this manuscript and Doris P. my princess. My appreciation also goes to Ben and Emmanuel, who fixed my computer. Thank you, Mom (Grace Partey), for teaching me to love Jesus. God bless my late pastor, friend, and brother, who was a general in the intercession movement, Rev. Alfred Adja Sai. I love you, my brother! Thank you also to Rev. Enock Dubgarty, Rev. Francis O. Candy, The late DCE, Mr. Andrews Teye, Brother Yohannes, Rev. Honest Etse, and many other intercessors. God bless you for your hard work. To Sgt. Abraham Sackey, a former police officer who has been my support-thank you. And Prophetess Comfort Darley Sackitey my great spiritual trainer. Rev. S.T. Apperty, Rev. Albert Osom, my great teacher. Rev. Humphry A. Tettey, Rev. Fr. Aburam. And finally, Rev. G. N. Kumasa my father, God bless you.

INTRODUCTION

Being converted in 1983, I responded to the call of God in 1986 and have engaged in evangelistic and healing ministry since then. As the anointing of apostolic intercession began to move to a higher degree from what it was in 1989, I became the first general secretary of the Manya-Krobo District Council of Churches; I held this office from 2000 to 2005. The council comprised more than two hundred churches. This book records many mighty works the Lord has performed through my ministry of prayer. Through these great works, the Lord has opened doors in the land, which was once in bondage. As the assignment of prayer warfare intensified, I felt the need to write a book concerning the matter at hand to stir up and wake the church. My mission in America is to intercede and train others to join forces with churches and create a concert of prayer ministries. Being part of KNOW Worcester and the prayer concert led by Rev. Len Cowan and Rev. Lou Soiles, who are doing a marvelous job in Worcester, Massachusetts, I feel the importance and the urgency to contribute. Being called as an intercessor for this and other nations, I have an obligation to present illumination on the subject of spiritual warfare to assist the body of Christ because I saw that many people are praying but do not know how to do spiritual warfare.

The Two Opposing Kingdoms

The opposing dominions are the kingdoms of God and of Satan. The kingdom of God is light. In contrast, Satan's jurisdiction is darkness. Jesus rejected the accusation of the Pharisees and the priests when they said He cast out demons by the prince of demons. It was through Jesus Christ that we came to know more about these two opposing kingdoms. Jesus exposed the secret and the difference between the two realms. Here's what He said:

> But when the Pharisees heard it, they said, "It is only by Beelzebul, the prince of demons, that this man casts out demons." Knowing their thoughts, he said to them, "Every kingdom divided against itself is laid waste, and no city or house divided against itself will stand._And if Satan casts out Satan, he is divided against himself. How then will his kingdom stand?_And if I cast out demons by Beelzebul, by whom do your sons cast them out? Therefore they will be your judges._But if it is by the Spirit of God that I cast out demons, then the kingdom of God has come upon you._Or how can someone enter a strong man's house and plunder his goods, unless he first binds the strong man? Then indeed he may plunder his house." (Matthew 12:24–29)

This book addresses the confusion that crippled the church concerning spiritual warfare. Satan's highest strategy is to keep the church in ignorance, and that's how he operates in his kingdom of darkness. Christ is the light of this world. To know Him is to have illumination and the keys of the kingdom of God.

Invading the Kingdom of Darkness
For the definitions of the key words *invasion, kingdom,* and *darkness,* refer to the glossary of this book.

The major text for this book is Colossians 1:13 (NLT): "For He has rescued us from the kingdom of darkness and transferred us into the Kingdom of His dear Son." The devil rules in darkness. He causes fear and torment. Satan's dominion reveals his character as evil. As a result, humanity is in constant and excruciating pain. Everyone wants out, but unless we pray against the evil forces that are in charge of this planet and enthrone Jesus, there will be no deliverance.

Serious Issues Plaguing Our World Today

This book's purpose is to inspire everyone who wants to see change through prayer. Many people pray only for their personal needs. Others pray for their communities and cities. That is great, but some of us are burdened to go beyond that. I challenge those who want to do more for the kingdom of God to go the extra mile in their prayer lives. Here's why. American leaders have turned their backs on God. The world is sitting on a powder keg. Terrorists have taken over. Youth are murdering one another. The police are rampantly killing the people they are supposed to protect. North Korea, Russia, China, and Iran are threatening nuclear war. The church is sleeping. The spirit of wickedness in high places and its territorial agents are in control of all these offensive actions. The world is plunging into constant darkness. No one can deny the rule of the kingdom of darkness based on all current and past affairs. Some of the root causes were what Paul the apostle referred to as a **"strongholds and high things"** that exalt themselves against God.

Pulling Down Strongholds

> For the weapons of our warfare are not carnal, but mighty through God for the pulling down of strongholds, casting down imaginations and every high thing that exalteth itself against the knowledge of God, and bringing into captivity every thought to the obedience of Christ. (2 Corinthians 10:4–5 KJ21)

Strongholds deal with two unique forms: (a) *arguments* and (b) *high things*. We must understand these terms to position ourselves rightly for the warfare we will engage in. If we fail to understand the nature of the stronghold we are dealing with, it will be difficult to invade this kingdom of darkness. Arguments are strongholds rooted in the mind-set of humanity. They are basically the choices, decisions, or beliefs of groups of people, individuals, or a nation. At the national level, it could be a treaty signed between two countries—for example, the covenant that the children of Israel made with the people of Gibeon when they were about to possess their land. The Gibeonites lied to the Israelites and signed a treaty with them only to realize after three days that they were their neighbors. Immediately the agreement created a stronghold, and they could not do anything otherwise. Here's the result.

> But all the princes said unto all the congregation, "We have sworn unto them by the Lord God of Israel. Now, therefore we may not touch them. This we will do to them: we will even let them live, lest wrath is upon us because of the oath which we swore unto them." (Josh. 9:19–20 KJ21)

Now the enemy has the legal right to torment the children of Israel, as God told them, "But if you will not drive out the inhabitant of the land before you, they will become pricks to your eyes, and as thorns in your side …" (Numbers 33:55 KJV). The enemy will use this stronghold for many years until they pull it down.

The "**high things**" are spiritual principalities in the form of territorial spirits. They do not originate from the mind-set of a person. They are rather from the invisible kingdom of darkness. They are cosmic powers established to rise against God. We see this idea working in many people in the twenty-first century like in no other generation. Many evil spirits control different geographical areas. George Otis asserted, and is quoted from Praying with Power by Peter Wagner. "Nested near the heart of spiritual mapping philosophy is the concept of territorial strongholds." C. Peter Wagner said, "Some high-ranking spirits are assigned to an individual territories, and they have the ability to postpone certain things God has willed" (emphasis added) Daniel revealed to us how the prince of Persia resisted the angel who was sent to help him until Michael came to liberate the angel. He postponed the answer sent to Daniel. Refer to (Daniel 10).

Intercede without Being Ignorant

As I visited many prayer concerts, groups and ministries, I noticed that only a few understood what spiritual warfare is. Although they prayed, they never engaged in the higher level of the battle. Someone said, "If you call the deep, the deep will come." It is clear that many Christians fear to invade the kingdom of darkness. Many leaders say gathering information or praying against the enemy is to glorify Satan. They choose only to honor Jesus Christ. Unfortunately, Jesus's problem with the Pharisees and the Scribes was not that He was praising God. It was rather the fact that He was casting out demons, breaking the strongholds, and setting people free. The religious leaders of His day did not understand spiritual warfare, so they opposed Him. Before Christ came on the scene, they had never heard anything about demons or evil spirits. Apostle Paul said in 2 Corinthians 2:11 (KJV), **"Lest Satan should get an advantage of us: for we are not ignorant of his devices."** It is this passion that compelled me to write this book to open the eyes of many intercessors and all Christians. This book reveals my experience as a prophetic and apostolic intercessor since 1989. You will read the stories of how God invaded spiritual kingdoms and delivered cities in Africa through strategic prayer.

Dealing with the Prince of Persia through Prophetic Prayer

Every state and nation has a prince who controls the spiritual affairs of that particular jurisdiction he occupies. According to Daniel, there was a prince of Persia (Iran) and a prince of Greece. "Then he said, 'Do you know why I have come to you? But now will I return to fight against the prince of Persia; and when I go out, behold, the prince of Greece will come'" (Daniel 10:20 KJ21).

During some spiritual warfare I engaged in, the princes of individual countries or states interjected. There is a Prince of America who tried on several occasions to fight me because we were knocking down his works. Details of the confrontation are in this book. Secondly, during the Taste of the Nations in our church 2014–2015, the worship night of all nations, as we were praying through worship for revival, the angel of the Lord came to me and said, **"We have just met with the prince of Massachusetts in the city of Worcester. He allowed the people to go and serve God."** The message is prophetic that revival is coming. Remember—Worcester is the heart of Massachusetts. Massachusetts is the spirit of America. Now the idea is clear that the stronghold of this state is in the city of Worcester. Meanwhile, Massachusetts is also a stronghold to America. Many first things done in the U.S., started in this state, mostly in Worcester MA. When I first came to this city, I could sense the powers of thick darkness hovering over the region. As God began to raise intercessors, today the light of the kingdom of Christ has invaded the darkness. The angel of the Lord came to me with the result of their battle with the prince of the region. God promised to fulfill all the prophecies. In 2016, about fifty churches, pastors, businesses, and organizations joined Convoy of Hope, led by Pastor Brian, and Robert Wood had a massive outreach campaign. The community felt the love of Christ. Many churches and intercessors are coming together to seek God. We can attest to this, that our prayers were answered. There was no unity in the body of Christ in the past years. This book is also full of teachings concerning spiritual warfare. Read it all for its worth. It is a book intended to create awareness and strengthen the hands of the intercessors and every believer.

Some Princes in Africa Invaded

To fulfill the Great Commission through revival prayer, Evelyn Christenson said, "We must be very careful not to substitute the means for the end. Our means—our ministry—should become stepping stones, the open doors, for actual evangelizing ... Prayer is the very important means in the salvation process."

It was 1993. As we embarked upon the spiritual warfare before hitting the street during our outreach campaign, the Lord showed me in an open vision the heartbeat of Jesus concerning a great soul captured by the prince of darkness of the Kroboland. The story of the conversion of Okumo (the chief priest of Dipo, the secret society) is in chapters 7 - 9 of this book. The story was covered by Vans Azu and recorded in the *Saturday Mirror* (a major Ghana newspaper).

Summary
This book will guide you in how to invade the kingdom of darkness. It is intended to motivate, inspire, and encourage. It teaches the importance of connecting to the frequency of heaven, doing battle according to the revelations and prophetic directions. It not only teaches about praying but learning to hear, see, and discern the strategic plans of the Holy Spirit as He takes you through the school of the Spirit. This book is designed to stir an awakening and empower intercessors to pray for their communities, countries, and the persecuted churches around the world. Two-way praying and the United Concert of Prayer are powerful, but we must go deeper than that. David Bryant said it best: "Revival praying, biblically understood is the highest form of spiritual warfare, because when God answers, revival leads the church into powerful advances in fulfilling the Great Commission." Do warfare! "After you do all to stand, stand, therefore ..." (Ephesians 6:10–12 KJV).

Are you ready for the spiritual ride? Then let's go!

PART I
THE POWER OF THE SECRET PRAYER CLOSET

CHAPTER 1

THE SECRET PLACE
OF THE MOST HIGH

He that dwells in the secret place of the Most High
shall abide under the shadow of the Almighty.
—Psalm 91:1

Under the Mosaic Law of the Old Testament, there was a tent called
the Tabernacle. It had three sections.

1. The outer court—this is where the congregation worshipped.
2. The holy place—here all the priests carried out their religious
    duties.
3. The Holy of Holies—this place was separated by a fourteen-
    inch curtain. Whoever touched the curtain would die. The
    high priest went there only once a year to offer sacrifices
    before the mercy seat of God.

The Levitical law had outlawed anyone entering the Holy of Holies
except the high priest. The high priest could not go in there without
blood. The congregation entered the outer court with fear and
trembling because there was no relationship with God as a Father.
Being the Lamb of God, Christ shed His blood as an ultimate sacrifice,

He entered the heavenly Holy of Holies in the Tabernacle with His own blood once and forever. Now there is an open heaven for such as are willing to seek Him passionately.

Those who enter will see the glory of God. He will protect them from harm. In the New Covenant, believers in Christ have the confidence to enter the holy of holies by His blood. Those who enter into this secret place have a close relationship and an uninterrupted communion with the heavenly Father. Not all in Christ enjoy such benefits. In the Old Testament, the worshipers entered the inner sanctuary, but not all of them dwelled in the Holy of Holies. Sometimes, they ran toward the altar. Their sporadic experience gratified them, so they could not seek habitually to remain in His inexplicable presence. Jesus paved the way on the cross when He said, **"It is finished," (John 19:30 KJV). A**nd the veil was rent. Most believers today still stand far off, gazing at the curtain that separates them from the presence of God. In 2 Corinthians 3:15–18 (NIV), it says,

> "Even to this day when Moses is read, a veil covers their hearts. But whenever anyone turns to the Lord, the veil is taken away. Now the Lord is the Spirit, and where the Spirit of the Lord is, there is freedom. And we all, who with unveiled faces contemplate the Lord's glory, are being transformed into his image with ever-increasing glory, which comes from the Lord, who is the Spirit."

I like how King James put it, "Now the Lord is that Spirit: and where the Spirit of the Lord is, there is liberty. But we all, with open face beholding as in a glass the glory of the Lord, are changed into the same image from glory to glory, even as by the Spirit of the Lord." I paraphrased this next verse. "When you seek Me in prayer and worship, you will find Me available to you if you seek Me with all your heart." ("You will seek me and find me when you seek me with all your heart" [Jeremiah 29:13]). "But if from there you seek the LORD your God, you will find him if you seek him with all your heart and with all your soul" (Deuteronomy 4:29).

A multitude of believers pray in a religious spirit but never enjoy the secret place of the Most High. They either believe in prayer but do not exercise it or don't believe in prayer but say they believe in the word of God. They question the results of prayer but believe in science. They worship in the spirit of religion but deny the power thereof. They pray but never in expectation of a miracle. But the seekers and the searchers of God's presence meet Him in the secret place through constant prayer and the attitude of worship. Such are those who benefit from the secrets of the Lord. They know what God is going to do next. "The secret of the Lord is with those who fear Him ..." (Psalm 25:14). The intercessor knows the heart of God. The mind of the Master is clear to His followers. They feel His heartbeat for souls. They know the season of intercession for the lost world is now. They understood the harvest is plentiful, but the workers are few. They determine to intercede in their closets until they hear, "Well done, faithful and good servant." They come together from different denominational, ethnic, and cultural backgrounds, yet they have one goal and intercede with one accord. Those warriors have the kingdom mentality. They know that "to live is Christ and to die is a great gain." They know that many followed Christ wherever He went. They pressed on Him hard, they touched Him, yet they never had any personal encounters, but the intercessors are determined to know their Lord. Today many believers go from church to church. They are looking for the greatest pastor, a powerful sermon, and beautiful worship. They compare pastors to pastors or prophets to prophets. But only those who *dwell* in the *secret place* of the Highest shall have their spiritual eyes opened to see the veil split up, the mercy seat revealed, the covering cherubs divulged, and the presence of the Almighty discernible.

Clark asserted, "These, like Simeon, have the Holy Ghost upon them, and like Anna they depart not from the temple; they are the courtiers of the Great King, the valiant men who keep watch around the bed of Solomon, the virgin souls who follow the Lamb whithersoever he goeth, of them it is truly said that their conversation is in heaven." The outer-court worshipers do not know what is in the holiest place. They don't know they lack something great. They never have an idea of dwelling in the secret place. But if they rise with passion and consistently to seek His presence, they will find Him. God desires those who seek Him with all their hearts. The Highest shows His secret to those who abide in Him. They know that you cannot be spiritually blind or deaf in that secret place. Everyone sees the scheme of the adversary openly, and nothing hides from them in that realm. It is a place of unbroken fellowship. Everything is crystallized; there is no presumption. The power God is kept here for those who come there. It is the lodging space of victory where the Shekinah glory shines, the home of the revelatory ministry of the heavenly vision and dream. It makes the life of the intercessor unique. It is in the realm of this secret place that one ascends and descends with the angels. The gates of heaven are open, and the Almighty stands at the gate, waiting to welcome the prayer of His dearest intercessors, His coworkers in the vineyard. I am hearing a voice in my spirit right now as I write. It says, "Come up with me, and I will show you deeper things that eyes have not seen nor ears heard, nor has come into the heart of men." Here's God divine telephone number to get into that place—Jeremiah 33:3, "Call unto me, and I will answer thee, and shew thee great and mighty things, which thou knowest not." Your prayer life will never be the same again if you desire to practice and make His presence your dwelling place. In the secret place of the Most High, there is power, revelation, and the glory of God. In this place, you are clothed with glory, signs and wonders follows those who dwells there. They never pray witout hearing and seeing, they never hear without taking action.

The Three Secret Places of the Prayer Closet
I found three secret places where we can pray without any excuse. It depends on how desperate one is. It's about passion, desire, and enthusiasm. King David observed,

"One thing I ask from the Lord, this only do I seek: that I may dwell in the house of the Lord all the days of my life, to gaze on the beauty of the Lord and to seek him in his temple. Then my head will be exalted above the enemies who surround me; at his sacred tent I will sacrifice with shouts of joy; I will sing and make music to the Lord." (Psalm 27:4, 6 NIV)

In Christ Alone
The name of the Lord is a strong tower; the righteous run to it, and they are safe. Christ is our hiding place from all fears and attacks. "I am the vine, ye are the branches: He that abides in me, and I in him, the same brings forth much fruit: for without me ye can do nothing" (John 15:5).

The Prayer Closet
The prayer closet is the secluded and solitary place you set apart to meet with God. It should be a place where no one can disturb you. Your mind will be at peace, and your spirit can focus on the Lord. That place is where the eyes and ears of the One who sees the hidden hearts and motives are open.

Pray Anywhere in the Spirit
About 95 percent of Americans spend most of their lives at work; they spend more time there than at home or church. What happens to the prayer life of the Christian who desires to pray but is caught up in the busyness of life? Most people lose the fire of prayer because of tiredness. The moment they start praying, sleep welcomes them. One secret that most believers don't know is that the devil will do anything to keep us from praying. People often feel sleepy when they are praying or reading the word of God, but the moment they finish, they are awake. The same person can watch a movie until the next day. One needs to understand that the tactic of the enemy is to distract. He can also take over your tongue if you are sleeping in prayer and will use your mouth against Jesus or you.

I remembered something that happened in 1987. We were always fasting and in prayer all night. One night, during a prayer service, a brother was falling asleep; he began to curse Jesus in the name of the devil. He then realized how dangerous it was to pray sleepy. The scripture admonishes us to be vigilant in prayer. Be conscious when praying.

Turning Break Time To Your Midday Prayer Closet
Please use wisdom. One may pray silently in spirit while working. You may pray at lunchtime or during your last ten-minutes break. You need to find a way and create a space.

One can pray as the Spirit prompts him or her to pray anywhere and anytime. Hide and pray in the car during breaks or lunch. The Jews prays three times a day. The Muslims prays five times a day. When it is time to pray, they will rather chose to lose a customer and his money. They are faithful but the Christians takes prayer for granted. They will decide to take advantage of their prayer time to do business or whatever they want. If you see a believer who make comment like, "it's just a prayer meeting or only a Bible Studies," you should be aware of that person. He is on his way to the spiritual cemetery. Without self-discipline, prayer and Bible study becomes burdensome. That's exactly how the devil wants you to feel. The key to praying publicly or secretly comes when your passion becomes stronger than the circumstances around you. It's not about where you pray. The main issue that Jesus was dealing with was the motive behind prayer. Do people want to be applauded by others when they pray? Yes, and that's what Jesus calls hypocritical prayer. I organize Christians at any job I work. We use our last fifteen-minute break. We also use our lunch break at noon for prayer and sharing on Tuesdays and Thursdays on our Nationwide Prayer Networks prayer line. It connects sisters and brothers in and out of the States to pray for America, Jerusalem, and the nations. It's powerful. Rev. Peter Lopez Jr. asserted in his book *No More Excuses*, "Holding on to excuses is what keeps your past in front of you and not behind you."

So When Do We Have to Pray? Part 1

John 4:21–24 (NIV) says,

> "Woman," Jesus replied, "believe me, time is coming when
> you will worship the Father neither on this mountain nor in
> Jerusalem. You Samaritans worship what you do not know;
> we worship what we do know, for salvation is from the Jews.
> Time is coming and has now come when the true worshipers
> will worship the Father in the Spirit and truth, for they are
> the kind of worshipers the Father seeks. God is Spirit, and his
> worshipers must worship in the Spirit and truth."

While the Samaritan woman was struggling with the place to pray,
she was also seeking the coming of the Messiah. She believed in the
prophecy of the Old Testament. The Lord knew her hunger and thirst
and revealed Himself to her. It was at the well of personal encounter,
a transition that brings spring of living water. It flows into the season
of prayer. It was a well of the Father's where the old-time revival in
a fresh anointing flowed. Out of that belly, spiritual thirst for the
kingdom of God and His righteousness are quenched. It is a well of
the sincere heart of those who seek the Messiah. He will not leave
them until they are saturated and satisfied. When anyone signs up
as a faithful intercessor today, the Lord is glorified and will beautify
them.

Jesus continued His teaching. "'Woman,' Jesus replied, 'believe Me,
time is coming when you will worship the Father neither on this
mountain nor in Jerusalem.'" To answer the question where do we
worship, if we use the woman's statement in a prayer context, then
the question will be where do we have to pray? Read on.

The Time Is Coming; the Time Is Now

Jesus told her the "time or season is coming …" Yes, the season was
coming, because at the time, she did not know who was speaking to
her. She hadn't had an encounter yet. She was in expectation, waiting

for the *future*. Jesus was in the *now*. He said, "You don't know who you worship, but we are aware whom we worship." If you know who you worship, you will recognize Him when you see Him. You will know His voice when you hear it. You will understand that *now* is the season to pray. Many believers go to church, but do all know the Lord?

The Samaritan woman met the right person at the right time. Jesus proceeded, "Yet **a** *time* is coming and has **now come** when the true worshipers worship the Father in the Spirit and truth, for they are the kind of worshipers the Father seeks. God is Spirit, and his worshipers must worship in the Spirit and truth."

The time was coming and had arrived. Many people complain that they go to church but don't feel the presence of God. But I say that the mature do not have to feel; they know their father's presence and His fragrance. The spiritual eye of the woman received illumination. We are to pray now and anytime the Spirit prompts us to come into His presence. She had an encounter with the Messiah. She ran, called the whole city, and testified to them that the Messiah they were expecting was already there. When we believers have such encounters, we will not wait until Sunday or Wednesday church services before praying or witnessing. We will pray anytime the Holy Spirit prompts us. Are you changing your attitude toward prayer?

Intercessory prayer is for all believers. It's not the job of a few old folks who might be boring, so they sign up for that position in the church. Our Savior is the first intercessor. He prayed when He was here on earth. If our Lord is still interceding for us, who are we to desert such an august privilege? O believer, whether you like it or not, the battle is at your gate. The enemy hates you with a grievous hatred, so you better put on all the armor of God and get in the fight. You cannot fight this war with the weapon of words. You can only fight with the weapons of the knees. The curiosity of a man led him to see something he had never anticipated. On a snowy day in the middle of the war that defined this great nation, he saw the father of our great country, President George Washington, on his knees, pleading to the Almighty God. The Lord heard his prayers and not only stopped the war but also made the United States of America the greatest nation on earth. This is my own saying to energize every prayer warriors. *"Prayer works so let's pray until prayer prays us. Pray until prayer eats you up."* That means let's pray until we have no more strength to pray. When I made this statement at one of our midweek prayer services, I didn't know how powerful that sounded until my prayer warriors later told me how that statement impacted their lives.

Great People Need Great Prayer
One problem I have with many Christians is that they are quick to judge and condemn. But the intercessor is called to pray and not to accuse. The only accuser we know is the enemy. Many Christians never show compassion when someone falls. When a great man of God falls, they will crucify him and then give him up to the media and the world to destroy him. It is the spirit of greediness and jealousy. This is what someone said, "When you go down, then my church goes up." Look, the army believes in the motto "No soldier left behind." They will certainly do anything to bring their fallen fellow soldier home, even if he dies. The soldiers know the dignity of their fellow soldiers and the wickedness of their enemy. Why do we the church behave in the opposite way? Are we not acting as being "holiest than thou?" that means, I am holier than you. All these calls for repentance and prayer for the church to undo heavy burdens that no one can carry. Mercy and grace must have a voice in our hearts. We are all in one Kingdom, Paul the Apostle asserted,

"There is one body and one Spirit, just as you were called to one hope when you were called; there is one Lord, one faith, and one baptism, one God and Father of all, who is over all and through all in all." (Ephesians 4:4-6).

We must cover and defend one another. If we have the same burden of prayer, we will unit, care and stand in for one another.

Samuel T. Padmore

Pray for Those in Authority

The scripture commanded us to pray for our leaders and not to inculpate them. We must take this wake-up call to intercede more for the next president. Remember the souls of Presidents George W. Bush and Barrack Obama requested prayer in the spirit realm during the difficult times in their presidency. But their requests were not public, so you must attune to the spirit to hear the next president crying for help. We need God to come back to America.

A few months after the presidential campaign of 2016 kicked off, the Lord told me that Mr. Donald Trump would win the election and would be the next president in 2017. I was skeptical, then the Lord linked me to another prophetess who had the same message. So only the two of us had that message at the initial stage. I don't remember her name as I saw her on youtube. We were praying for a strong Christian but, lo and behold, "What is written, is written." In another open vision, I gazed in astonishment a rumbling Tornado. The dark clouds formed a tunnel, at the ingress stood Mr. Donald Trump with his hands outstretched to balk it. The Lord also said to me, "This man wants to stop darkness, but he himself is in darkness so it will take prayer to help him to rule."

> First of all, then, I urge that supplications, prayers, intercessions, and thanksgivings be made for all people, for kings and all who are in high positions, that we may lead a peaceful and quiet life, godly and dignified in every way. This is good, and it is pleasing in the sight of God our Savior. (1 Timothy 2:1–3)

Our call is to pray and not to judge or criticize our leaders and those in authority. Many Christians do the opposite. They call the president the Antichrist and many other titles. If we are called to bless, how is it that we have turned to take the place of the accuser of the brethren? Pray fervently and effectively for your president in whatever country you are in. I know some pastors or Christians stand for election, but no one votes for them, yet if an unbeliever stands, Christians will vote for him or her and then later start complaining. Let's wake up. We have more important work to do than this. It's time to intercede faithfully for our leaders. So join the spiritual army.

CHAPTER 2

THE PRAYER CLOSET (PART 1)

But when you pray, go into your room (enter thy closet) close the door and pray to your Father, who is unseen. Then, your Father, who sees what is done in secret, will reward you (openly).
—Matthew 6:6, 9–10.

There are several forms of prayer.

- **Prayer closet** - It is the private or secret form of prayer, a personal moment one sets apart to commune with God. Many intercessors pray in secret for their families, communities, cities, states, and nations. Some also pray on their behalf. During this prayer, one can pour out one's heart to God concerning personal issues. There have been many cases when people were voicing their individual needs to God during cooperate prayer and later were criticized for what they were asking God. For example, someone was asking God for a husband. After that prayer, some people who had their fiancés in that group marked her. They didn't want her to talk to their guys. "Worry for nothing, for in all things with prayer and supplication, let your request be made known unto God ..." (Philippians 4:6, paraphrased) so I taught her how to do Hannah-like prayer and then later received the Holy

15

Spirit Baptism. Why do we need a prayer closet? It is a season where you can pray, wait, be silent, and listen to the voice of the Spirit of God. Prayer is a two-way street. **The Wind-Word of the Spirit** - Sometimes, He speaks through the wind as He carries you away to where He wants you. Other times, you will hear the still, small voice. He can also enable your eyes to see open visions, trances, or even dreams. This kind of prayer is different from cooperative prayer where it's hard to hear God's voice directly unless you concentrate deeply in the Spirit. Cooperative prayer is when the entire group or congregation gets together to pray. These prayers have two sides.

- **Pop-up prayer** - (popcorn prayer) is the time when all the people can lift their voices and pray one after the other. Sometimes, it goes from one person to another. But mostly, it pops up from who is feeling the need to pray at the moment or whom the Spirit moves to pray. It is more of an orderly prayer session.

- **Cooperate prayer** - is when particular people are selected to give the directives and lead the congregation to pray. With this, everyone lifts up his or her voice and prays at the same time. It might sound confusing, but it generates more power when we all pray together. The apostles commonly practiced it, according to Acts 4:23: "They all raised their voice and prayed, and the place was shaking ..." You can read Acts 4:23-29. As the leader allows the Holy Spirit to use him or her, everyone prays in the same direction but different ways as led. We must listen; sometimes people flow as the Spirit gives them utterance on the same subject but in a more profound way. It energizes the group, and God speaks in that way. People are allowed to pray in the Spirit as led.

- **Prophetic praying and declaration** - When a pastor, prophet or person who is mature in the Spirit leads by confessing the word in prayer and the people follow. As he or she declares the prophetic words, the congregation or the audience repeats them. It's very compelling and rewarding. This prophetic declaration is very powerful, and afterward, the group is allowed to pray more in their way using the prophetic words. Many people catch fire by this kind of prayer if led by the Spirit. It's profound; try it.

A Set Time

When we set time alone with God, we must be consistent. It creates discipline, which eventually forms a prayer attitude and then transforms into a character and then a lifestyle. When this happens, one transitions from a praying person to a person of prayer. The Israelites and the church had an appointed time for prayer. Everyone at the individual level needs to create a moment with God, and it must be consistent. We have learned from our Lord as Mark observed, "And rising very early in the morning, while it was still dark, he departed and went out to a desolate place, and there he prayed" (Mark 1:35). One must be committed to this process in order to mature.

What Is Prayer?

Prayer is the soul's sincere desire,
Unuttered or expressed,
The motion of a hidden fire
That trembles in the breast:
Prayer is the burden of a sigh,
The falling of a tear,
The upward gleaming of an eye,
When none but God is near
Prayer is the simplest form of speech
That infant lips can try;
Prayer, the sublime strains that reach
The Majesty on high:
Prayer is the Christian's vital breath,
The Christian's native air,
His watchword at the gates of death,

He enters heaven by prayer
Prayer is the contrite sinner's voice,
Returning from his ways,
While angels in their songs rejoice,
And say, Behold he prays!
The saints in prayer appear as one,
In a word, indeed, in mind,
When with the Father and the Son
Their fellowship they find
Nor prayer is made on earth alone:
The Holy Spirit pleads;
And Jesus, on th' eternal throne,
For sinners intercedes
"O Thou, by whom we come to God!
The Life, the Truth, the Way,
The path of prayer Thyself hast trod,
Lord, teach us how to pray!

By Montgomery

When You Pray

Jesus said, ***"When you pray …"*** It's a must that every believer pray. It is not **if** you pray but *when* you pray. There was a young man who walked by a riverbank to school. As it continued to happen, he wondered what this senior had been doing there with his hands lifted up toward heaven in the same spot. His curiosity drew him to inquire from the top man what he had been doing in this place. It was a happy moment to have one disciple at last. The man answered the young man's question. "I pray here every day." The young man was intrigued and requested the man should teach him to pray like him. To his amazement, the man took him into the river and held his head deep in the water until the young man couldn't breathe and was gasping for air. He took him out of the water and asked the young man, "Do you still want to pray?"

The young man said, "I did not ask you to teach me to swim; I just want to learn to pray like you."

"How desperately did you need air?" the man asked him.

"Very desperate," he replied.

"In order to pray fervently and more efficiently, you need to be as desperate for God as for air."

Believers must be desperate for prayer. Their hunger and thirst after God must grow stronger each day. Christian complacency is like a zombie movie. As breath is the life for the living, so is a prayer to the believer. The moment you stop your intimacy with God, you stop living your spiritual life. Jesus, teaching His disciples, said, "When you pray ..." *When* is referring to a definite or specific season, moment or time of prayer. Many prayers are not valid because they are only from the head and not coming out of the spirit. You connect with the heart and not with your head. To connect with God, one must pray with passion and desperation. You must pray with the burden of God. You must set a time and place where you will meet with God.

Don't Pray Like the Hypocrites
"And when you pray, do not be like the hypocrites..." (Matthew 6:5 NIV) A *hypocrite*, Clark observed, is "a stage-player, who acts under a mask, personating a character different from his own; a counterfeit, a dissembler; one who would be thought to be different from what he is. A person who wishes to be taken for a follower of God, but who has nothing of religion." I added, except to the outside world, he doesn't live the prayer life within. This person only prays in public and never in private.

Jesus Dealing with Some Specifics
He was dealing with the *motives*, the *place*, and the *time* the Jews prayed. Matthew 6:5 says, "And when thou pray, thou shalt not be as

the hypocrites are: for they love to pray standing in the synagogues and the corners of the streets, that they may be seen of men. Verily I say unto you; they have their reward."

According to Barnes, "The Lord was speaking about prayers done in public places. The word 'synagogues,' here, apparently means, not the location of worship of that name, but places where many were accustom to assemble—near the markets or courts, where they could be seen by many" (paraphrased). Jesus did not censure prayers in the synagogues. He was against the pretentious prayer, and yet they had nowhere to do secret prayer. The Jews habitually prayed in public places. The Muslims practice the same style. They pray at particular times of the day for public recognition. As you read this book, know that it's not about what people do but about you. Jesus asserted, *"But you, when you pray, enter into thy closet, and when you hast shut thy door, pray to thy Father which is in secret; and thy Father, which sees in secret shall reward thee openly"* (Matthew 6:6).

"Enter into thy closet"—every Jewish house had a place for private devotion. The roofs of their houses were quiet areas, well adapted for walking, conversation, and meditation (Matthew 9:2). Professor Hackett (*Illustrations of Scripture*) observed, "On the roof of the house in which I lodged at Damascus were chambers and rooms along the side and at the corners of the open space or terrace, which often constitutes a sort of upper story. I observed the same thing in connection with other houses." There was a place adopted as a secret and solitary place in every house, which was the porch of the entrance. This room projected a story above the whole building. It was at this location the religious Jewish person prayed. Although no one would see him or her on his or her knees, God, who sees the secret heart, would reward him or her openly. During the communion with His disciples, Jesus Christ, our Lord, assembled in this place, which Brother Luke mentioned it in the book of Acts as the "upper room," but in the Gospel, it is the "prayer closet or place for secret prayer." Where is your prayer closet, O believer?

The Prayer Closet of the Believer

The excuse that many believers give is they have no time to set apart because of constant traveling, working, and running errands, so consequently they have nowhere to hide and pray. You see, that's what the devil has designed for you, to prevent you from getting into that secret place of the armor and the arsenal of the Lord. Well, here's a question that demands an answer. What drove Jesus to the mountain to pray in the solitary place every morning despite His busy schedule? Mark 1:35 NIV says, "Very early in the morning, while it was still dark, Jesus got up, left the house and went off to a solitary place, where he prayed." The answer is passion and desperate dependence on His Father. How about today's church? If the apostles couldn't do it without prayer warfare, how could we? Battles we are dealing with today are even more sophisticated than those in their era. In those days, there were nothing like internet and polluted movies that will entrap and entice their children like the thwenty first century challenge. We are facing the worst enemy in the end time of our days.

Intensive Desire

It was His love, strong desire, and desparation to commune with His Father. Jesus wanted an unbroken fellowship. He purposed to know the will of His Father and His agenda for each day before the day began. This passion and the burden of assignment will constrain you to search for a secret place. It does not matter where one finds oneself. The revelation about the prayer closet is to create a secret place wherever we may find ourselves to be alone with our God. Barnes says it best: "It should be some 'place' to which we may resort where no ear will hear us but 'His' ear and no eye can see us but 'His' eye. Unless there is such a place, secret prayer will not be long or strictly maintained." Remember—our Lord Jesus Christ was divine but a man as well. He went through all the busyness of life. Jesus was always working, yet He created a secret place of prayer. His lifestyle was constant secret communion with God the Father. The challenge the majority of believers have is the consistency of prayer. Many people have the habit of starting an intense prayer life because they read a book or heard a sermon but later going back to the lukewarm lifestyle. If you have the burden of Christ and the heartbeat of God, you will not give yourself rest or give God rest until He finishes through your prayers what He has begun. Do you have a burden? Do you pray passionately with such a burden? Many people of old prayed with passion and tears in their eyes. Jeremiah was called the weeping prophet. He asserted, "Oh that my head were waters, and my eyes a fountain of tears, that I might weep day and night for the slain of the daughter of my people!" (Jeremiah 9:1).

Pray with me now!

Father, forgive me for my lukewarm prayer life.
Deliver me from the power of the flesh and the busyness of life that takes my eyes from you.
I oppose you, the spirit of inconsistency in prayer. Devil, you have no more power to distract me. I rebuke the spirit of procrastination.
Holy Spirit, fill me with the Spirit of consistency in my prayer life.
I am bold like a lion, burning with a blazing fire from within.
I am fervent in Spirit and cannot be lazy anymore.
Thank You, Father, for setting me free in the mighty name of the name that's above any other name, even in the name of Jesus Christ of Nazareth. Amen and amen.

CHAPTER 3

SATAN'S RULE

Satan rules from the second heaven to the first heaven and then into the earth realm. He rules through an organized hierarchy, which is operated by his high-ranked agents. There are levels of operations set up in the chain of command, which is set over tribes, cultures, and nations in the earth realm to control human affairs. They control the natural government in the supernatural world. Every non-God-fearing ruler or president is under the supervision of a principality known as the powers of darkness in high places. Here's the devil's chain of command.

The Hierarchy

1. **The commander in chief is Satan.** He is the king of all evil, both spiritual and natural.
2. **Dominions or lordships.** These are in charge of kingdoms and have ascendancy or supremacy over the natural rulers.
3. **Thrones are the class of celestial beings (evil angels).** Thrones are also worshiped as gods, which control cultures and traditions. They are unyielding, intransigent, relentless, and inexorable spirits that dominate the hearts and the beliefs of the people. They work hand in hand with the ranks in the next section.

4. **Principalities and powers, or rulers and princes,** are satanic, higher-ranked demons or unholy angels strategically structured to manipulate monarchal ruling, political kingdoms, and systems of nations and governments through deceptions. High-level wicked princes are set over nations and regions of the earth realm. They are commanding generals over Satan's fallen army.

5. **Powers and authorities** are demons dispatched to mislead those in authority. The apostle admonished the Christians to pray for all those in authority for the purpose that we may live peaceful and quiet lives.

6. **Rulers of Darkness** of this World are demonic forces that operate in the realm of the spirit of darkness through the human leaders. They initiate some great kings and presidents, lawmakers, judges, banking CEOs, and many in the higher ranks of the Illuminati and many other cults, which are controlled by these demons. Demonic agents are sent out for deception and ruination or wrecking through manipulation of natural elements and systems.

7. **Spiritual wickedness in high places** (heavenly places are the first and second heavens) refers to demons deployed to inflict pain, destruction, murder, and all kinds of afflictions on the human race. They enjoy places of commotion and torment. Satan has set these demonic forces against the church through cunningness, craftiness, and schemes. He uses them to throw fiery darts into our minds. They infiltrate the church, manipulate doctrines, and mislead many. They are the types of demonic spirits that hinder Christians from Bible study and prayer to keep them ignorant and prayerless. As a result, they become powerless. Then they can afflict them and torment them with fear. These spirits are Satan's troops and operate in unity. Lukewarm spirit is controlled by Satan himself and is very dangerous for a Christian to be in that state. Pray and break that chain.

Different Levels of Spiritual Warfare

- **Informed intercession** - is a battle between Satanic forces and the intercessors, the army of God, those called to stop the invasion of the devil in the earth realm.

- **The ground level prayer** - is the process in which the Men and Women of God helps individuals who need to be free from demonic oppression. These kind is known as spiritual clinic or deliverance from the seven strongholds of the strongman, namely, regression, repression, suppression, depression, oppression, obsession, and possession.

- **The Strongman**—this entity is a spirit that keeps people from believing in Jesus Christ the Savior. The Christian has the power to destroy satanic strongholds that keep individuals and cities in bondage by binding the strongman. Every member in the kingdom of God has the authority and warrant from Jesus Christ for the arrest of the demonic forces. Believers must rise to the place of power to be able to bind the strongman. Unfortunately, many believers are running from place to place, looking for deliverance, whiles others are rejecting the idea of spiritual warfare. Intercessors must learn how to bind and loose and cast out demonic forces. Obey the spiritual rule. You are not allowed to bind Satan and the principalities. We are commanded to cast them out and then bind the demons and the strongman in charge of supernatural invasion.

- **Prayer warfare** - is the demonstration of spiritual warfare at a higher level to open doors for the gospel of our Lord Jesus Christ. It is a battle in the realm of the spirit, but sometimes, it can occur in the natural. The warriors must expect to attack and combat, offend and defend. Those forces never give up; they will try to oppose vigorously. Their attacks can be dramatic, but if you do not give up, they will flee.

In my early life as a spiritual warrior in 1986, during one of my training sessions in the Spirit as the Lord taught me, He took me to a quiet place and left me. It happened more often. When He was gone, an angel came to talk to me. He was so handsome, and he started talking to me. It has been about thirty years now, but I can still remember it as if it were yesterday. In those days, fasting and prayer were my normal lifestyle, and in fact, I hated to eat. Then the angel who came to talk to me said, "Oh, as for you, there's no need for you to fast and pray anymore because you have reached the higher level. You are more spiritual and very powerful, so don't pray anymore." The moment he said that, the Holy Spirit gave me discernment and I saw that this was Satan, operating as an angel of light.

I screamed at him, "You are Satan! I rebuke you in Jesus's name!" Immediately, he transformed as an ugly and vicious man ready to attack. We began wrestling and continued for hours. He was tired, and I was tired, but whoever gave up first would lose the battle. As I was mentioning the name of Jesus, he was doing the same. The Lord was still standing somewhere behind me but did not help me. He was watching the fight and enjoying it knowing that I was not going to lose the fight. I was suddenly taken over by the Holy Spirit and rebuked the devil. "The Lord rebuke you, even the one who died and resurrected, in the name of Jesus Christ of Nazareth." And he fled. Afterward, the Lord came over and took me. He taught me three lessons:

1. He taught me how to discern between the angels of light and the true angel of God.
2. He also explained the importance of persistence and longsuffering in the spiritual battlefield.
3. He advised me not to listen to the praise of demons or men. It creates pride and arrogance in the spirit, which causes spiritual shipwreck and heresy. If I had truly accepted the accolade Satan was giving me, I would after that moment have started teaching a heresy that fasting and prayer were not necessary. He would have destroyed me. Men and women of God, intercessors and prayer warriors must be on guard against the cunning and craftiness of the Devil.

- **The strategic level** - is the tactical, operational, and strategical intercession of confronting demonic forces who are in charge of particular cities, cultures, and peoples.

- **Territorial spirits** - are demonic spirits that have gained control over a territory to dominate and have dominion over the people through their beliefs in the hierarchal order in the culture, which mostly involves protective deities linked to homes, tribes, temples, clans, cities, valleys, and nations at large.

There are three types of strongmen:

1. **The strong spirits** that rule over principalities or vast geographical areas in the earth realm.
2. **Demons** who rule over people, families, churches, and communities and keep them in bondage or strongholds. There was a strong demon fighting the first church I pastored. After I took over in 1989, I went to pastoral college in 1993. There, the Holy Spirit revealed to me a python with seven heads. The angel of the Lord gave me a sword, and I cut off all the heads and killed the serpent. When I went home that weekend, I recounted to the founder everything that had happened and the directions the Holy Spirit gave me to transform the church. She agreed and allowed the transition, and I moved the church to a different location. The church was liberated. Many churches are being controlled by this strongman while the pastors are in spiritual darkness. They might be in a form of certain religious beliefs such as dos and don'ts.
3. **The princes** are in charge of principalities. They are known as the strongmen. These princes are the gods and goddesses of the supernatural world and yet rule the affairs of humanity.

You are learning these secrets to help you fight the strategic warfare. The Greek word *Nikao* means "overcome"! It is an admonishment to make spiritual war and overcome. I pray that you will grow stronger to overcome.

CHAPTER 4

WHEN DO WE PRAY?

Pray when you need God the most.
Pray when you want to hear His voice.
Pray when you have no one to comfort you.
Pray when you face your giant.
Pray when the battle is at your gate.
Pray when the battle has not yet begun.
Pray when you want to get closer to God.
Pray when you want the Lord to use you mightily.
Pray when you want signs and wonders.
Pray when you want the Holy Spirit to save a soul.
Pray when you want God to employ more coworkers in His vineyard.
Pray when you want to make a difference.
Pray when your community, city, state, country, and the world need God the most.
Pray when you feel like praying.
Pray when you don't feel like praying.
Pray when everybody is praying.
Pray when nobody wants to pray.
Pray when you want to survive the storm.
Pray when you need revelation of knowledge of Christ.

Remember, all these desire births revival first in your heart before it takes over the nations.

Don't forget there are tons of reasons you should pray.

Prayer is the breath of the believer. Prayer is the relationship builder between God and His sons and daughters. The source of a believer's spiritual life is prayer. Pray until you can't pray anymore. Pray until prayer prays you. It means pray until you have no more strength to pray, and you begin to roar like a lion in the wood.

Why a Prayer Closet?

It is the secret place of intimacy with the Father. In fact, intimacy results in reproduction and that brings responsibility. Engagement brings maturity. Intimacy without fruitfulness is intimidation. Spiritually speaking, intimacy is a deeper connection with our heavenly Father. Intimacy is the highest and deepest level in a relation between couples. It's an atmosphere of emotional consummation. It's an experience that leaves a mark. That's the level where blood chemistry is exchanged and mixed. It's the moment of knowing the real person. Someone observed the word intimacy is "into-me-see." When we are in constant prayer fellowship with the Father, into-us-He-sees. King David asserted, "Search me oh God and know my heart; Try me and know my thoughts." (Psalm 139:23. AKJV) As I get closer to Him, I can now say "into-Him-I-see."

Spiritual Intimacy

Jesus said, "I am in My Father, and My Father is in Me, and you are in Me." Someone asserted, "You have a bowl full of water and a bottle of water. As you put the bottle of water into the bowl of water, you will then say, 'The water is in the bottle, and the bottle is in the water.'" Here's how I feel about spiritual intimacy as I write. When we fall in love in the attitude of prayer, praise, and worship, we are cultivating a higher level of intimacy with God. Our relationship deepens as we spend more time in this spiritual act. If we do it with a good conscience, not looking for any applause from humanity, He reveals His heartbeat and tells what He's going to do next. Before God moves, He will touch somebody's heart to pray. Jesus said, "My sheep know me. They hear my voice, and follow me. We will know Him better and recognize His voice if we consistently spend time with Him. John 10:14–15 says, "I am the good shepherd; I know my sheep, and my sheep know me—just as the Father knows me and I know the Father—and I lay down my life for the sheep."

Jesus's goal in the next verse was that the unbeliever after salvation would have to know Him. The believer can hear and know His voice. He or she must follow the Lord exactly as He knew and obeyed His Father. It is unfortunate that almost every Christian says they hear from God yet, a common humility, they do not have.

John 10:16 says, "I have other sheep that are not of this sheep pen. I must bring them also. They too will listen to my voice, and there shall be one flock and one shepherd."

There is an efficient process to help cultivate a deeper relationship in prayer with God.

- Strive to pray in season and out of season. Join the prayer ministry in your church.
- Don't wait for D-day.
- Set a goal to know Him better by studying the word. The more word you have in you, the easier prayer becomes.
- Study the word. Firstly, learn to know Him through His word. Go to Bible Studies in your church. "Study to show thyself approved to God, a workman who needed not to be ashamed ..." (2 Timothy 2:15).
- Learn to spend more time in prayer, praise, and worship.
- Pray with the word of God and pray in the Spirit.

The enemy has already heard all prayers from Adam's to John the Baptist's, but now the Kingdom of God suffers violence and the violent men take it by force. The word of God is the two-edged sword that stands as a weapon to defeat our enemy. It is a weapon to offend and defend according to Ephesians 6:10-18; Hebrews 4:12. Use it wisely.

Wait on the Lord.
Meditation is the most powerful moment of prayer. It is the time when God speaks to you. Pray briefly and wait, spend more time in His presence and He will speak to you. Be silent for an extended period. When meditating, your mind must not be left blank. It needs to be preoccupied with the word. You might even doze off or fall asleep during a long meditational prayer. Don't worry about it. Be in expectation, and He will speak to you. I do tell my people who are desperate to hear from God that God would not speak when you are speaking. He is a gentle Spirit. Again, I said, "God is constantly speaking, but you don't hear. So your prayer is not to ask God to speak. Rather, ask Him to open your ears to listen to what the Spirit is saying to you and your eyes to see what He is showing you."

Pray regularly in the Spirit. Although the enemy hears all the prayers, when you speak in tongues, there's nothing but confusion in the camp of the devil. Brother Jude asserted the other day, "But you, beloved, build yourselves up [founded] on your most holy faith [make progress, rise like an edifice higher and higher], praying in the Holy Spirit" (Jude 1:20 AMP).

Building a life of prayer takes a long time; you need to exert more energy. While many people want to have overnight success, the building continues over time. Making a deeper spiritual and prayer life is never an easy journey. There is nothing like a shortcut in the kingdom economy. You have to be like gold that goes through the seventh process of the fire. In the end—note this, not at the beginning but the end—it becomes pure and precious gold. Too many Christians are microwave Christians. Too fragile and delicate but the real Christian life is a fight.

Trust and Obey

Jesus observed, "Anyone with ears to hear should listen and understand" (Mark 4:9 NLT). Most of the time, we hear but don't listen. Listening comes with obedience.

"He who has an ear, let him hear what the Spirit says to the churches" (Revelation 2:29 NASB).

If you observe these two scriptures carefully, you will notice in the Gospel of Mark, our Lord was speaking about individuals receiving the message for themselves. In the book of Revelation, the message was for the churches. When you receive a message from God, your personal messages must transform you and build you up first. I am not saying you should wait until you are perfect. It's a process, but you need to assimilate the message first.

Obey and Act

When the Lord speaks, one must work it out immediately. Delayed obedience is disobedience. People who hear from God have more responsibility than those who do not hear at all. But the advantage of receiving from Him is far greater.

CHAPTER 5

CONCEPTS OF THE COMBAT (PART 1)

According to the truth already established, we have seen that Adam's contract with the devil concerning the earth is still dynamic even though Christ died for us. God cannot alter His word. He gave the earth to man, and man sold it out. God will not do anything on the earth realm except we give Him permission. God can deliver us from whatever we go through, but He said, "Call unto Me and I will show you great and mighty things that you don't know about" (Jeremiah 33:3). He also said, "If my people who are called by My name will humble themselves and pray ... I will heal their land ..." (2 Chronicles 7:14). God said it again in another place: "And I sought for a man among them, that should make up the hedge, and stand in the gap before me for the land, that I should not destroy it: but I found none" (Ezekiel 22:30). You are God's ambassadors on earth so He can't do anything without you deploying Him. There's a powerful atomic energy that works from the earth realm. It works in you and through you.

The Angel Possess Authority in the Earth
The secret code of this battle against the angel was that he had no legal right on the earth. The devil has the authority over this world

because Adam sold it to him. One thing we must understand is that the enemy is legalistic. He always wants to see someone trespassing so he can accuse him.

Let's observe these scriptures. Daniel 10:12–13, 20–21 says,

> Then he said to me, "Do not be afraid, Daniel, for from the first day that you set your heart on understanding this and on humbling yourself before your God, your words were heard, and I have come in response to your words. "But the prince of the kingdom of Persia was withstanding me for twenty-one days; then behold, Michael, one of the chief princes, came to help me, for I had been left there with the kings of Persia … Then there touched me again one whose appearance was like that of a man, and he strengthened me … Then he said, "Do you understand why I came to you? But I shall now return to fight against the prince of Persia; so I am going forth and behold, the prince of Greece is about to come. However, I will tell you what is inscribed in the writing of truth. There is no one who stands firmly with me against these forces except Michael, your prince."

The angel of God was kept in custody because the spiritual prince of Persia (Iran) thought that he was trespassing in the earth realm. The prince of this world knew that his contract with Adam was still in full force, but something was about to happen once the angel set his foot on the earth realm. In verse 18, the Son of Man came to the meeting the angel had with Daniel. In verse 20, the angel said to Daniel "… but I shall now return to fight against the prince of Persia …" Note what happened here between the angel and Daniel:

1. The angel set his foot on the ground in the earth realm.
2. He touched Daniel.
3. He possessed authority from the earth realm when he made contact with Daniel.

By observing verses 10 through 18, one will realize that the angel laid a hand on Daniel three different times. The first touch might be from the angel who was sent to speak to him, but Daniel felt weak. The second and third were from the Son of Man. When the angel touched Daniel the first time, he derived power from him for activation of authority in the earth realm. The purpose was to fight the princes of Persia and Greece. This spiritual act was the reason the Son of a Man appeared on the scene.

Who was that Son of Man? The Lord Jesus Christ. He restored power and authority to Daniel. But He didn't fight for the angel because He had already finished the fight before the foundation of the world. The angel was temporary legalized to operate on the earth. He gained authority over the globe when he touched Daniel. He told Daniel, "I am now returning to fight," referring to the princes who thought they had power over Persia and Greece. Daniel, being a human, had more authority in the land than the angel because it was his jurisdiction. But after the angel associated himself with Daniel, he received the dominion to deal with the princes of Persia and Greece. The devil was fighting because of the concealed prophecy of Jeremiah, which God wanted to reveal to Daniel. His plan was to keep the children of Israel in exile forever.

Here's another clue to clarify the point I am trying to establish. When Moses died, Michael had nowhere to derive authority in the earth realm to deal with the devil. So when he faced Satan, he said, "The Lord rebuke you, Satan, even the Lord, who chose Jerusalem" (Jude 1:9). There are certain dimensions that demand a higher level of supernatural operations in the earth realm. God gave this world to Adam so He has no legal authority and He can do nothing except humans permit Him. It was Michael who kicked the devil and all his angels from heaven. He had the legal right to the presence of God because that was his jurisdiction.

Jesus Possessed a Human Body to Access the Earth Realm
For God to have dominion on earth, Jesus had to have a human body to enter the earth realm. The only legal process for a passage to the planet is to come through the womb of a woman. The blood of the man will contaminate the seed. The legalities are that only man can deal with the devil here in the earth realm because that's his jurisdiction. Jesus had a legal right on the earth by possessing the human body.

> Therefore, since the children share in flesh and blood, He Himself likewise also partook of the same, that through death He might render powerless him who had the power of death, that is, the devil, and might free those who through fear of death were subject to slavery all their lives. For assuredly He does not give help to angels, but He gives help to the descendant of Abraham. Therefore, He had to be made like His brethren in all things, so that He might become a merciful and faithful high priest in things pertaining to God, to make propitiation for the sins of the people. For since He Himself was tempted in that which He has suffered, He can come to the aid of those who are tempted. (Hebrews 2:14–18)

Receiving Keys in the United States
In 2006, the Lord spoke to me about my mission in America. Why didn't You bring me in the time of peace and prosperity?" I asked.

"America didn't need you then, but now America needs you the most. I brought you to intercede for the land," he replied.

In 2006 and 2007, President G. W. Bush came to me two times in my night vision and asked me, **"Please pray for me."**

I met President Obama on many occasions in the realm of the spirit, he is always quite and alone. He told me, **"Please pray for us."**

In 2012, President Obama gave me his car key and walked me to the car. He then said to me, "Drive." He also gave me a large golden key in 2014. It was at a time when a catastrophe occurred in this nation. There were many dead bodies brought from the street. They laid them on the floor in a big arena, and there were many dignitaries around him. Everyone was broken and crying. He gave me a large golden key and told me to pray for America. "Please pray for America." These were all prophetic visions, which are being fulfilled right now as I see the spiritual bankruptcy, a nation that rejects God, and the walking dead in the spiritual cemetery—schools are prohibited to pray or have Bible, the police and black men killing one another, motivated by racism; there is a divided government, terrorists destroying many lives; and many Christians in apostasy destroying the Bible they once believed. They are now saying it is not the word of God. They deny the divine birth, death, and resurrection of Jesus Christ our Lord. All this is happening in America today.

The keys the president gave represent authority, and his car signifies this nation. When he said drive, that means take your position and do your work as an intercessor. Fight these battles until victory permeates the defeat. Chapter 18 of this book teaches concerning the importance of the keys of the kingdoms. So why was I given the keys? Read more.

Confrontation with the Principality / Prince of America

I am called to intercede for my country, the United States. Because of the nature of the intercession, I need supernatural permission to enter into certain realms of spiritual America. Every country, state, and city has its duplicate in the supernatural world as well as its rulers. In 2006, I met the principality of this nation, who wanted to destroy the United States. As I was fasting and praying, he confronted me. He said to me, "What are you doing here? I will kill you!"

I told him, "You can't kill me because the Lord sends me with a purpose."

He said, "I will break your arms."

I told him, "My hands are anointed for healing this nation so you cannot touch me. The scripture said, 'Touch, not My anointed and did My prophet no harm.' I trample you under my feet. You can do me no harm."

He said, "I will deal with you."

"I rebuke you in the name of the Lord Jesus Christ," and he fled. The next day while driving, suddenly I had a near-fatal accident. It was a head-on collision, which totaled both cars. The police had to cut the doors to remove the lady in the other car. I am grateful that she survived. I had just a minor injury. Within 2006 to 2013, there were series of attacks. But the devil lost the battle. The intercessor possesses the keys of his country or any nation the Lord sends him. The spiritual warrior needs to declare boldly to the enemy, "I have the keys of the kingdom to delivering the land freely without your permission despite your attacks or obstacles."

Another Secret Revealed about the War against America
I am shaking in every fiber of my being since I received this vision. I got up 5:00 a.m. this morning, Monday, July 11, 2016. I was editing this manuscript before publishing. The battery of the computer was running out at 6:00 a.m. I don't like using it while it's on charge. I left it and went to seek my Daddy's face. I asked Him to clarify some stuff for me. That means we are going to have a swift flight on a long journey again. The Lord took me up in the Spirit. It was from 6:00 a.m. to 6:30 a.m. We soared across the Pacific Ocean. It was dark. I was afraid, so He said, "Do not fear because I have to show you this." It was a long flight in the air, but we were so close to the surface of the water. We were soaring horizontally, but as we were approaching the shoreline, He began to raise me up vertically until He set my feet on the dry land. I was standing, watching what was going to happen. He lifted me up to another location and left me there. He then got to

a spot and called me, "Son, come closer to the water and see this, but don't be afraid." I went there. There were grasses and trees. I stood and watched what He was going to show me. I saw a lot of birds and hawks flying. I saw an eagle too. As I was beholding the eagle, the Lord said, "Join your two hands and lift them up in the form of prayer posture."

When I did, the eagle sat on my hands. My hands were still in the air, and I was not supposed to lower them down while the Lord was teaching me. My left side was facing the north, toward the Pacific Ocean. I heard the voice of the Lord above me. He said, **"Look to your left."** That place was full of papyrus. As I was watching, here came Secretary of State Hilary Clinton, followed by Donald Trump, and the third person was Bernie Sanders. Then the voice told me, "Secretary of State Hilary Clinton, Donald Trump, Bernie Sanders, and the pastors are not praying."

As the voice was speaking to me, suddenly, they all disappeared. The voice continued while my hands were still in the air with the eagle resting on them. At this time, I could not see the eagle, but I could feel that she was still there. The voice said, "Look in front of you." There I saw a creature like a porcupine. It had a hole underground, but it was sealed. It opened and entered the hole and then closed it. The creature did not see me, but my spirit was following it. I saw a lot of underground tunnels. When the animal was getting ready to start a secret attack, to shoot its sharp quills, but instantaneously the angels of the Lord started throwing arrows at the porcupine. Arrows were flying from every direction, and they were all aiming at his neck and head. They pinned him to the wall. I began to ask questions.

"What is this Lord?"

The Lord came back. He said, "The enemies of the United States knew that they could not defeat her from the air because America has air supremacy, so they are working to attack from underground. They want to find a way through the Pacific Ocean and dig underground tunnels and then send missiles, but before they strike, the Lord will release His angelic warriors to fight. That is why He is raising intercessors not to hold their peace. God still loves America."

The porcupine represented spiritual Prince of Russia who wants to destroy America. The eagle represents America, which desperately needs prayer. The United States can only survive by prayer, and that is why she was set on the prayer-postured hands. Why are most of the pastors compared to the politicians? Many of them are busy competing with one another while the devil is taking territories. Any place abandoned will be occupied by the enemy. So God sees many pastors as politicians. This is sad. Politicians and pastors both need to pray but especially the pastors. God will still save our beloved country if we don't, yet it is expedient that we take this information and intercede. God will do nothing except somebody prays.

The Lord also told me in a separate encounter that Donald J. Trump will win the election but he will need prayer like no other president in history. This prophecy came three month after he announced his presidential candidacy in 2016. No one will believe so I only told my intercessory group. We have labored in prayer from day one of the campaigns for God's choice to be realized. As I always says that, an intercessor must not tied to a particular party because we are called to intercede for all those in authority. We must fight a common enemy as theLord unfolds the secret plans of the enemy. What I saw about Mr. Donald Trump presidency was scary. I gazed in astonishment a rumbling Tornado. The dark clouds formed a tunnel with a frightening storm. At the ingress of the tunnel stood Mr. Donald Trump with his hands outstretched to balk it. I heard the voice above me, "Lift up your eyes," I am not permitted to say what I heard. But there is one reason why this man will win the election. In him is found boldness but he need spiritual guidance and prayer to lead this nation. Looking at the strategies of Russia, they will create division in the American government, turning Mr. Trump against many and many will turn against him. Every kingdom divided against itself shall not stand. Do we as intercessors and prayer warriors have job to do? Absolutely. We must intensify our prayers and do not stand aloof and watch on. The prince of Russia and other enmies are digging the underground tunnel. We must activate the angelic warriors to set the battle in array.

Underground and Secret Plans of the Enemy
This revelation has twofold meaning. The spiritual and natural.

1. Inevitably, our national security and the navy must keep extra-watch beyond the Pacific Ocean concerning Russian's activities. They will dig a very long and deep tunnel from where the U.S, cannot monitor. We must pray that our satellite be able to pick up any hidden actions by our enemies.
2. Spiritually speaking, the tunnels that the enemy is digging to launch their nuclear bombs are the issues that are befalling our nation.

Research on Cyberattacks on the Electrical Energy of the United States
After the vision concerning underground attacks, I began to look for more information on the matter the Lord revealed to me. According to *USA Today*, "Some of the worst fears of those in charge of the power grid's security came true shortly before 1:00 a.m. on April 2016, when the unknown attack on Pacific Gas & Electric's Metcalf substation in Northern Califonia was attacked. The attackers severed six underground fiber-optic lines before firing more than 100 rounds of ammunition at the substation's transformers, causing more than $15 million in damage."

So Badly Broken
The report continued, "Between 2011 and 2014, electric utilities reported 362 physical and cyber attacks that caused outages or other power disturbances to the US Department of Energy. Of those, 14 were cyber attacks and the rest were physical in nature."

Russia and the United States

According to the Israeli news, Russia's weapon is an electromagnetic pulse (EMP), which is an electromagnetic discharge that fries sensitive circuits within minutes, and this is planned to target the US Energy Power Grid. If this happens, the nation will black out in seconds, and then every appliance that has an electromagnetic circuit will not work. The militarily sophisticated weapons will not function, and then the enemies will surround this land and invade. We must not ignore this wake-up call. Intercessors need to take it seriously. God still loves the United States, but the sins are too great, so we need to cry aloud for repentance until we receive grace.

Shut Down the Islamic Jihadists/ISIS

They are breaking the strength of America. When I said the battle is more spiritual than natural, I mean that chanting, "Death to the United States," is to make both Christians and the nation's leaders ignorant of their devices. Some of the strategies are the following:

- to demean the fear and the love of God in the land
- the racial profiling, the police shootings of black men, the threat of civil war
- blacks killing cops and everyone walking in fear
- American citizens transforming into terrorists, making them difficult to detect or identify

We must agree that the strength of America rests on four words, *"In God we trust."* Now our nation has rejected the God who made the United States great. We forgot the One who gave our founders wisdom and bravery to make this country powerful. A man's curiosity led him to discover something he never anticipated. On the day of a snowstorm, he saw President George Washington, the father of this nation, on his knees, praying to God for mercy to win the war that defined this great nation. In a documentary, it was also noted that whenever Congress was in session, he would take his vice president to church for three hours to pray for the nation. How did our leaders forget so quickly?

The second issue is the unity. America is strong when we stand together, but now the racial profiling has divided this nation. Every country that divides against itself will not stand. Prophetically, God will save our beloved country. We must not rest until we deliver America.

Pastors and Politicians to Pray

The pastors and politicians who will lay a hand on this book will have to take this information seriously. These prophetic messages are classified top secrets. Everything that comes about already occurred in the realm of the spirit. That is why God reveals them to His prophets before they manifest in the natural world. We need both spiritual and natural leaders to connect to God concerning the war against the United States. I was asking the Lord from which ocean is the enemy planning to attack? I heard, "The Pacific." I remembered the three oceans that border the United States—the Pacific, Atlantic, and Arctic. Anyone who will get a copy of this book will have to share the information with other prayer warriors. There is a bunch of secret information that the Lord is revealing concerning this land, but I can't share everything in this book. We will have to raise some altars at these oceans.

We need to protect ourselves by taking over the airways, land, and seaways in the realm of the Spirit. Surely, the Lord will rescue America, but He will do nothing except someone prays. The Lord said,

"For Zion's sake will I not hold my peace, and for Jerusalem's sake I will not rest until the righteousness thereof goes forth as brightness and the salvation thereof as a lamp that burns ... I have set watchmen upon thy walls, O Jerusalem, who shall never hold their peace day nor night." You that makes mention of the Lord keep not silence, and give Him no rest till He establishes, and till He makes Jerusalem a praise in the earth. (Isaiah 62:1, 7–8 KJ21)

The Police to Avoid Generational Curses
Every bit of blood that drops to the earth cries for revenge. Cain killed his brother, and his blood and the earth that received it called God to punish the one who shed it.

"The Lord said, 'What did you do? The voice of your brother's blood is crying to me from the ground. You are now cursed from the ground that opened its mouth to take your brother's blood from your hand" (Genesis 4:10–11).

"Whoever sheds man's blood, by man shall his blood be shed; for in the image of God, He made the man" (Genesis 6:6).

A Pastor Fought Generational Battle
A message to the "Police, Do not Bring Your Family to a Malediction." A man of God was sick to the point of death. He prayed for healing but did not receive one. He began to ask God the cause of the infirmity. The Lord told him to ask the oldest man in the family concerning his grandfather. The man said, "Your father's father killed an innocent man, which he not supposed to do. The man asked him not to kill him, but he insisted. The guy requested to say his last words. He said, 'I am forty years old. If you kill me, no one younger than me will grow beyond my age.' Your grandfather did not stop but ended the man's life. Since then, no youth have been able to live past that age. The curse of premature death became part of this family."

What will happen to the police who are killing the innocent black men? Because of ignorance on the part of the police, they are creating generational curses for their children and beyond. I invite you to join us in praying for the police and their families.

Fight for Your Families
There is enough available arsenal at the disposal of the intercessors to fight with for our cities, States, and countries at large. If the enemy

crushes America, there will be no hope for the rest of the nations of the world. Let's do everything in our power to fight for America fervently in our prayers. The Intercessors are the bridge builders and gap-standers for our God to liberate the land. The one thing an intercessor must understand is there are many personal attacks, obstacles, and setbacks against him or her. The attacks will rise against his or her family, health, church, and finances. But these things must not be foreign or a surprise. The apostle Paul acknowledged that he received "… surpassingly great revelations. So to keep me from becoming conceited, I was given a thorn in my flesh, a messenger of Satan, to torment me" (2 Corinthians 12:7, Berean Bible).

The Lord, who called us, will protect us and will be with us. Be strong in the Lord and the power of His might. Fight for your sons, daughters, wife, brothers, sisters, homes, cities, states, and the nations at large. Nehemiah admonished the warriors and the builders in this regard.

> Then I stationed men in the lowest parts of the space behind the wall, the exposed places, and I stationed the people in families with their swords, spears, and bows. When I saw their fear, I rose and spoke to the nobles, the officials and the rest of the people: "Do not be afraid of them; remember the Lord, who is great and awesome, and fight for your brothers, your sons, your daughters, your wives and your houses. (Nehemiah 4:13–14, NASB)

As Nehemiah encouraged his people who were building the walls of Jerusalem, the enemies continued to devise secret plans. Fortunately, God revealed all the secrets of the enemies to stop them from overthrowing Nehemiah. But look at how Nehemiah set the warriors and the builders up in order to complete the work. Some of the builders were holding weapons in one hand and then building with the other. There were also warriors who were protecting the workers. Let's take a look at Nehemiah 4:15–18. (NASB):

When our enemies heard that it was known to us and that God had frustrated their plan, then all of us returned to the wall, each one to his work. From that day on, half of my servants carried on the work while half of them held the spears, the shields, the bows and the breastplates; and the captains were behind the whole house of Judah. Those who were rebuilding the wall and those who carried burdens took their load with one hand doing the work and the other holding a weapon. As for the builders, each wore his sword girded at his side as he built, while the trumpeter stood near me.

We might be extremely busy, but there must be a time allotted for this special intercession. If possible, start a group in your community and city immediately. Gather other brothers and sisters who are like-minded. The Lord will reward our works. It's not as unto men but Him. If we pray in secret, He will reward openly.

PART II
INVADING THE
KINGDOM OF DARKNESS

CHAPTER 6

THE PRAYER CLOSET (PART 2)

Wisdom Keys and Prayer

Invading the kingdom of darkness through the power of secret prayer is the battle that the enemy cannot withstand. To have a successful prayer life and results, here is some wisdom to apply. Your spiritual path is decided by your "vision" and accomplished by your "consistency." God will openly reward the routine of secret and strategic intercessions. An ordinary method will never produce an extraordinary expectation of a prayer life.

The disciples prayed but couldn't cast out the demon in the child. You must possess a growing faith with constant prayer and a fasting lifestyle to be able to do the works Jesus did. Matthew 17:19–21 KJV says,

> Then came the disciples to Jesus apart, and said, why could not we cast him out? And Jesus said unto them, because of your unbelief: For verily I say unto you, if ye have faith as a grain of mustard-seed, ye shall say unto this mountain, Remove hence to yonder place, And it shall remove, And nothing shall be impossible unto you. Howbeit this kind goeth not out but by prayer and fasting.

Successful prayer life only dies after its habit dies.

The prophet Elijah chose not to confront Jezebel as he confronted the prophets of Baal. If he did, he would not have run for his life. If you start the spiritual warfare, finish it. The unfinished business will always come after you. Whatever you fail to kill will hunt your children or the next generation. The fact that Elijah failed to deal with Jezebel when John the Baptist came in the Spirit of Elijah, the spirit of Jezebel arose in Herodias and requested for the beheading of John the Baptist as a comeback battle in cold-blood. Mark 6:22–24 says,

> And when the daughter of Herodias herself came in and danced, she pleased Herod and his dinner guests; and the king said to the girl, "Ask me for whatever you want, and I will give it to you." And he swore to her, "Whatever you ask me, I will give it to you; up to half of my kingdom." And she went out and said to her mother, "What shall I ask for?" And she said, "The head of John the Baptist." ...

If there is anything that did not help you succeed yesterday, repeating the same thing will not contribute to making it any better tomorrow. If being lukewarm could not assist you yesterday, turn to a prayerful lifestyle. There must be a constant fire in the closet. "Any tree that is not planted by my Father will be rooted out," J. Konrad Hole asserted, and I add, "It is impossible to break away from something that is not working. Ineffective, prayerless, ungodly, and mediocre people, until you disconnect from the excuses you are using to tolerate them, whatever delays you will crush you if you pay attention to it. Wrong choices will drain you as if you associated with bad people."

Prune them because they can paralyze your prayer life. Champions of intercessors are recognized by the burden they carry to intercede. They are formed by the heartbeat of God concerning people, cities, or nations on the journey of prayer life. The spiritual champions can only be recognized on the spiritual battlefield and not on the couches. They are built tough for the storm. They stand firm, and after they do all to stand, they stand, therefore. Anything that influence the journey of prayer will decide how effective that prayer life will be. Balaam was not successful even after he raised fourteen altars and sacrifices against them until he was eventually able to turn the Israelites against God by letting them sin and activate the anger of the Lord (Numbers 31:8, 16).

Although he wished to die the death of the righteous, Balaam died as a "sorcerer" because he knew the will of God but chose not to follow. Let the will of God's glory dominate your life. And Jesus, because of the glory set before Him, endured the cross. Let's prune all that doesn't want us to finish strong and achieve an excellent result for prayers. Pray now and activate the fire of the Holy Spirit to invade anything that is slowing or weighing down your prayer life and passion.

Pray this prayer.

Father, thank you for shedding the blood of your Son, Jesus Christ, on my behalf. I come against anything that has dominated my life but left me prayerless and weak. Father, root out the spirit of being lukewarm that has overpowered my prayer life. I command any tree in my life that is not planted by my Father to be rooted out right now. I cut off and flushed out the spirit of Jezebel that has infiltrated the generational bloodlines of my parent in Jesus's name. Oh, you demon of inconsistency in prayer, break your holds in my life. I take authority over you in the name that is above all other names. Holy Spirit, fill me. Saturate me. Set me on fire to finish the intercessory business in Jesus's name. Amen and Amen.

The next chapter will also show you how the power of God mightily blew over the Krobo Land in Ghana. You will read a brief history of the people of Adangme in order to appreciate what God has done through the power of the Holy Spirit. Please don't put this book down. You will learn about how the demons have deceived generation after generation until God said, "Enough is enough." Read on.

CHAPTER 7

THE HISTORY OF DIPO (SECRET SOCIETY INITIATION)

Before you proceed to the next compelling chapters about the deliverance of Okumo from the powers of darkness, I want to explain the stronghold the enemy set in the land of our fathers in Africa. The Dipo initiation rite is the tradition of the ancestors, which the goddess introduced to them. She has no genealogy and has no grave.

The Administrative Structure
The family is the strong foundation that makes the Africans unique. The tribe consists of all clans in the community. Thus the administrative functions of the social and tribal organization are enhanced by the heads of the tribes and the families. In Ghana each clan has a god, which protects them from their enemies. There are three principal gods worshiped by the Krobo tribes:

1. Yehowah Mau—the God of heaven, the supreme King (Jehovah God)
2. Kloweki—the earth goddess, the wife of the heavenly god, the mother of the tribes, and all worship must go through her to the god of heaven.
3. Nadu—the bloody war god, invoked only at the time of war

Thrones govern six clans. In the past, the priests of these gods were the rulers of the tribes. The separation of religion and politics became a necessity and not an option when British colonialism enforced the central power of the nation of Ghana in 1951. The heads were set up as *wetso matseme*, divisional chiefs, and must come from the direct bloodline of the priest. Under the chiefs are *asofoatseme* or community fathers or subchiefs, and under them were *weku-matseme* or the heads of the families. The priests rule through the kings down to the family heads and have their sacred emblems or symbol of authority engraved on the chief's stool or throne. The throne was then sanctified and become sacred and spiritually empowered the gods.

These divisional chiefs rule under the highest in rank, and he is the paramount chief, the **Konor.** The Konor is the president of the six divisional chiefs. Each divisional chief has his spiritual leader, the priest. The konor's spiritual leader is the **Okumo Madjanor Atreku.** He is the highest chief priest and has the power to install or dethrone the konor. He serves the sky or the heavenly god directly through the earth goddess Kloweki. Spiritually speaking, the Okumo is the supreme authority in the land.

Don't put this book down. Before you read about the power of God that captured Okumo, I want you to know the history of Dipo first, rituals in Africa then you will appreciate the work God did.

Rituals
According to Monica Wilson (1954:241), as cited in Turner ([1969]2009:6), "Rituals reveal values at their deepest level ... Man express in ritual what moves them most, and since the form of expression is conventionalized and obligatory, it is the values of the group that is revealed. I see in the study of rituals is the key to an understanding of the essential constitution of human societies."

Secret Society in Africa—Sande Spirit
Many African rituals come with spiritual initiations. Liberia, Guinea, Sierra Leone, and Ghana have similar traditions. In Liberia, every

year, young girls prepare for their introduction into the women's secret society. The list continues—the Ndebu of Zambia (Turner 1967), the Bemba of Zambia (Richars 1982), the Kaguru of Tanzania (Beidelman 1997), and the Gisu of Uganda (La Fontaine 1972). Some of the societies also have initiation ceremonies for girls and boys.

One of the major organizations is called Sande Society. It operates mostly in Guinea, Sierra Leone, and Liberia. The primary spiritual practice as part of the initiation is that the young women are led to take a vow of secrecy after weeks of training in the forest. The girls are forbidden to tell the uninitiated girls or men what has happened to them. They give the girls new names. The deepest part of this initiation is the pain associated with the process. They mutilate the girl's clitoris. The tribes call it female genital mutilation (FGM). This create dissatisfactions in the sexual life of many which the devil controls.

Most of the Liberia's ethnic groups, which are not limited to Kissi, Bassa, Mende, and Gola and others, regard the rules of this historic secret as critical. They deem it a centuries-old society, which they cannot abolish. The society chooses older women to perform these ceremonies. According to the women who talked to me, it's secret and they are not allowed to discuss it openly. They made the young women believe that the spirit of Sande would guide them into womanhood. Any woman that has gone through these rituals and initiations needs and must seek for deliverance.

Ancient Greek Goddess
In my research, I have come to a conclusion that the goddess Diana of Rome is the same goddess who infiltrated every nation and culture in different forms and by different names. The Canaanites call her Ashtaroth. The Egyptians know her as **ISIS.** Greeks calls her as Aphrodite, and the list continues. One of the Haitian goddesses was Aido Quedo, Loa of fertility and snakes.

Now let me take you to Ghana. There is a tribe in Ghana that practices female mutilation as part of their initiation process in the

Volta Region. It was at the time of the HIV/AIDS pandemic that the former president J. J. Rawlings stopped it, took the girls from the shrines, and built schools for them.

Dipo Initiations in Ghana

The Dipo ceremony is an initiation rite to mark the coming of age of young women. For many Ghanaian cultures, it is one of the most significant events in an individual's life. This type of initiation rite is practiced in most Ghanaian traditional cultures. The events that mark this occasion, however, differ from place to place. The Akans call it the *Bragoro* while the Ga-Adangmes call it *Dipo*.

Krobo Girls

The strongest decree given to the Krobos by Kloweki is the Dipo initiation. Dipo has become the most important aspect of life. It's a must that all girls go through the process to make them real women. Its purpose is to bind all Krobo girls to the racial ideology of womanhood. The head of the families bring the girls to the institution. The grade levels changed from puberty age to two years old or less.

Kloweki and the New Light (The Coming of the Cross)

According to history, during the migration from South-western part of Nigeria by the GA-Adangme tribes, all the tribes separated at one point in time. As the Krobos journey toward the Eastern part of the Gold Coast, they were obstructed by a river and were troubled as how to navigate their way. The goddess Kloweki appeared to them and led them to cross the river they were afraid of and brought them to the mountain, which became their home. She became their goddess. According to a German missionary, this goddess saw a vision of the cross and prophesied the coming of a new light, and that meant her time with them had expired and she must leave. She made the symbol of the cross in her hand and held it; then she disappeared. It was not long before the German Basle missionaries came with the cross in their hand. When the paramount chief saw them, he said, "These are my Dwarf gods (my white gods)," and he accepted them and allowed them to build a church near the shrine across the street from the Palace at Odumase Krobo. That Presbyterian chapel is still there with the shrine today.

The Challenge for Christians

According to what we studied, we realized that each home has a god. Spiritually speaking, the belief system splits family houses, although they live together. There are pagans on one side and Christians on the other. The problem is that this practice has weakened a lot of Christians, and they are confused with wavering opinions.

Elijah confronted the same situation on Mount Carmel. In 1 Kings 18:21, it says, "And Elijah came to all the people and said, 'How long will you falter between two opinions? If the LORD is God, follow Him; but if Baal, follow him.' But the people answered him not a word."

Between the first and the seventh day, there are behind-the-scenes activities of the Dipo initiations, which are purely demonic and unacceptable to God. The idea was good, but the process was not. The rites were significant in preventing teenage pregnancy and sexual promiscuity until girls were of age and ready to be married. However, with the increasing number of younger participants way below puberty age, that was a clear sign that Dipo had lost its significance. The Secret Society or Dipo custom has become a thorn in the flesh of the Christians. The Christian who is firm in his faith might have a spouse whose foundation is not strong. She might struggle to keep the faith or obey her parents' advice to send their daughters to be initiated secretly without the knowledge of the man. Many people have been trapped each year. Some of the girls are taken secretly without the knowledge of the spouse, and before he realizes it, the girl undergoes the initiation. There are a lot of instances where the girls who are on *fire* for God will rebuke the fetish priests and fight their way out. It has become a stronghold and a battle. Not only does Dipo defile people but the decrees of the goddess and other laws the inhabitants have to obey are not accepted by the church, and for that reason, there's a constant spiritual battle. The Christians considered the kings, queens, and chiefs as pagans and had nothing to do with them. There's a wall between the traditional rulers and the Christians, but God has begun something different. A new way to save the traditional leaders and the fetish priests is to establish a relationship with them instead of condemning them.

The Jealous God

Leonard Ravenhill, in his book *Why Revival Tarries*, said many are asking, "Where is the God of Elijah," but he said, "Where are the Elijahs of God?" I want to provoke someone to rise like the man who was fashioned like us but did one powerful thing that we hesitate to do and the Holy Spirit summarized in two words, **"He Prayed."**. Someone has to stand up. Yes, the church is doing a tremendous work against this stronghold, but most church members equivocate and perform this Dipo rite. They bind themselves to other unacceptable teachings of the elders that defile the word of God. The fear that their daughters will not get a husband and also will not be accepted by society has entrenched weaker Christians. It's a snare, and they fall into it. They are between two opinions and don't know what to believe. The scripture said it in 1 Kings 18:21, "And Elijah came to all the people, and said, 'How long will you falter between two opinions? If the Lord is God, follow Him; but if Baal, follow him.' But the people answered him not a word." Yes, the people said nothing because they didn't know whom to vote for but the Lord our God showed up on May 24, 1993, and snatched the chief priest of Dipo, who was the overseer of this traditional rite and destroyed the works of the enemy. "For this reason, the Son of God was manifested to destroy the works of the devil" (1 John 3:8). It was on the Day of the Lord and in the acceptable year, the year of divine favor. The Spirit of the Lord came upon a young man burning with fire on the streets of Kroboland near the headquarters of the stronghold of the shrine of Dipo, which had bewitched the people for many years. He preached, saying, "The Spirit of the Lord is upon me because the Lord has anointed me. He has sent me to preach good news to the poor, to proclaim release to the prisoners and recovery of sight to the blind, to liberate the oppressed, and to proclaim the year of the Lord's favor" (Luke 4:18, 19).

It is a year to set the captives free and open the eyes of those who were spiritually blind—a season to declare freedom and the year of jubilee to those who were in bondage. Through the power of consistent intercession, the Lord had anointed one that no one could regard, one who had humility and in the natural had nothing to alarm anyone. He had nothing to call the attention of the spiritual giants of the land. Goliath thought he was going to waste his strength and the power of his spear throwing it at the young man David. He thought he need not waste energy; he thought he could just use words by invoking his gods to finish the job. But Goliath had no idea that the battle had changed its form from the natural into the supernatural. He was not aware that the fight was now between the gods. If it were natural, David would have used the armor of King Saul and requested some of the troop to join him. He was rather not comfortable in the king's armor or with his spear. In 1 Samuel 17:38–40, it says,

> Then Saul dressed David in his tunic. He put a coat of armor on him and a bronze helmet on his head. David fastened on his sword over the tunic and tried walking around because he was not used to them. "I cannot go in these," he said to Saul, "because I am not used to them." So he took them off. Then he took his staff in his hand, chose five smooth stones from the stream, put them in the pouch of his shepherd's bag and, with his sling in his hand, approached the Philistine.

How long should the intercessors, the spiritual invaders of the cities, continue to rely on the arm of flesh and the help of man? May it be known from today that the battle of 2015 and beyond is not in the natural but in the spiritual. It's a war between the gods. We must declare it with confidence; the fight is the Lord's.

In 1 Samuel 17:43–47, it says,

He said to David, "Am I a dog, that you come at me with sticks?" And the Philistine cursed David by his gods. "Come here," he said, "and I'll give your flesh to the birds and the wild animals!" David said to the Philistine, "You come against me with sword and spear and javelin, but I come against you in the name of the Lord Almighty, the God of the armies of Israel, whom you have defied. This day the Lord will deliver you into my hands, and I'll strike you down and cut off your head. This very day I will give the carcasses of the Philistine army to the birds and the wild animals, and the whole world will know that there is a God in Israel. All those gathered here will know that it is not by sword or spear that the Lord saves; for the battle is the Lord's, and he will give all of you into our hands."

Something terrific happened in the Krobo State. It was a shock. The gods didn't see it coming. Neither the priests, nor the kings, nor the people were at peace when the Lord visited the land. There was a spiritual invasion of the large shrine of Kloweki, and God broke the power of Dipo. The Holy Spirit arrested the supreme authority of the priests of Dipo. He heard the message of the voice of the one who cried on Krobo-Mampong Main Street, saying,

Forasmuch then as we are the offspring of God, we ought not to think that the Godhead is like unto gold, or silver, or stone, graven by art and man's device. And the times of this ignorance God winked at; but now commandeth all men everywhere to repent: Because he hath appointed a day, in the which he will judge the world in righteousness by that man whom he hath ordained; whereof he hath given assurance unto all men, in that he hath raised him from the dead. And when they heard of the resurrection of the dead, some mocked: and others said, We will hear thee again of this matter. (Acts 17:29–32)

If you want to know more about what happened, then proceed to the next chapter and observe what the Lord has done.

CHAPTER 8

THE INVASION OF THE HIGH PRIEST OKUMO OF DIPO

The Supreme Leader of the Secret Society

The heartbeat of Jesus was revealed during evangelistic intercessory prayer.

I had just taken over as a senior pastor after the pastor in charge left the church. Being twenty-five years old at the time, I started a youth outreach ministry. I was preaching on the street while the outreach team was singing. We always prayed in our church before hitting the street. After each prayer, the Holy Spirit would show us where to go, which spot to stand on. On May 24, 1993, while we were praying, I saw an open vision above the altar on the wall the sacred heart of Christ pierced with the thorns and the blood was percolating. When I was looking, the Lord spoke to me. He said, *"My heart is broken because there's a soul suffering, you need to go and rescue him."* I can still see that vision clear today as I write. After the vision, I told my team, and then the Lord sent us out onto the Street. Being led by the Holy Spirit, I stood at a spot to preach. Halfway through the message, there came some young men, about twenty of them. They stopped and listened. I marked a special person among them in white lining with a white headband who was barefoot. I had never met him, but I knew who he was. I did not ask if he wanted to accept Christ at that moment because the Holy Spirit was moving in wisdom.

I went to him and asked if he enjoyed the message. He replied with joy. I said to him, "Do you mind if I come to your house to study with you?" He agreed. I set up an appointment with him right away. After prayer and fasting, I started the hundred-hour war. Catch it or lose it. Leaving nothing to chance. He was the prince of Dipo, the chief priest, the one in charge of the whole Kroboland. If you read the history of the people of Krobo, you will see that the spiritual head of the paramount chief, the konor is the Okumo, whom we are about to uncover. He revealed his secret name, Nene Okumo Madjanor Atreku. It was a powerful and sacred name that you couldn't just mention. We carefully planned my visit to his house, which I started on May 25, 1993.

The Tactical Plan of the Holy Spirit for Okumo's Deliverance
My visit was private, and when I finished studying with Okumo, he left, and then his young men started coming for the Bible studies. The reason was that his armor bearer and the elders would kill whoever attempted to convert him with the gospel. I never carried a large Bible with me. I had a small Gideon's pocket Bible. During the Bible studies, he said to me, "I have four questions; if you can answer satisfactorily, I will never let this month of June pass me by without giving my life to the Lord in honor to my mother who died in June." He said, "I asked many preachers who came to me the same questions, but no one was able to answer with confidence."

I replied, "I don't have the answers, but Jesus Christ does." Knowing that this was a defining moment, I prayed immediately in my spirit. I couldn't afford to fail because he had asked a lot of preachers already, but their answers didn't work for him. If we trust in our wisdom and knowledge, we will fail but effective, fervent prayer never fails. In 1 Corinthians 2:1–5, it says,

And I, brethren, when I came to you, did not come with excellence of speech or of wisdom declaring to you the testimony of God. For I determined not to know anything among you except Jesus Christ and Him crucified. I was with you in weakness, in fear, and in much trembling. And my speech and my preaching were not with persuasive words of human wisdom, but in a demonstration of the Spirit and power, that your faith should not be in the wisdom of men but in the power of God."

Please read his questions and answers.

Okumo's Questions and Deliverance from the Power of Darkness
Question 1: "Will I die if I give my life to the Lord and quit the fetish (Voodoo) priesthood practice because I had a covenant with the goddess? What should I do to be saved?"

Answer: "If you die, I'll throw my Bible away, and I will never serve my God again. It will mean that Christ did not rise from the dead. 'For this reason, the Son of God was manifested on the cross to destroy the works of the enemy' (1 John 3:8). Hebrews 2:14–18 (NIV) says, 'Since the children have flesh and blood, he too shared in their humanity so that by his death he might break the power of him who holds the power of death—that is, the devil—and free those who all their lives were held in slavery by their fear of death. For surely it is not angels he helps, but Abraham's descendants.'"

Question 2: "Would I not be insane or perish if you remove my headband? It is not supposed to touch the ground. It must not fall. No hand should touch it. And also nobody is allowed to see my head. I might even die."

Answer 2: "'We bring into captivity every high thing that exalts itself against the knowledge of God …' (2 Corinthians 10:3–6 NIV). 'For though we live in the world, we do not wage war as the world does.

65

The weapons we fight with are not the weapons of the world. On the contrary, they have divine power to demolish strongholds. We demolish arguments and every pretension that set itself up against the knowledge of God, and we take captive every thought to make it obedient to Christ. And we will be ready to punish every act of disobedience, once your obedience is complete.' Any evil spirit assigned to provoke that judgment is shut down by the power of the blood of Jesus."

Question 3: "Where would I stay if I give myself to Christ because I don't want to go back to that shrine again after my salvation?"

Answer 3: "'The Lord had prepared a place for you already before He called you' (John 14:1–3 NIV). 'Do not let your hearts be troubled. You believe in God; also believe in me. My Father's house has many rooms; if that were not so, would I have told you that I am going there to prepare a place for you? And if I go and prepare a place for you, I will come back and take you to be with me that you also may be where I am.' Before God sent me to you, He had me prepare a room for you and your wife in our mission house. 'All things are possible to those who believe.' Do you believe?"

"Yes, I do," he said.

Okumo Converted

Question 4: "How am I going to survive if I quit the priestly office? The Dipo celebration is a thriving business that takes care of my family. I might become unemployed. What do I do then?"

Answer 4: "'The young lion does hunger and thirst, but those who fear the Lord shall never lack any good thing. His name is Jehovah Jireh. The Lord, who provides, He will meet your needs according to His riches in glory in Christ Jesus' (Romans 10:11–13). As the scripture says, 'Anyone who believes in him will never be put to shame.' For there is no difference between Jew and Gentile—the same Lord is

Lord of all and richly blesses all who call on him, for, "Everyone who calls on the name of the Lord will be saved.""""

Then he told me that many believers said the only way he could receive his deliverance was through fasting. I said that was not true. "God is not expecting your fasting. God wants you to believe and accept Jesus Christ as your personal Savior and Lord. John 3:16 says, 'For God so loved the world that he gave His one and only Son, that whoever believes in Him shall not perish but have eternal life." We are fasting for you because The Lord saw your tears and showed me that you need to be saved as soon as possible."

The Okumo accepted the Lord and was baptized. The Lord answered all his questions immediately, and God was glorified in the city.

Invading the Kingdom of Darkness with the Power of Secret Prayer
The battle has just begun. Pastor Thomas Muthee said it best, "Before the ground troops win the battle, the battle must be won first in the air." That means prayer warfare must be activated. That night was a successful moment.

Okumo's First and Second Visit to My Residence and His Deliverance
The first visit was a short visit and prayer because he didn't want his people to be alarmed. At the second visit, I took him to the auditorium and started praying for him. It was around 4:00 p.m. The Holy Spirit took over during the short prayer, but it turned into a major deliverance. While I was praying for him without touching him, his headband fell to the ground. He always wore the headband, and no one was supposed to see his hair. Then he asked me with perplexity and trembling. "Pastor! Did the headband fall?"

"Yes, it did!" I replied.

Then he said, "Am I still alive? Am I still alive?"

I said, "Yes, you are alive in Jesus Christ because the devil is the liar from the beginning."

After the deliverance around 4:00 p.m through 5:00am. that whole night turned into a night of victory. His elders didn't know what the Lord was doing. After the headband had fallen to the ground by itself through the power of the Holy Spirit, I took it and burned. It was dangerous. By the power of the blood of Jesus Christ, the devil lost the battle.

The Night of Victorious Celebration on June 4, 1993

When my spiritual mother heard of the deliverance that was going on in the church, she came to join me to pray while the man (Okumo) went to the shrine to bring his clothes. Two hours later, we heard a shout of victory from afar on the Main Street. I said to her that this praise was coming right here in the auditorium. We were still praying. Half an hour later, the youth group of about fifty-five was being led when Nene Okumo Madjanor Atreku with his clothes in his hand arrived. Their fetish culture didn't allow anything manufactured from abroad. So he never had a bag to carry his clothes.

He never wore shoes or sandals. If it rained, he never went out. Can you see the enslavements? He walked without shoes on his feet even when it was hot. He had no choice. So the victorious shout came to our church. My spiritual mother and I were still doing spiritual warfare. None of the youth could touch any of his clothes to help him carry them because they were all afraid. The third trip was the end of his footprint in that shrine. During the travel, something amazing occurred. At each trip, the number of the people following him multiplied. At first, fifty-five youth followed him. The second trip increased to about 150, and by the end of the third voyage, the number had increased to about 300 people. It was 5:00 a.m. the next day. Can you imagine, I did not plan that his visit starting at 4:00 p.m. would extend to the next day. The entire house and the church were full. Revival broke out.

A Satanic Agent Cannot Stand the Power of God

The executioner (laabia) was the Okumo's armor bearer and weighed about 350 pounds and was about six feet tall. He came with the elderly priestess, who was sent to bring me with them to the shrine; it was around 9:00 a.m. I came downstairs to see who was looking for me. I said to them, "Shalom. Peace be with you."

The executioner said, "I have no peace with you."

I told him, "Then I have nothing to discuss with you," and I started praying with power under the unction of the Holy Spirit. It was like I threw a bomb at him the moment I said "In Jesus's name." He ran away as if somebody was chasing him violently from the house. He couldn't come into the house; he stood outside at the roadside. He could not look into my face. The priestess was scared but couldn't run because she was old. She respectfully and humbly told us that their grandmasters wanted us to come with them to explain why we had converted Okumo. She also said that the king, Nene Tekpernor Addipa II, the then acting president, the paramount chief of the entire Manya-Krobo State wanted to see us. My spiritual mother told her that we had nothing in common with the kingdom of darkness, and therefore we couldn't go to their grandmasters or chief priests, but the king was our king, and we would see him. At our visit, the King didn't send for us. But he said, "I need to baptize but will call on you when I am ready." He gave us money and sent for a taxi; he paid for the rental. It all happened June 5, 1993. The king was speaking prophetically.

The Baptism of Abraham (Okumo)

The baptism of Okumo occurred on Saturday June 12th, 1993. The Okumo was given a new name (Abraham). The convoy of the trip to the Volta River at Kpong was three cars. They were all singing and drumming. Being the biggest market day in the region, news broke out that the Okumo died, and the pastor who baptized him also died. That was their expectation and fear. While I am writing this story, the

Holy Spirit just prompted me to say that "Yes, the Okumo died that day; he died to the devil and all his worship as they proclaimed and is now alive for Christ." It did not surprised me that the devil made them confess because it was their fear and belief that anyone in that high rank of office of that demonic priesthood would die if he or she ventured to quit his or her position and denounce his or her faith to serve the Lord because it happened to many people.

As I am writing this story, twenty-three years later, I confess with a boldness that Abraham is still alive today. Glory and honor to God in the highest. His deliverance shocked the entire region and prolonged the revival that began in the 1970s and which was ending in the 1990s. To God be the glory, great things He has done. God answered all his questions instantly the moment he gave his life to Christ.

Prophetic Answers to Serious Decision and Questions
If you recall the four questions Abraham asked before he gave his life to Christ, you will remember that God did not disappoint me for trusting that He would make a way.

Okumo thought that he would die by giving his life to the Lord because of the goddess he promised to serve. Now the first question was answered; he did not die (John 3:8).

Okumo was scared that he would become insane if the white headdress fell to the ground. "No," I said, because of Galatians 3:13. The amazing thing that happened first during the deliverance was the white headband. Thank God I did not touch him, but the Holy Ghost did. That was his greatest fear. When it fell, it was a powerful experience because he was expecting that something terrible would happen to him if the headdress touched the floor.

When he saw the white headband on the floor under my feet, he shouted with a loud voice, "Pastor! Did it fall?"

"Yes, it fell," I said.

He asked again, "Am I alive? Am I still alive?"

"Yes, you are; because Jesus lives, you will live also."

Then he was filled with the Holy Spirit instantaneously.

The Lord answered the third question. Okumo was wondering how he was going to survive and financially support his family. The answer was that God would not leave or forsake him. King David said in Psalm 37:25, "I have been young, and now am old; yet have I not seen the righteous forsaken, nor his seed begging bread."

The prophetic answers were fulfilled right after Abraham's baptism on Saturday. The next Sunday, a friend of mine visited us when he heard the news. He was the manager of the Implegilo Construction Company at the time. He signed a check of 10.000.00 GHS. It was a lot of money in those days. He also offered Abraham a job right away. The Lord had blessed him and after the company closed down, this man became the MP, (Member of Parliament). He served in that Office over twenty years, and no political opponent could defeat him. God used MP Michael Teye Borboryo Nyaunu to answer His servant. Praise Jesus, none of my responds to Okumo's questions went unfulfilled.

As for the fourth question, "Will I get a place to reside with my wife?" this issue was also solved. We gave Abraham a room in our mission house. He almost lived in the church. A month later, the Roman Catholic charity sent him to a driving school. The man who had never in his life sat in a car became a bus driver. Was that a miracle? God had set everybody and everything in motion to serve His purpose. It was as if everyone was waiting to fulfill his or her part in the process of Abraham (Okumo) salvation. His deliverance glorified God, but it shocked the kingdom of darkness in the land.

Praise God. Prayer works.

Revelation 12:9–11 (NIV) says,

> The great dragon was hurled down—that ancient serpent
> called the devil, or Satan, who leads the whole world astray.
> He was thrown to the earth and his angels with him. Then
> I heard a loud voice in heaven say: "Now have come the
> salvation and the power and the kingdom of our God, and
> the authority of his Messiah. For the accuser of our brothers
> and sisters, who accuses them before our God day and night,
> has been hurled down. They triumphed over him by the blood
> of the Lamb and by the word of their testimony; they did not
> love their lives so much as to shrink from death.

CHAPTER 9

JUDGMENT ON THE PRINCE OF THE LAND

Salvation of the Grandmaster of the Secret Society, Judgment on the Priestess of the Secret Society, and Judgment on the Prince of the Land

The spiritual warfare turned physical when the devil could not prevail against us. We had services day and night. One night, I was preaching in our church at Odumase Krobo. Suddenly the prince of the land appeared. The late paramount chief Nene Azu Mate-Korle II was the supreme King over the entire traditional area. He was a very powerful king. His son the prince came to me with two swords drawn in his hand, pointed them at me, and walked toward me to slay me while I was preaching. He was furious. He was questioning why I had converted Okumo.

The people in the service were scared, but I stretched out my hand toward him and commanded the church to pray. I was not scared but rather filled with boldness. I was even ready to die for my King, Jesus. I rebuked him in Jesus's name with my finger pointed at him. By the time I opened my eyes, he was standing in front of me very close, about one yard away. He was hitting the ground with the two swords in his hand.

He asked me why I had converted Okumo, the head of the priests of their gods. I rebuked him, and he turned away and went home. The next day, he came back, but this time under the judgment of God. He apologized with his face covered with saliva and tears. He began rolling on the floor and crying that I should pray for his forgiveness. I prayed for him. The Lord decided not to heal him but to make him a sign to the people. He was stricken with insanity or madness and suffer to this day. I am not sure if he is still alive. Here's what Apostle Paul did. Acts 13:7–11 (NIV) tells us,

> Who was an attendant of the proconsul, Sergius Paulus. The proconsul, an intelligent man, sent for Barnabas and Saul because he wanted to hear the word of God. But Elymas the sorcerer (for that is what his name means) opposed them and tried to turn the proconsul from the faith. Then Saul, who was also called Paul, filled with the Holy Spirit, looked straight at Elymas and said, "You are a child of the devil and an enemy of everything that is right! You are full of all kinds of deceit and trickery. Will you never stop perverting the right ways of the Lord? Now the hand of the Lord is against you. You are going to be blind for a time, not even able to see the light of the sun." Immediately mist and darkness came over him, and he groped about, seeking someone to lead him by the hand.

Judgment on the Priestess

We changed Okumo's name to Abraham. Abraham asked me if we could visit one of the grand masters who loved him and took care of him as his son. We went there one night and in the dark, ministered unto the senior man with a little lamp because they didn't use electricity. He was shaking in his recliner. The moment he started confessing Christ as his personal Savior, the priestess came there suddenly because the demons felt the threat in their domain. When she saw Abraham and me, she shouted with a loud voice. It was in their community near the shrine. The laabia (executioner) came with a very sharp machete ready to attack us. The whole place was immediately full of the multitude, and they all had stones and rods in their hands. Acts 17:1–9 says,

> When Paul and his companions had passed through Amphipolis and Apollonia, they came to Thessalonica, where there was a Jewish synagogue. As was his custom, Paul went into the synagogue, and on three Sabbath days he reasoned with them from the Scriptures, explaining and proving that the Messiah had to suffer and rise from the dead. "This Jesus I am proclaiming to you is the Messiah," he said. Some of the Jews were persuaded and joined Paul and Silas, as did a large number of God-fearing Greeks and quite a few prominent women. But other Jews were jealous; so they rounded up some bad characters from the marketplace, formed a mob and started a riot in the city. They rushed to Jason's house in search of Paul and Silas to bring them out to the crowd. But when they did not find them, they dragged Jason and some other believers before the city officials, shouting: "These men who have caused trouble all over the world have now come here, and Jason has welcomed them into his house. They are all defying Caesar's decrees, saying that there is another king, one called Jesus." When they heard this, the crowd and the city officials were thrown into turmoil. Then they made Jason and the others post bond and let them go."

I was on fire, ready to die for Jesus, and I was not afraid of any threat. But to my surprise, Abraham was full of the Holy Spirit and said to them, "We are ready to die for the cause of the gospel because even Paul, Stephen, and the apostles were stoned and killed."

I opened my mouth to speak a word to the priestess who stopped the salvation of the man, but the Holy Ghost said to me, "Don't say a word. I will take care of her."

So I held my peace. Then some of the Good Samaritans in the community came begging us to leave. We left, but the next day, the Lord visited that priestess, and for three days, she did not leave her room, and that was her end.

The Grandmaster Accepted Christ

We did not stop there; we went further. Abraham said, "I can't see my elders who cared so much about me perish." We went to the grand chief priest, who was about eighty years old. He was the man who sent the laabia and the priestess the day after the conversion of Abraham. He wanted us arrested and for me to explain why I converted the Okumo. I refused to go at that time, but Abraham and I went to him with the gospel. He lived in a different community. This grandmaster accepted the Lord and confessed Jesus as his Lord and Savior. He trembled with fear. We visited many of them, and some of the elders gave their lives to Christ. They became aggressive and hostile against us, but the fire of revival was still burning in us.

I was twenty-five years old at the moment of Okumo's conversion, and God covered and protected me. I walked to and fro through that community near the shrine where Abraham used to stay. The Satanists never knew me or saw me because sometimes, the wind was activated. Many believers started to preach around that community early in the morning, condemning those satanic worshippers. These pagans attacked the Christians and destroyed the church of Pentecost that was in that community; they kept harassing them until the members stopped using the church facility for a while. I don't believe that condemning people will help them give their lives to Christ. The apostle Paul said we should preach the gospel with love. It is the Holy Spirit that convicts the sinner. We need to understand that Christ did not come to judge the world but to save it. My strategy, was to win through relationship. The gang leaders started following me because of the love I was showing to them when the entire community disowned them.

The next Okumo who was installed to replace Abraham died because God manifested Himself. All believers rallied together in their churches, interceding. Thus God was magnified in the land. Intercessory prayer works and brings glory to God. Don't be weary praying; the result you are expecting may not happen now, but sooner or later, God will show up.

Attacks from Other Pastors

There were a series of attacks from some of the churches and pastors; they wanted the glory. They said they had preached to Okumo. They visited Abraham on so many occasions while he was still in our mission house after his conversion, and they wanted to take him to their church. The devil was busy using them to confuse Abraham.

On the other hand, other churches and pastors were fasting and praying all night to shut down the worship of idols in the land. After his baptism, I went with Abraham from church to church to show that he was alive and not dead as they had heard. Their strongholds were rooted deep in the heart of the indigenous people. The powerful tool they used was (and still is) fear. Honestly, those who quit the idol worship without any deliverance and strong teachings, guidance, and prayers, either go back through severe attacks or death. The devil has been in charge for a long time, but his days were numbered when the believers began to pray. I joined Krobo Pentecostal Fellowship in 1994. (K.P.F.) was a fellowship of Pentecostal churches and pastors who came together once a month to host all-night prayers and three-day fasting and prayer sessions. I became an organizing secretary. We also founded the Manya-Krobo Council of Churches, which comprised all the churches and pastors of which I was the general secretary from the year 2000 until I moved to the United States in June 2005. The hardest thing to do was to bring pastors together for a common purpose, but I went from house to house and city to city. I went from Odumase to Kpong, Akuse, and other towns, even Assesewa, trying to sell the idea of John 17:21, "That they may be one" to the pastors. Most of the churches in the land came together, and we became united. The church triumphed. Programs were organized to learn more about Dipo and how to deal with other controversial issues from the spiritual perspective. There's now no ignorance concerning those Satanic schemes; they're high in awareness and deliverance.

CHAPTER 10

TWO KINGDOMS COLLIDED

The Kingdom of God Comes with Power

When one is moving in the prophetic, one sees and hears secret things that no one will imagine in the natural. It is this prophetic intercession that makes the warfare more compelling. The devil's secret plans are at the fingertips of this warrior. A person with this mighty power does not talk; he takes action, according to the directions of the Holy Spirit, who is the radar for the battle. "For the kingdom of God is not in word but power" (1 Corinthians 4:20). "For I determined not to know anything among you except Jesus Christ and Him crucified. I was with you in weakness, in fear, and in much trembling. And my speech and my preaching were not with persuasive words of human wisdom, but in a demonstration of the Spirit and of power" (1 Corinthians 2:2–4). "For the Kingdom of God is not meat and drink, but righteousness and peace and joy in the Holy Ghost" (Romans 14:17).

The Battle against the Throne God

The god in our family house is known as Throne god. There was an inexplicable spiritual battle with the high priest of the throne of the kingdom of darkness after the death of my grandfather.

I moved to our mission house in 1986 because of this idol worship. In 1996, just after my grandfather passed away, in the vision of the night, the Lord took me up in the Spirit and brought me to my grandfather's house. There I saw my stepgrandfather slaughtered and lying on the floor in a pool of blood. The place was where they killed sheep for the purification of the community and sacrifices were made on their behalf. That place was a spiritual altar, which they constantly used for the Throne god. Every intercessor needs to understand the dynamics of the spiritual altar. You need to recognize its spiritual and physical implications. They laid my stepgrandfather on the altar there. It was in the center of the house. The Lord sent me to destroy the evil plan of the enemy.

Then He said to me, "Your stepgrandfather will die if you don't pray." Since the king's command was in haste, I went the same day to organize the Christians in the house. Often, we Christians think for God and do things that we believe He wants. I figured He wanted me to bring all the Christians in the house together to pray. Everyone agreed to fast and pray the next day, including the pastors, deaconesses, and church elders in the house. When Africans talk about family, it includes the extended family. We have a large family. Half of the people were Christians and the other half pagans. The greatest challenge was the family heads were compelled to enforce the pagan belief despite their Christian faith. They were afraid that they would die.

The Eight-Hour Operation Spiritual Desert Storm
Sometimes, God's way of saying no breaks us. It surprised me when I went the next day to my grandfather's house and all the people who assured me had failed. Those who wanted to take part in the fasting did not join me on the agreed-upon date. They all had excuses. Then the Holy Spirit prompted me, "I've called you to intercede; I have not called you to call them. So go and sit right where I have shown you and pray."

I sat on that spiritual altar where the demons had their blood covenant with the family and the entire community. It was a huge house with about thirteen rooms and could accommodate over two hundred people during ceremonies. I did not talk to anybody, and nobody dared to ask me anything until I finished praying. I sat quietly and prayed silently from 6:00 a.m. and 2:00 p.m. It was the Operation Eight-Hour Spiritual Desert Storm. The Christians knew what I was doing but were afraid to join me. The unbelievers in the family and the priest of the Throne god (Se Wornor) knew it was a spiritual battle. They said nothing to me. Neither did they ask what I was doing. It was Jeremiah's style of dealing with some prophetic acts. After this operation, I returned to the mission house where I was residing as senior pastor. When I left, the priest of the throne and the elders of the community did sacrifice a sheep on the altar at the spot. It was the place where I sat, and that same night, because he knew what would happen, the devil vehemently attacked me. I then understood why the Lord didn't allow anybody to join me in that strategic intercessory prayer. The reason was that the believers who wanted to join me were not robust enough to do that kind of spiritual warfare.

The Priest of the Throne and the Power of God
In the night vision, the Holy Spirit took me back to the house. The moment I entered the house, I was going to my grandfather's room. I saw him sitting in the living room, and he was beckoning me. He wanted to inform me of the ambushing of the prince of the throne. They set this attack because of the Operation Eight-Hour Desert Storm prayer. I ignored the call because I said to myself, "He is dead, and I have nothing in common with him." After I refused my late grandfather's call, suddenly everybody ran away from the house. I didn't know what was going on. When I turned, there came up behind me the prince of the throne, who was killing the people. He was half naked and had a piece of red cloth around his waist. He had a gun and a rod in his hands. That red fabric was the attire they used for aggressive spiritual warfare and the performance of rituals. The rod in his hand depicted his power. If they pointed that wand at you, you would become static or be weak until they defeated you. Whenever they would go out with that stick, people panicked. Woe to anyone if the king sent a messenger to his or her house with that rod.

When I saw him, I moved to the hallway to get out, but he locked the door and then he pointed the staff at it. He shot at me several times. I kept declaring the name of Jesus Christ at any gunshot. As I point my finger at him, the bullets then turned into ashes. The entire hallway was full of smoke, and then a few of the ashes touched my neck. I knew the battle was fierce, and I could not be passive about it. Yet the Lord did not allow me to fight him, so I commanded the door to open. Instantaneously the door opened, and I went out then closed the door against him. When I woke up around 4:00 a.m., I couldn't turn my neck. It was painful. My neck was stiff, and I started wondering what was happening. Then the Holy Spirit reminded me, "It's the warfare." With just one word, the pain fled. I remembered what Martin Luther said to the devil when many of his enemies were threatening to take his life. One night, he heard noises in his room. Luther lit a candle and checked, but the doors were locked. As he turned, he saw the devil sitting in a chair with a wicked smile. "Oh! Is it only you?" said Luther, and he blew out the candle and returned to bed. That's how we can make the devil feel at times. He was disappointed. When our action tells him that we are not afraid of him and we don't even care about him, yet we are tactical and wise to deal with Him, he will leave us alone. When I knew my attack came because of the warfare, I engaged. With one word, I rebuked him, and he instantly fled. You can do likewise.

God Rewarded My Secret Prayer Openly
Within six to twelve months, the eight-hour silent prayer broke down the walls of the high priest of the Throne god. There was a huge crack in the wall of his room. He and his family evacuated. The house of the Throne also fell apart. That's the power of prayer warfare. I invite you to read more about his salvation and death in the next section.

The Salvation and the Death of the Prince of the Throne
Around 1997–98, I received another message from the Lord. (I will use a different name here for privacy purposes.) He said, "Nene Kwame, the prince of the throne *dies* tomorrow. Go and save him." I

went quickly to visit him only to find him sick with stroke. Nobody told me. I spoke to him. He accepted Christ and denounced the throne god and the devil. He surrendered his life to Christ and was baptized by Rev. S. T. Tettey. Once the Lord has overthrown the spiritual prince of the Throne god, it is easy to deal with the man who occupied the office. It is imperative to take action whenever you hear the voice of the Lord. Hallelujah! Jesus reigns!

The Effective, Fervent Prayer in Secret
The effective, fervent prayer of the righteous person avails much.

- ➤ It establishes the will of God on earth.
- ➤ It brings the kingdom of heaven to earth and into the hearts of man.
- ➤ It changes circumstances.
- ➤ He or she will receive a reward from God publicly.

The Prophet-Activated Kingdom Power

"[36]And it came to pass at the time of the offering of the evening sacrifice, that Elijah the prophet came near, and said, LORD God of Abraham, Isaac, and of Israel, let it be known this day that thou art God in Israel, and that I am thy servant, and that I have done all these things at thy word.

[37]Hear me, O LORD, hear me, that this people may know that thou art the LORD God, and that thou hast turned their heart back again.

[38]Then the fire of the LORD fell, and consumed the burnt sacrifice, and the wood, and the stones, and the dust, and licked up the water that was in the trench.

[39]And when all the people saw it, they fell on their faces: and they said, The LORD, he is the God; the LORD, he is the God." (1 Kings 18:36-39)

The Old Altar Rebuilt

Elijah knew one secret, which the priests of Baal didn't know. According to 1 Kings 18:36–39, Elijah knew that the old altar was a place of the covenant between the fathers of Israel and the living God. If he wants to win the battle, he has to fight it from the root. God instructed Jeremiah to break down and destroy the kingdoms of darkness. "See, I have set you this day over nations and kingdoms, to pluck up and to break down, to destroy and to overthrow, to build and to plant" (Jeremiah 1:10). As Elijah activated the altar and spiritually broke the altars of Baal, God came down. The fire went before Him and then swept the sacrifice and the stones. Something remarkable happened that day. Water is an enemy to fire and is supposed to be a setback or resistance. Here, in this case, the water turned into fuel. Is there any problem that looks insurmountable? Is it not the time to give up on doubt? The same situation will be a set up for your miracle. Don't give up yet; just believe and pray one more time. The Lord is with you.

We are in the world today as if it were the time of Elijah. Who is willing to stand as God's Elijah today? Are you ready to rise to the ruling power and dominion of Baal? Heaven has to respond because we stand for His name. Here's the difference between Christians and other religious people. We don't defend our God. He protects us, but the Muslims and other religious people will kill for their god. Gideon's father told the city, "If Baal is a god, let him defend himself because Gideon breaks down his altar." He couldn't defend himself.

PART III
THE STRATEGIC LEVEL
OF SPIRITUAL WARFARE

CHAPTER 11

THE LASER FOCUS ON THE PRAYER TARGET

Using Spiritual Mapping

Survey the enemy's camp with the radar of the Spirit. For clarity of what mapping in the spirit is all about and why it is necessary for intercessors to intercede more accurately, we can study the US and our allies' war techniques in Iraq. We knew that we were going up against a nation who had the most modern, up-to-date weapons. The combat was on two levels. The first tier was known as Desert Storm or Desert Shield. The United States watched all the movements, strengths, and weaknesses of the Iraqi forces through their air operation. They gathered all necessary information with reconnaissance flights over Iraq. As the United States and our allies tried to avoid civilian casualties, the highest military action was to bypass the radar system of the enemy. We achieved our plan by using stealth bombers, which enabled us to mount an attack without being detected on their radar. On the first night of the assault, the major bombardment was almost over before Iraq even realized what had happened. The air strike was successful because of the strategic knowledge that our military intelligence had. Operation Desert Storm and air war phase 1 were powerful. Phase 2 had to do with the one-hundred-hour war of the ground assault. We as intercessors are to mount similar strategies in the area of spiritual warfare.

An influential teacher on spiritual warfare Pastor Harold Caballeros from Guatemala talked about X-rays and smart bombs. He said, "What an X-Ray is to a physician, the spiritual mapping is to intercessors." Here's how Pastor Bob Beckett described it. He is also using what happened during the first Persian Gulf War when Saddam Hussein launched many Scud missiles but did minimal damage to the allied forces. It would be like the leader of a country who is using the scud missiles to fight those who have the modern technological smart bombs. He would have to depend on the most popular TV, for his confirmation of any damage he did to his enemies. This is exactly how many people pray today because they are not aware of the devices of their enemies.

Beckett contrasted the Scud missiles with the smart bombs of the allies. They would enter through the smokestack or a window or door of the place at which they were aimed. The reason they could do this was that before the air war began, a small number of experienced reconnaissance specialists went behind the enemy lines, located the high-priority targets, and programmed the targeting coordinates into the computers on the smart bombs. Bob said, "We have had all too much Scud-missile praying in our churches. We need more smart-bomb praying!" By Peter Wagner book entitled *Praying with Power*. He is my favorite teacher on spiritual warfare.

Deliverance minister, Pastor Boat from Ghana gave his testimony when the Lord healed him. That attack came as a result of the curse from his grandparents' bloodlines, which took the lives of many of his family members from generation to generation. He said no one passed the age of forty in his family. When it got to his turn, he was near to death, but he didn't want to die so he was praying with tears, asking God about the cause. One day during his prayer, he saw a man who came to him and told him to go and request the oldest person in his extended family tell him what he knew about his grandfather. When he asked, the senior man narrated what his grandfather had done. He had killed an innocent man because of wickedness. In those days, there were a lot of wars. Every stranger was a suspect. He told him that his grandfather had met a man whom he thought was an enemy and proceeded to kill the man. The man said that he wasn't an enemy, but he refused to let him go. The man begged, but mercy lost its importance and he rejected his plea. The man finally agreed to die, but he said, "I have something to tell you before you kill me." The man was forty years old. He said, "If you shed out this innocent blood, no one in your family will exceed my age." But his grandfather killed the man and that was why premature death did not depart from his family before they hit the age of forty. When Pastor Boat got the message, he went on his knees and repented for the sins of his fathers and asked God for forgiveness. After that, he took the battle to the camp of the enemy and bombarded his strongholds. He was delivered and healed and is still preaching the gospel to this day. He broke the power of a generational curse of premature death.

Considering these three scenarios, if we want to intercede effectively, we need to research, investigate, or survey the cause of the problem or what kind of agent the devil is using against that situation. That is what spiritual mapping is all about. When you get the right and strategic information that the enemy might be using against you, it gives you boldness to plan an attack against his stronghold. It becomes helpful in hitting the right target with the assurance that you are not missing the point. To deal with the situation, we need to go to the root. Note, the secret that destroyed the fig tree was the word Jesus spoke. He said to the fig tree, "No one will eat fruit on you." Mark 11:20 says, "In the morning, as they went along, they saw the fig tree withered from the roots." Speak to any root of the fig tree, and it will no more occupy a vantage place. It is clear that the word Jesus spoke clung to the *roots* of the fig tree and cut all its sources of supply. If the roots lost the ability to extract nutrients from the soil, the tree, the branches, and the leaves would automatically wither and eventually the tree would die.

Defining Spiritual Mapping

My definition of *spiritual mapping* is to "study and view the nations as they exist in the spiritual world, and not what we see in the natural." In his work *The Last of the Giants* (Chosen Books), George Otis said, "One of the ways of the spiritual dimension would be as familiar to the average believer as the sea is to mariners." That's not so. He said, "The problem seems to be that many believers—particularly the Western Hemisphere—has not taken the time to learn the language, principles, and protocols of the spiritual dimension."

Stalking Valuable Information Concerning the Adversary

Osama bin Laden would still have been alive if the Navy SEALs did not get the right information. Any information the warrior receives is his or her power. That helps to create a strategic plan to hunt down the enemy. The United States is always dominant when it comes to tracking down information from their enemies.

There were important yearly celebrations for a god called Nadu celebrations in Ghana in the Eastern Region, but now they are abhorred. No one remembers even the name or its celebration anymore because the Christians regularly prayed for years until some vital information was obtained through the knowledge learned about spiritual mapping in the mid-1980s to the '90s. Then churches started coming together, praying and fasting and doing all-nights, prayer walks and Jesus marches. We always organized this prayer warfare before the yearly celebrations. Suddenly the Nadu Priest died, and there was no successor. That was the end of that celebration and the worship of the so-called mighty war god. Although fasting and all-night prayers were paramount, the information from the enemy's camp was like a treasure.

God could have told Moses all the information he needed about the enemy whose land they were going to possess, but He urged him to send twelve spies to the Promised Land. Numbers 13:2 says, "Send some men to explore the land of Canaan, which I am giving to the Israelites. From each ancestral tribe send one of its leaders." The most important information Moses needed was in Numbers 13:17–20.

When Moses sent them to explore Canaan, he said, "Go up through the Negev (North) and on into the hill country. See what the land is like and whether the people who live there are strong or weak, few or many. What kind of land do they live in? Is it good or bad? The nature of the towns they dwells? Are they unwalled or fortified? How is the soil, is it fertile or poor? Are there trees in it or not? Do your best to bring back some of the fruit of the land." (It was the season of the first ripe grapes.)

Information Needed
The detailed information they received was valuable; it affects the way the warriors will handle or prepare for their battles. After Joshua succeeded Moses, he also sent two spies to Jericho, and they brought a real report. When they went, they realized that the hearts of the men in the city melted, and there was no strength in them. We as the church, as Apostle Paul put it, "wrestle not against flesh and blood, but against principalities, against powers, against the rulers of the darkness of this age, against spiritual wickedness in heavenly places" (Ephesians 6:12).

Ed Silvoso said, "In active warfare, the most critical information is not what you know, but what you don't know. Especially if your enemy knows that you don't know." For lack of knowledge, my people perish. He continued, "Generally speaking, the church today is dangerously ignorant of the scheme of the devil. In fact, some people make it a point of pride not to know much about the devil and his devices. They haughtily declare that they will focus exclusively on Jesus and forget the evil." That is a graveyard. You can ignore the devil, but he will not ignore you. He takes pride in fighting ignorant Christians because they are easy targets.

The Enemy Also Does Spiritual Mapping on Us
The devil is angry with us. Whether you are an intercessor or just a believer, you are a prime target. Whether you like it or not, the battle is at your gate. Hell must know you. In 2006, while I was conducting spiritual exercise through prayer and fasting, the devil, being the prince of this land, came at me confrontationally. He said, "What are you doing here? I am going to kill you."

I told him, "You can't kill me because the Lord sent me here for a purpose, and until God fulfills His purpose, I am not dying. Here's what the word of God says, 'Come together, all of you, and listen: Which of the idols has foretold these things? The Lord's chosen ally will carry out his purpose against Babylon; his arm will be against the Babylonians'" (Isaiah 48:14).

Then the devil said to me, "I will break your arms."

I told him, "You can't, because my hands are for healing the sick nations. The Lord rebuked you saying, 'Touch not mine anointed, and do my prophets no harm'" (1 Chronicles 16:22).

Then he told me, "I will deal with you."

I rebuked him and declared that the word of God says, "When the enemy shall come in like a flood, the Spirit of the LORD shall lift up a standard against him." And he fled. After that spiritual confrontation, the next day, I had a terrible accident. It was a head-on the colision. Both cars were totaled. I only had a minor injury. Between 2006 and 2013, it was a real battle with the beast, as Paul put it. The enemy lost the battle.

Known in Hell
While this was going on, I received a letter from a medium from the Netherlands. She was an older lady mentioned every detail of what I was going through at that time. Then she added, "I have been trying to reach you and help you but couldn't get closer to your soul

because where you are, I cannot come there. I was freezing to death the more effort I made to get to you." She said, "I cannot reach your soul because you are protected." She gave me some directions to perform. She also wanted me to send her some information about myself that would enable her to help me. Do you see the devil's trick? She was doing spiritual mapping on me to get more information. After the principality failure of several attempts to fulfill his predictions during our confrontations, he sent an agent who wanted me to give her permission to afflict my soul. I took everything she sent, anointed it, and trampled it underfoot, and I activated the fire of the Holy Spirit to consume it. Since then, I have won the battle. Victory belongs to the King of kings. Glory and honor be onto the Ancient of Days! Don't forget that every situation you go through has originated from the spiritual realm. If you cannot win in the realm of the spirit, you will lose the battle to the enemy in the natural realm. We are known in hell because we are at our Father's business as intercessors and soul winners.

Is It Possible to Enhance This Spiritual Mapping?
Yes, it is possible if we know what we want and are passionate about delivering the land and the people. It will not matter what it costs. In 2002, I led a missionary group from Nigeria. One of them was from my town and is my friend in the vineyard. Rev. John Nartey was the leader of the group and asked me to lead them to the Imam (the leader of the Muslim community). I was then the general secretary of the Christian Council of Churches in the Manya-Krobo State. We also went to some of the traditional rulers and the fetish (Voodoo) priests. It was an enjoyable visit. I will talk later about the imam and how he and his family challenged the power of God in my life and the judgment that came upon them a couple of years before this visit. Pastor John also had some of the group members visit the sociofinancial department and other areas. To do aggressive intercession for the Kroboland, he wanted us to do the spiritual mapping. This state is a case study, and every piece of information obtained here can be modified and used for the furtherance of the kingdom.

Samuel T. Padmore

The Three Key Questions We Asked
Is there a problem this community is facing?

Something was terribly wrong with this community, and somebody had to rise and bring deliverance to the city. Most of the pastors in the land were interested in delivering the land from the kingdom of darkness. Was there a cause? It's not easy to just conclude that this was the answer. Sometimes it got complicated. Did the founding of the city affect the way things were going or the situations that started happening later on? The wrong assumption would mislead the intercessors. Sometimes the conditions were caused by natural means. Was there any solution to this situation?

C. Peter Wagner, in his book *Praying with Power*, gave us details about how to handle this information. He said there's a frequent transition made from the spiritual mapping researchers to the spiritual warfare practitioners. They are not the same. He said X-rays are to the surgeon what the spiritual mapping is to the intercessors. When the X-ray technician finishes his or her job, he or she gives the information to the physician who ordered the X-ray. The physician is the only one allowed to interpret the results for the patient and then decide what procedure is necessary. Some surgeons are not capable of operating the sophisticated X-ray equipment in their hospitals; only the trained technicians know how. In the same way, intercessors need the patient, spiritual-mapping researchers. At this juncture, there's the need for mediators with the gift of discernment to understand the implications of what the researchers have found and how to deal with it. As I used my experience for a case study, the information we obtained from the traditional rulers and the study of the Krobo history gave us enough evidence of the situation of the land. Our intercession team had a much easier way to handle the issues. We knew what to deal with, what to attack, and how to strategically wage this warfare.

94

CHAPTER 12

DIFFERENT TYPES OF COVENANTS

Covenant (תירב / διαθηκη),
In the Hebrew Bible, the covenant (Hebrew: *berit*) is the formal agreement between Yhwh and His people, the children of Israel, in which both party agrees to a set of commitment toward the other. The language and understanding of covenant is based on ancient Near Eastern treaties between nations.

The Bible understands covenant from two different perspectives. The unconditional or eternal covenant (Hebrew *berit ʿolam*) between Yhwh and Israel/Judah presumes that the covenant can never be broken, although it does allow for divine judgment.

The Godly and the Seven Covenants of the Bible.
God made several covenants with His people in both the Old Testament and in the New Testament. In these covenants, God promised to bless His people if they would obey His word. The most difficult thing people can do is to follow their creator. They broke His covenant over and over again. God gave the contracts with conditions, and if they did not carry it out as expected, He responded to their disobedience with punishment.

95

The Edenic Covenant

The Edenic covenant was the dispensation of humans' dominion over creation. It was a charge and a test at the same time. Every position and blessing comes with responsibility. God blessed Adam and Eve and made them king and queen of this world (Genesis 1:26–31). The condition attached to the blessing was only one word, *obedience*; they were not to eat from the tree of the knowledge of good and evil.

> And the Lord God commanded the man, saying, You may freely eat of every tree of the garden; But of the tree of the knowledge of good and evil and blessing and calamity you shall not eat, for in the day that you eat of it you shall surely die … And the man and his wife were both naked and were not embarrassed or ashamed in each other's presence. (Genesis 1:16–17, 25)

Adamic Covenant

The sin entry point into this world was when Adam and Eve broke that covenant (Genesis 3:15–19, 22–24). It was necessary for the discipline of the human race and hope for the generations that inherited such punishment.

Noahic Covenant

In Noah's era, humanity exhibited a higher level of wickedness, which called for greater discipline. In Genesis 6–9, we saw how God punished and also gave humanity a second chance at a fresh start.

Genesis 6:3 says, "Then the Lord said, My Spirit shall not forever dwell and strive with man, for he also is flesh; but his days shall yet be 120 years."

Genesis 9:1–17 tells us,

> Behold, I establish My covenant or pledge with you and with your descendants after you. And with every living creature

that is with you—whether the birds, the livestock, or the wild beasts of the earth along with you, as many as came out of the ark—every animal of the earth. I will establish My covenant or pledge with you: Never again shall all flesh be cut off by the waters of a flood; neither shall there ever again be a flood to destroy the earth and make it corrupt. And God said, This is the token of the covenant (solemn pledge) which I am making between you and Me and every living creature that is with you, for all future generations: I set My bow [rainbow] in the cloud, and it shall be a token or sign of a covenant or solemn pledge between Me and the earth. And it shall be that when I bring clouds over the earth, and the bow [rainbow] is seen in the clouds, I will [earnestly] remember My covenant or solemn pledge which is between you and Me and every living creature of all flesh; and the waters will no more become a flood to destroy and make all flesh corrupt. When the bow [rainbow] is in the clouds, and I look upon it, I will [earnestly] remember the everlasting covenant or pledge between God and every living creature of all flesh that is upon the earth. And God said to Noah, This [rainbow] is the token or sign of the covenant or solemn pledge which I have established between Me and all flesh upon the earth.

God's plan to save man has been in motion since before the beginning of this world. It was God's plan to establish a covenant. Observe verse 17 above. He launched an agreement with a promise of the *seed* of the woman in Genesis 3:15. This seed was the Redeemer who would crush the head of the serpent (the devil). God would keep this promise regardless. God's unconditional covenant with Noah brought about a principle for human government, comprised of the virtue of human life. The man is forbidden take another man's blood; rather he is to be his brother's keeper. God promised that He would never curse or destroy the earth again with a flood. The relationship between the beasts and humanity is reestablished in Genesis 8:22 and 9:2. God now commanded humans to eat meat but without the blood in it. The sons of Noah would replenish the continent; they were the only survivors of the human race.

Abrahamic Covenant

This type of covenant is unconditional. Through many of Abraham's dreams, God established an unconditional covenant with him and his seed forever. Genesis 12:1–3 (AMP) says,

> And the Lord said to Abram, Go for yourself [for your advantage] away from your country, from your relatives and your father's house to the land that I will show you. And I will make of you a great nation, and I will bless you [with abundant increase of favors] and make your name famous and distinguished, and you will be a blessing [dispensing good to others]. And I will bless those who bless you [who confer prosperity or happiness upon you] and curse him who curses or uses insolent language toward you; in you will all the families and kindred of the earth be blessed [and by you, they will bless themselves].

God promised Abraham the land of Canaan (Genesis 13:14–17). Read all the scriptures to have a better understanding. God imputed righteousness to Abraham because of his faith in the Lord (Genesis 15:6). Abram, renamed Abraham, became the father of many nations. God gave him a conditional covenant that required circumcision. This covenant must be practiced through Isaac, the promised child, according to Genesis 17:1–27. God reassured Abraham he would have a son. Read Genesis 18:1–15.

Isaac was born, but Ismael was not allowed to be a joint heir. If Abraham allowed the illegitimate son in the house, he would have created confusion in the distribution of the land (Genesis 21:1–13). The Lord God confirmed His covenant after Abraham obeyed God in the sacrificing of his son Isaac. Read Genesis 22:1–18.

Abraham became the father of many nations. The Lord God promised Abraham that his seed would be as uncountable as the sand of the seashore (Genesis 22:16–18). His seed would be as the stars of heaven (Genesis 15:5).

In Genesis 22:16–18, the multiplication of the seed as the sand on the seashore referred to the natural children of Israel, and according to Genesis 15:5, the seed would be like the stars of heaven. The stars represent the church. According to Matthew 16:16–18, Peter received a promise from Christ. "I will build my church, and the gate of hell shall not prevail against it. Jesus Christ was the seed of the woman in Genesis 3:15 and then from Genesis 12 to 22, God continued to mention "your seed." God confirmed His covenant with Isaac and Jacob.

Mosaic Covenant
The Mosaic covenant has a prerequisite. This contract was not complete without the law and the priesthood. Deuteronomy 7:12–13 says, "Then it shall come about because you listen to these judgments and keep and do them, that the Lord your God will keep with you His covenant and His lovingkindness which He swore to your forefathers …" Exodus 19:1–8 tells them if they obeyed and kept the commandments, he would bless them. It was a contract or agreement between God and His people.

The Covenant Proper
Exodus 34:10 says, "Then the Lord said: 'I am making a covenant with you. Before all your people I will do wonders never before done in any nation in all the world. The people you live among will see how awesome is the work that I, the Lord, will do for you …" Please, read the rest of the scriptures to verse 27, as well as Exodus 20:19 and 34:1–9, 15–28 and Deuteronomy 5:1–33.

Moses, like Jesus Christ, was the mediator between God and man. Exodus 34:8–9 says, "Moses bowed to the ground at once and worshiped. 'Lord,' he said, 'if I have found favor in your eyes, then let the Lord go with us. Although this is a stiff-necked people, forgive our wickedness and our sin, and take us as your inheritance.'" Hebrews 9:22 says, "And almost all things are by law purged with blood, and without shedding of blood is no remission." Moses introduced the law with blood. Here's what Paul has to say in Romans 3:19–24:

> Now we know that what things soever the law saith, it saith to them who are under the law: that every mouth may be stopped, and all the world may become guilty before God. Therefore by the deeds of the law, there shall no flesh be justified in his sight: for by law is the knowledge of sin. But now the righteousness of God without the law is manifested, being witnessed by the law and the prophets; Even the righteousness of God which is by faith of Jesus Christ unto all and upon all them that believe: for there is no difference: For all have sinned, and come short of the glory of God; Being justified freely by his grace through the redemption that is in Christ Jesus."

Please read 2 Corinthians 3:7–9, Hebrews 10:1–10, and Galatians 3:10–25.

The Davidic Covenant

The Davidic covenant established the kingdom of David. It had the following components:

i. His throne would be established forever.
ii. David could not build the temple he wanted to erect for God, but rather, his son would.
iii. God promised to bless or discipline his descendants.
iv. The Lord promised that the Messiah would come through the lineage of King David (1 Chronicles 17:9–15 and 2 Samuel 7:10–17).

The New Covenant (Grace)

The New Covenant is an eternal, unconditional promise. It is the agreement that establishes the father-son/daughter relationship. Here God pledged to impart His word or law into the hearts and minds of His people. He offers restoration of favor and blessing for His people, sanctification, atonement, and ultimate forgiveness, along with expiation, which refers to the removal of our sins, and propitiation, which relates to the elimination of God's wrath through the blood of Jesus Christ. The promise of the Father is that the Holy Spirit will live in us and the temple will be rebuilt (Ezekiel 37:26, 27). There will be an end to war and the establishment of the global peace.

The Blood of the New Covenant

Matthew 26:26–28 (AMP) says,

Now as they were eating, Jesus took bread and, praising God, gave thanks and asked Him to bless it to their use, and when He had broken it, He gave it to the disciples and said, Take, eat; this is My body. And He took a cup, and when He had given thanks, He gave it to them, saying, Drink of it, all of you; For this is My blood of the new covenant, which [ratifies the agreement and] is being poured out for many for the forgiveness of sins.

Read Luke 22:19–20 and John 6:53–63.

The words of Our Lord Jesus Christ depict the covenant proper. Read Matthew 28:18–20, John 12:47–50, and Hebrews 1:1–3 and 2:1–4. Moses, being the mediator of the Old Covenant, prophesied about the mediator of the New Covenant, which is Christ Jesus in Deuteronomy 18:15–19.

Christ administered the requirement of the New Covenant from His office of mediation. Read Hebrews 1:3, Romans 14:9, 1 Timothy 2:5, and Acts 2:33.

The Greek word *diatheke* is used thirty-three times in the NT and is translated as "covenant." It's also used interchangeably to denote the term "testament," which is used thirteen times in the New Testament.

These are the seven covenants of God with His people. Are there satanic covenants? Yes, there are satanic covenants, which bring the anger of God to the earth.

Satanic Covenants Defile the Land and Bring Curses
Psalm 106:34–40 says,

> They did not destroy the [heathen] nations as the Lord commanded them, But mingled themselves with the [heathen] nations and learned their ways and works. And served their idols, which were a snare to them. Yes, they sacrificed their sons and their daughters to demons And shed innocent blood, even the blood of their sons and of their daughters, whom they sacrificed to the idols of Canaan; and the land was polluted with their blood. Thus were they defiled by their works, and they played the harlot and practiced idolatry with their deeds [of idolatrous rites]. Therefore was the wrath of the Lord kindled against His people, insomuch that He abhorred and rejected His heritage.

After the children of Israel had possessed the Promised Land, they forsook God and polluted the land with the particular sin that God warned them not to commit. They covenanted with the devil and sacrificed their children. Many people did not understand the effect of bonds through sacrifice. There's no covenant without sacrifice. In every nation, there was and are still promises and sacrifices. Unfortunately, many people think that idol worship occurs only in Africa. The devil is fooling many individuals in the elite countries, and they take the serious business of the enemy to be what they call "fun." Someone asked me about four years ago why there were demons in Africa but not in America. To understand the answer to that question in a deeper sense, read the following concerning altars and sacrifices. I have tried to study satanic altars in different countries. I can write down some of them so you can learn and strategize your prayer.

CHAPTER 13

ALTARS

Different Type of Altars

An altar is a place where people offer sacrifices, even if it is not an event involving slaughter. Mostly, altars were built by humans with building materials, such as stone, earth, metal, and brick. According to *Baker's Dictionary*, we have found altars in Palestine dating back to approximately 3000 BC. They used natural rocks as well (Judges 6:20). Altars are sometimes isolated or stand in the courtyard of a shrine. Satanic altars might also not be built with any material but the area could be dedicated to the devil by blood or drink offering. Godly altar could also be raised by anointing oil and prayer.

Altars were imperative in human survival. They were, therefore, the places where the divine and human worlds interacted. Altars were places of spiritual transaction, influence, communication, and exchange. Altar activities move God faster than any prayer offered because it's the seal of a covenant transaction. In the interaction between Yahweh and Baal, as Elijah contested with the prophets of Baal, God responded because Elijah found the old altar, which was the place of the covenant between God and the patriarchs.

The Significance of Altars

An altar is a venue of contact between humans and the spiritual world. It is a location designated to offer sacrifices to Yahweh of the Old Covenant, to gods, idols, or spirits. It is a place of worship. The land upon which they build the altar becomes part of the covenant. We have already established the fact the agreements are legally binding between man and Yahweh or other gods. An altar is a place of activation of spiritual powers upon the land by sacrifices through fellowship or communion.

Noah Built an Altar

God smelled the aroma and found it pleasing. He responded to Noah's action by declaring that he would never again destroy all living things through a flood.

> And Noah built an altar unto the Lord; and took of every clean beast, and of every clean fowl, and offered burnt-offerings on the altar. And the Lord smelled a sweet savor, and the Lord said in his heart, I will not again curse the ground any more for man's sake; for the imagination of man's heart is evil from his youth; neither will I again smite any more everything living, as I have done. While the earth remaineth, seedtime and harvest, and cold and heat, and summer and winter, and day and night shall not cease. (Genesis 8:20–22)

The Altars of the Patriarchs

Abraham built three altars to Yahweh, and at each instance, Yahweh responded to Abraham.

> God appeared to Abram and said, "I will give this land to your children." Abram built an altar at the place God had appeared to him. He moved on from there to the hill country east of Bethel and pitched his tent between Bethel to the west and Ai to the east. He built an altar there and prayed to GOD. (Genesis 12:7–8)

The Lord said to Abram after Lot had left him, Lift up now your eyes and look from the place where you are, northward and southward and eastward and westward; For all the land which you see I will give to you and your posterity forever. And I will make your descendants like the dust of the earth, so that if a man could count the dust of the earth, then could your descendants also be counted. Arise, walk through the land, the length of it and the breadth of it, for I will give it to you. Then Abram moved his tent and came and dwelt among the oaks or terebinths of Mamre, which are in Hebron, and built there an altar to the Lord. (Genesis 13:14–18)

And He said to him, I am the [same] Lord, Who brought you out of Ur of the Chaldees to give you this land as an inheritance. But he [Abram] said, Lord God, by what I shall know that I shall inherit it? And He said to him, Bring to Me a heifer three years old, a she-goat three years old, a ram three years old, a turtledove, and a young pigeon. And he brought Him all these and cut them down the middle [into halves] and laid each half opposite the other, but the birds he did not divide. And when the birds of prey swooped down upon the carcasses, Abram drove them away. When the sun had gone down and a [thick] darkness had come on, behold, a smoking oven and a flaming torch passed between those pieces. On the same day, the Lord made a covenant (promise, pledge) with Abram, saying, To your descendants, I have given this land, from the river of Egypt to the great river the Euphrates. (Genesis 15:7–11, 17–18)

Land Secured with Special Sacrifice

For Abraham to be sure the land was secured, God showed him the particular animals he needed to sacrifice. We find those animals in the preceding passage. The token to ensure that the Promised Land was secured have to be the blood of the birds and animals sacrificed. God told him to lay the pieces in two rows and He would pass through.

After the presence of Yahweh had gone through the sacrifice in the form of the smoking furnace and a flaming torch, He assured Abraham with an oath that He would give the land to his descendants.

The Altar of Isaac

> And there was a famine in the land, other than the former famine that was in the days of Abraham. And Isaac went to Gerar, to Abimelech king of the Philistines. And the Lord appeared to him and said, Do not go down to Egypt; live in the land of which I will tell you. Dwell temporarily in this land, and I will be with you and will favor you with blessings; for to you and your descendants I will give all these lands, and I will perform the oath which I swore to Abraham, your father. And I will make your descendants multiply as the stars of the heavens, and will give to your posterity all these lands (kingdoms); and by your Offspring shall all the nations of the earth be blessed, or by Him bless themselves, For Abraham listened to and obeyed My voice and kept My charge, My commands, My statutes, and My laws. So Isaac stayed in Gerar ... And the Lord appeared to him the same night and said, I am the God of Abraham your father. Fear not, for I am with you and will favor you with blessings and multiply your descendants for the sake of My servant Abraham. And [Isaac] built an altar there and called on the name of the Lord and pitched his tent there, and there Isaac's servants were digging a well. (Genesis 26:1–6, 24–25)

God reaffirmed His promise to Isaac concerning the land He would give to Abraham's descendants. In response, Isaac built an altar and sacrificed to his father's God, Yahweh.

Jacob Built Three Altars

> And he dreamed that there was a ladder set up on the earth, and the top of it reached to heaven, and the angels of God

were ascending and descending on it! And behold, the Lord stood over and beside him and said, I am the Lord, the God of Abraham your father [ancestor] and the God of Isaac; I will give to you and your descendants the land on which you are lying. … And Jacob awoke from his sleep, and he said, Surely the Lord is in this place, and I did not know it. He was afraid and said, How to be feared and reverenced is this place! This is none other than the house of God, and this is a gateway to heaven! And Jacob rose early in the morning and took the stone he had put under his head, and he set it up for a pillar (a monument to the vision in his dream), and he poured oil on its top [in dedication]. And he named that place Bethel [the house of God], but the name of that city was Luz at first.

Note Genesis 28:20–22: "Then Jacob made a vow, saying If God will be with me and will keep me in this way that I go and will give me food to eat and clothing to wear …"

There's a startling truth here. Jacob made a vow that if God blessed him, he would give Him a tenth of everything he owned. In Malachi 3:8, God told the children of Israel, "You are cursed with a curse because you are robbing Me." It could mean that God was saying they were cursed for not fulfilling the vows of their fathers. Whatever happens in the lives of the parents affects the future generations. You might notice that the land promised to Abraham was not inherited by him. At that time, the patriarchs were still strangers in that land. They bought portions for their usage. Our generations are suffering today because of the covenants, altars, and sacrifices our ancestors made to the devil. We will go deeper and see how God plans to deliver us.

When Jacob came from Padan-aram, he arrived safely and in peace at the town of Shechem, in the land of Canaan, and pitched his tents before the [enclosed] town. Then he bought the piece of land on which he had encamped from the sons of Hamor, Shechem's father, for a hundred pieces of money. There he erected an altar and called it El-Elohe-Israel [God, the God of Israel]. (Genesis 33:18–20)

As we carefully observe the actions of Jacob, we realize that he did four things that his predecessors didn't do in the following scriptures: Genesis 28:12–13 and 17–19 and 33:18–20.

Jacob undertook four actions:

1. He anointed the land
2. He changed the name of the land.
3. He vowed a vow in the land.
4. He offered a drink offering to God.

Jacob moved in the prophetic act. He took complete ownership of the land with these actions. Remember you can only change the name of something or give a name to something that belongs to you or you have absolute control over. Adam named everything in the garden because he was in charge. In Africa, especially Ghana, in the tribe where I came from, if a man had a child with a woman he did not marry, he had no power over the child, and for that reason, the child could not bear his name. He changed the name of the child after he performed the adoption.

> And God said to Jacob, Arise, go up to Bethel and dwell there. And make there an altar to God Who appeared to you [in a distinct manifestation] when you fled from the presence of Esau, your brother. Then Jacob said to his household and to all who were with him, Put away the [images of] strange gods that are among you, and purify yourselves and change [into fresh] garments; Then let us arise and go up to Bethel, and I will make there an altar to God Who answered me in the day of my distress and was with me wherever I went ...

So Jacob came to Luz, that is, Bethel, which is in the land of Canaan, he and all the people with him. There he built an altar, and called the place El-bethel [God of Bethel], for there God revealed Himself to him when he fled from the presence of his brother ... And God said to him, I am God Almighty. Be fruitful and multiply; a nation and a company of nations shall come from you and kings shall be born of your stock; The land which I gave Abraham and Isaac I will give to you, and to your descendants after you I will give the ground. Then God ascended from him in the place where He talked with him. And Jacob set up a pillar (monument) in the place where he talked with [God], a pillar of stone; and he poured a drink offering on it, and he poured oil on it. And Jacob called the name of the place where God had talked with him Bethel [house of God]. (Genesis 35:1–3, 6–7, 11–15)

With careful observation, you will realize that Abraham built three altars, Isaac erected one, and Jacob raised three. In total, there were seven altars constructed in the land. Seven is a prophetic number, and that had sealed the deal. The land had gone through a constant attack from generation to generation. But because of the voice of the seven altars and the sacrifices, no one succeeded in claiming the Promised Land from them.

The 21 Altars of Balaam and Balak
Balaam understood the secret of the seven altars. His prophetic insight unveiled the secret code of the patriarchs to secure the land. When Balack asked him to curse the children of Israel, he was aware that if he could build fourteen altars, he would be able to invert or reverse the promise and then stop them from possessing the land. When the fourteenth one was not able to attack the original seven, he proceeded to build another seven making it twenty-one in total. But there was one thing that Balam didn't know until his third-set of seventh altar sacrifice after Balak built them. He heard the sound of

the King among them and the blessings of the God of their fathers. He shouted to King Balak, "How can I curse whom the Lord has blessed? Let me die the death of the righteous." The Righteous One Balam was talking about was the King of kings, the seed of Abraham. He cannot be cursed, and enchantment had lost its power over him. Balaam also saw the nature of the lion among the children of Israel. Who did all these descriptions fit? It was the vision of the Lion of the tribe of Judah. He was and is and shall be the King among His people. He is the only Righteous One. His death and resurrection were the perfect sacrifice on the altar of the holy of holies. It was a sinless sacrifice to redeem both the land and the people.

> And Balaam said to Balak, Build me here seven altars, and prepare me here seven oxen and seven rams. And Balak did as Balaam had spoken, and Balak and Balaam offered on each altar a bull and a ram. And Balaam said to Balak, Stand by your burnt offering, and I will go. Perhaps the Lord will come to meet me, and whatever He shows me I will tell you. And he went to a bare height. God met Balaam, who said to Him, I have prepared seven altars, and I have offered on each altar a bull and a ram. And the Lord put a speech in Balaam's mouth, and said, Return to Balak and thus shall you speak. Balaam returned to Balak, who was standing by his burnt sacrifice, he and all the princes of Moab. Balaam took up his [figurative] speech and said: Balak, the king of Moab, has brought me from Aram, out of the mountains of the east, saying, Come, curse Jacob for me; and come, violently denounce Israel. How can I curse those God has not cursed? Or how can I [violently] condemn those the Lord has not denounced? ... Surely there is no enchantment with or against Jacob; neither is there any divination with or against Israel. [In due season and even] now it shall be said of Jacob and Israel, What has God wrought! Behold, people! They rise like a lioness and lift themselves up like a lion; he shall not lie

down until he devours the prey and drinks the blood of the slain. (Numbers 23:1–8, 23, 24)

Elijah Repaired an Old Altar for the Deliverance of the Land

Then Elijah said to all the people, "Come here to me." They came to him, and he repaired the altar of the Lord, which had been torn down. Elijah took twelve stones, one for each of the tribes descended from Jacob, to whom the word of the Lord had come, saying, "Your name shall be Israel." With the stones he built an altar in the name of the Lord, and he dug a trench around it large enough to hold two seahs of seed. He arranged the wood, cut the bull into pieces and laid it on the wood. Then he said to them, "Fill four large jars with water and pour it on the offering and the wood." At the time of sacrifice, the prophet Elijah stepped forward and prayed: "Lord, the God of Abraham, Isaac, and Israel, let it be known today that you are God in Israel and that I am your servant and have done all these things at your command. Answer me, Lord, answer me, so these people will know that you, Lord, are God and that you are turning their hearts back again." Then the fire of the Lord fell and burned up the sacrifice, the wood, the stones and the soil, and also licked up the water in the trench. When all the people saw this, they fell prostrate and cried, "The Lord—he is God! The Lord—he is God!" (1 Kings 18:30–33, 36–39)

Did you see the power of altars? When the presence of the Almighty God was in the valley of decision and the original altar was in motion to speak, the counterfeits could not counteract it. In the patriarchal era, altars were markers of a particular location, commemorating an encounter with God. Abraham built an altar where he pitched his tent between Bethel and Ai. Presumably at that platform, he called on the name of the Lord. Sacrifices were an important process of exchange in altar transactions. The priestly code of Leviticus devotes a significant amount of space to the proper sacrificial procedure and to what sacrifices are appropriate in various circumstances. Sacrifice was the highest form of a spiritual act of external worship. Unlike the divinities of nations surrounding ancient Israel, the deeper level of communion with Yahweh and Israel's survival depended on the sacrifices (Exodus 30:21). The act of sacrifice moved the offering from the profane to the sacred, from the natural to the supernatural and from the visible to the invisible world. By this action, the worshiper sealed a contract with God. Blood, believed to contain the life of an animal (or a human being), was particularly important in the sacrificial ritual. They sprinkled the blood against the altar (Leviticus 1). They smeared the blood once a year on the horns of the altar of incense.

The Levitical Altar

And make the altar of acacia-wood, five cubits square and three cubits high [within reach of all]. Make horns for it on its four corners; they shall be of one piece with it, and you shall overlay it with bronze. You shall make pots take away its ashes, and shovels, basins, forks, and fire pans; make all its utensils of bronze. Also make for it a grate, a network of bronze; and on the net, you shall make four bronze rings at its four corners. And you shall put it under the ledge of the altar so that the net will extend halfway down the altar. And make poles for the altar, poles of acacia wood overlaid with bronze. The poles shall be put through the rings on the two sides of the altar, with which to carry it. You shall make [the altar] hollow with slabs or planks; as shown you on the mountain, so shall it be done. (Exodus 27:1–8 AMP)

An altar of earth you shall make to Me and sacrifice on it your burnt offerings and your peace offerings, your sheep and your oxen. In every place where I record My name and cause it to be remembered, I will come to you and bless you. And if you will make Me an altar of stone, you shall not build it of hewn stone, for if you lift up a tool upon it you have polluted it. Neither shall you go up by steps to My altar, that your nakedness is not exposed to it. (Exodus 20:24)

CHAPTER 14

SATANIC ALTARS

Satan's strategies never change. He has the attitude of counterfeiting and perverting the original principles of Yahweh. He knows the significance of covenants, altars, and sacrifices. Many continents and countries like Africa, Asia, the United States, Russia, China, and Europe are full of satanic altars. Unfortunately, most people are ignorant about the evil presence in the elite countries, and they think that Africa is the traditional place of such worship. The scripture says, "For lack of knowledge, my people perish." This book is intended to enlighten all believers and most substantially the intercessors. What I am writing comes from my personal, practical experiences; the revelations of the Holy Spirit; and also research on the experiences of many renowned Christian intercessors. Someone asked me why there is satanic worship in Africa but not in America. I told her that the satanic worship in America is stronger than in Africa, but it's civilized and professionalized. The Satanists, witches, mediums, and so on and so forth are professionals. They camouflage themselves with their positions and the people they know so that the law will favor them. People need to know what's going on today in America and the rest of the elite countries.

Pamela Rae Schuffert presents investigative journalism from a biblical Christian perspective. She wrote an article with this clear title, "Satanism in America Today: Asheville, NC." The subtitle is "Pagan Mecca of the Southeast." Here's what she has to say. "I am quietly crying as I write this article." Sister Pamela said the Holy Spirit instructed her to write this article to inspire intercessors to pray. She said, "And understand that what is happening in the Asheville region, is going on all over America, in city after city. And in your area as well. Most of you only don't know it. The highway to hell that leads to Asheville runs right through your city as well. I am wanting out, and wanting Jesus to forgive him." Sister Pamela cited the story of a young man who had recruited countless souls and sacrificed many on the Satanic altars in Asheville. He became aware after he sacrificed his girlfriend against his will. He had no choice.

My question is does America know? *No*, many Christians are naive about the satanic operations in America today. According to Sister Pamela, there's a group called the *"power people coven."* It has a variety of wealthy and prominent individuals in society as members, such as mayors, lawyers, judges, doctors, brain surgeons, nurses, doctors who perform abortions, district attorneys, teachers, principals, students, and many other influential people throughout every city in America.

Pamela stated, "I discovered that every city across America has its 'power people coven' that secretly rules over that town from behind the shadows. Asheville is but a microcosm of what is happening in many other cities and regions across America, in varying degrees. Every state has their 'Asheville.' It could even be your hometown, like Elyria, Ohio … or Lilydale, New York, or East Harrison, Indiana, all known regions of very hard-core Satanism that I have visited and prayed over or ministered. This terrible darkness is everywhere across America."

Pamela stated in her many years of research on the confessions of young people, youths, whom their mothers dedicated to Satan in the womb. As children, some were as young as four years old. The Satanists give them knives and force them to sacrifice infants that they brought before them.

The Undercover Satanism and Human Sacrifices

Some students, teachers, and principals in high schools play the game of pretending. Some people act as though they are students in the school, faking it all along in order to win some older students for sacrifice. Christian parents, please, it is important to pray for your kids as never before when they are going to school or playing with their friends. Unfortunately, it is not only students who play this game but teachers and principals in the night of the dark systems of schools in America. Some covens require gang-rapes for rituals. They have sacrificed many infants to Satan. Vampires are real and not just in movies. Parents be alert and be selective in what your kids watch.

Doctors, nurses, and many health workers also fake it. When my sister was going to have her daughter in the hospital, she began to feel incredible pain and the nurse that was taking care of her was doing some strange things, but my sister, being a woman of God, discerned and required that the nurse should not take care of her. A pastor friend and I were seriously interceding through the night for her. You can imagine what would have happened. What about people who don't know how to pray or have no one to pray for them? That's why we pray for those in hospitals, schools, and so forth.

Satanism in Massachusetts—The Bridgewater Triangle Rituals

The Bridgewater Triangle refers to an area of about 200 square miles (520 km²) within southeastern Massachusetts in the United States. Many have said that the habitats have had some mysterious occurrences, like UFOs (it's spiritual), poltergeists (a ghost or other supernatural being supposedly responsible for physical disturbances, such as loud noises and objects being thrown around), orbs, and mutilation of cattle. There were also thunderbirds and giant snakes.

There was a famous researcher who described Bridgewater and its boundaries. Loren Coleman, in his book titled *Mysterious America*, mentioned the "towns of Abington, Rehoboth, and Freetown [are] at the points of the triangle. Brockton, Whitman, West Bridgewater, East

Bridgewater, Bridgewater, Middleboro, Dighton, Berkley, Raynham, Norton, Easton, Lakeville, Seekonk, and Taunton are inside the triangle. Others made similar claims about an area in neighboring Vermont called the Bennington Triangle."

Historical locations and landmarks in Massachusetts include Hockomock Swamp. The name means "the place where spirits dwell." Another place found within the boundaries of the Bridgewater Triangle is Dighton Rock. There were numerous reports concerning the Freetown-Fall River State Forest about different occult activities, which included sacrifices, Satanists murdering people for rituals, suicides, and gangland killings. According to the research, I found out that the Native Americans cursed the swamp centuries before because of the colonial settlers' unfair treatment of them. According to unreliable sources, a great belt called the Wampum Belt, which belonged to the Wampanoag people, was lost in King Philip's War. According to the legend, this abnormal restlessness in the site can be attributed to the curses from the Indians, owing to the loss of the belt. Whatever this means, the truth of the matter is that there is a curse, and the devil is in charge, but that should come to an end with the intercessory prayer of the intercessors. We have a job to do. We can't rest until we finish our job and the will of the Father is done on earth as it is in heaven.

Satanism in Worcester, Massachusetts
In my research of Satanism in Worcester, here's one of the demonic invasion I had found. "Satan invade Worcester on their first ever tour of North America!! Supported by local speed metal maniacs SEAX who are returning from tour and making their Debut with new vocalist Ace Hammer!!! Also supporting this bill is Portland's Kings (and Queen!) of hard and dirty rock and roll HESSIAN!!!" I found out that music is one of the center points of Satanism and traps the youth not only in Worcester but around the world.

A Satanic Altar in Delaware

She described her first date with a Satanist, who took her to a satanic altar where they had a picnic at midnight. According to Bill Maher, Ms. O'Donnell on her first appearance on the political platform as a Republican candidate on a TV show in 1999 confessed this. She said, "I dabbled in witchcraft" but "I never joined a coven." She said, "One of my first dates was on a satanic altar, and I didn't know it ..." The results of my study confirm that such altars are real and spiritually dangerous. Unfortunately, many people in America still do not know. The ignorance of spirituality in America is heartbreaking. A lot of satanic operations are ongoing, yet the church is still not recognizing them. Intercessors or prayer warriors, it's time to take the battle to another level. Demons control locations of shootings, accidents, and haunted houses. These places need intercessors to invade and destroy altars and Satanic activities there. There are territorial spirits that cause accidents or deaths. If we fail to do something about it, spiritually speaking, the problem will continue from generation to generation.

CHAPTER 15

FAMILIAR AND MARINE SPIRITS

Marine and familiar spirits control the satanic altars in Worcester, Massachusetts, and other cities in America.

I saw two giant spirits fighting against the church and the people when I did the spiritual mapping and research on the City of Worcester's invisible realm. Those were marine and familiar spirits.

Jesus stood between a lady and me in the City of Worcester at the junction of Portland Street and Franklin Street across from the City Hall. He spoke to the woman for a while and then left. While Jesus was speaking, I saw Satan and three demons standing behind the woman, and as I was watching, the demons were making a lot of noise in her ears, so she didn't hear what Jesus was telling her. As soon as Jesus left, Satan stood right where Jesus had been standing. The woman didn't realize that Jesus had left and the devil was the one speaking. I was signaling her, but she didn't want to listen. The Lord taught me this lesson. Afterward, we left and walked toward the Main Street.

Another lady standing in front of the old post office told the woman who didn't want to listen that the familiar spirit that was controlling her could not stand the power of God. "Now I got power over you, and I am going to destroy you in Jesus's name," the other lady said. It is a critical message to the church and intercessors. Satan is using familiar spirits in disguise, but many Christians do not know the difference, so they move from one church to another. They are forever learning, but they never come to maturity. Pray that the eyes of the church will open and receive the discerning of spirits.

What Is a Marine Spirit?

From Latin *marinus, marine* means "about the sea or body of water" (*Thesaurus Dictionary*). Marine spirits dwell in bodies of water, like rivers or the sea. During creation, God divided the earth into three parts. Genesis 1:6–10 (AMP) says,

> And God said, Let there be a firmament [the expanse of the sky] in the midst of the waters, and let it separate the waters [below] from the waters [above]. And God made the firmament [the expanse] and divided the waters which were under the expanse from the waters which were above the expanse. And it was so. And God called the firmament Heavens. And there was evening, and there was morning, the second day. And God said, Let the waters under the heavens be collected into one place [of standing], and let the dry land appear. And it was so. God called the dry land Earth, and the accumulated waters He called Seas. And God saw that this was good (fitting, admirable) and He approved it.

The three divisions of the earth were the following:

- the sky or atmosphere, which we call heaven
- the sea
- the dry land

In verse 28, it says God created man and gave him dominion over the fish of the sea, birds of the air, and the animals that move upon the earth. Genesis 1:28 says, "And God blessed them and said to them, Be fruitful, multiply, and fill the earth, and subdue it [using all its vast resources in the service of God and man]; and have dominion over the fish of the sea, the birds of the air, and over every living creature that moves upon the earth."

The agent that controls the marine spirits is a female spirit known as the queen of the coast. This queen governs the water kingdom of Satan. Their strategy of operation is to possess women or men and use them to fulfill their purpose. There are two types of marine-spirit-possessed people: the conscious, those who are aware that they have the water spirit and have a legal contract with the devil; and the unconscious, those who are not aware of the agreement and for that reason don't know that marine spirits have possessed them.

How Do These Marine Spirits Work?
"The thief cometh not, but to steal, kill, and destroy ..." (John 10:10a). The marine spirits possess women more than men. Their primary purpose is to torment the head to destroy their homes.

How do we identify and defeat marine spirits? God created man with a purpose that he would have dominion over the spirits in the sea (marine spirits), spirits in the air, and spirits on land. Ephesians 6:12 says, "For our struggle is not against flesh and blood, but against the rulers, against the authorities, against the powers of this dark world and the spiritual forces of evil in the heavenly realms."

The people who are most easily possessed by the water spirits are women. Satan uses them to seduce men and break apart the homes. The scripture says, "Strike the shepherd, and the sheep will scatter." The man is the head and the leader or shepherd of his home. Sex is the preliminary strategy. They use whatever means to get to the man they want to destroy. Some single women are constrained by the marine spirits only to go after married men. The reason for this is to torment the victim through a broken heart, and once they succeed, depression sets in and the person can make wrong decisions. The victims are now under their control as they offered them sex. Here's the character of those mariners.

They are never committed too much time in relationships and are unreliable. They mostly pretend to be what they are not and change their attitude and voices, depending on the situation. These marine spirits contract spiritual marriages. It means that those people have married in the realm of the spirit world. Such people do have sex in their dreams with some people they know or don't know. The people who are married but still have this kind of experience mostly realize that they constantly have problems with their spouse naturally. The reason is that the spiritual wife or husband is always jealous and will create friction in the natural marriage. Some people wake up realizing that they have discharged without remembering that they had sex in their dream. The experiences vary. These skills are not limited to bishops; they affect pastors and church members as well as unbelievers. It is very dangerous. If you go through experiences like this, you need to seek deliverance.

Some of these marine spirits come from the bloodlines of your ancestors through the covenants that they had with the gods or witchcraft practices. Some of them came from sexual partners that people allowed in their lives. Others come from movies, books, pornography, and much more, as they open doors. If it is a bloodline issue, then the grandparents contracted that covenant and passed it on to their children. Your parents also passed it on to you. So you realize that no one has ever had a successful marriage in your family, and even you are falling into the same predicament. Whatever the parents refused to deal with, the children will have to face. You need to do something now before it's too late.

CHAPTER 16

THE ISLAMIC ALTAR VERSUS THE CHRISTIAN ALTAR

Muslims Attack on the Rejected Land Given to Build a Church

It was 2002 when I was looking for land on which to plant a church. Ben, one of our dedicated ministers, brought me to his grandfather, who gave us some land. The land was rejected for many years because they had used it for refuse in the past. It turned into a hill and was very nasty. It would take a visionary to see the beauty of that piece of land. I must have had a vision for reaching the Muslims and the unchurched because it was in the Islamic community. At that time, I had newly won three influential gang leaders, and when I shared with them what I wanted to do, they encouraged me and said that they would plow the land with the workforce. O God, bless my senior minister Comfort Tetteh of blessed memory. She was a businesswoman but served with her whole heart and also supported the work. She took care of all the logistics that were needed. Emphatically, when we started working on the land, people were saying, "Oh, this is a nasty place. What will you do with this rejected property?" Within two weeks, the entire nasty hill was leveled, and it was the most beautiful piece of land one could have. The same people who had been criticizing began to say, "Oh that is amazing! What are you going to do with it?"

"We will build church," we told them.

They said, "We will be part of the church."

We were beginning to win souls instantly, and then the devil struck.

Pastor Peter Lopez said it best: "When you are doing nothing, no one talks about you." Yes, no one cares when you are not making a difference. The great apostle put it this way in 1 Corinthians 16:9: "A great door and effectual is opened unto me, and there are many adversaries." The attack rises when you turn the ordinary into extraordinary. As soon as we turned a stinky, nasty, and bushy hill into a Beulah Land, the enemy interjected. The Muslims came upon us with sharp machetes, threatening to kill us if we didn't leave the land. Their mother instigated these guys. She was also a Muslim. While they raised their swords to attack us and were making a commotion, suddenly we were surrounded by mixed multitudes. It was around 9:00 a.m. My guys were standing behind me and were just waiting for my command as to what they should do.

Don't forget that God has just converted my new members from their lifelong careers as the strongest and most ruthless gang leaders who were a threat to the society. They were acquainted with violence, so they were ready to counterattack these satanic agents. They were only waiting for my command, but I told them to leave the Muslims alone. It was a severe attack because the Muslims came upon us with sharp machetes to slay us. We feared nothing because Christ was with us. Later on, one of my friends, Pastor Honest, joined me, and we raised an altar on the land. We walked around the ground seven times and anointed it. When we finished, they also came and set up theirs against ours. Now it became altar versus altar. It turned into a battle between the Gods. They had a bucket full of some black concoction and circled around, spreading it on the land. Later, secretly, we went and stood in the middle of the land and activated our altar to speak against their altar. It was real spiritual warfare happening live. Here's what the scripture says in Psalm 53:5: "There were they in great fear, where no fear was: for God has scattered the bones of him that encamps against you: you have put them to shame because God has despised them" (KJ21)

Within three days, the Lord brought judgment upon the house of our enemies who attacked us. They were thrown into confusion and rose against one another. The same machetes that were lifted up against us were used to destroy their mother, who incited them against us. Her sons attacked her, threw her out of the house, and never returned. We saw the house she went to dwell in; it was an abandoned and broken house. Thus we were avenged by the Lord who sent us. Psalm 27:1–3 says,

The Lord is my light and my salvation; whom shall I fear? The Lord is the strength of my life; of whom shall I be afraid? When the wicked, even my enemies and my foes, came upon me to eat up my flesh, they stumbled and fell. Though a host should encamp against me, my heart shall not fear: though war should rise against me, in this will I be confident. (KJ21).

The Rules of Raising Altars
In this book, you will study the definitions and the significance of altars. An altar is where humanity meets with divinity. It could be holy or satanic, depending on who is raising it and to whom and for what purpose. Most altars are visible while others are invisible.

Altars are strategic and must be kept secret. Joshua 2:1 says, "Joshua the son of Nun secretly sent two men out of Shittim as spies, saying, 'Go, view the land, including Jericho.' They went and came into the house of a prostitute whose name was Rahab, and slept there." The spies went secretly and did their transactions in secret. They also carried the promise Yahweh gave to Joshua. Joshua 1:3 says, "Every place that the sole of your foot shall tread upon, that have I given unto you, as I said unto Moses." As the spies walked on the land, they raised invisible altars. What were they doing in the night in Rahab's house? Consequently, they were praying. Because of the altar, they warned the woman to tie the scarlet thread upon her window. Lo and behold, the entire wall fell, but her house built on the wall was still standing because the altar was speaking. You need to keep it secret because the satanic or demonic human forces who understand what an altar is will attack if they see you raising one. Joshua 2:7 says, "The men pursued them the way to the Jordan to the fords: and as soon as those who pursued them had gone out, they shut the gate."

One must mature spiritually. Raising altars is not for kids. It's a serious business and must be carried out as such. One must be filled with the Holy Spirit and must be prayerful.

Faith is the key to success. Mark 11:24 says, "Therefore I tell you, whatever you ask for in prayer, believe that you have received it, and it will be yours" (NIV).

The word of God is the only weapon of which the enemy is afraid. Activation of the word of God in raising altars grants sure victory. When we use the word of God, heaven is deployed to do battle in the earth and the realms of the spirit. Isaiah 55:10–11 says, "So is my word that goes out from my mouth: It will not return to me empty, but will accomplish what I desire and achieve the purpose for which I sent it."

Fervent strategic prayer is the centrality of the raising of altars. Without prayer, forget about spiritual altars. In 1 Kings 18:36–37, it says,

> At the time of sacrifice, the prophet Elijah stepped forward and prayed: "LORD, the God of Abraham, Isaac and Israel, let it be known today that you are God in Israel and that I am your servant and have done all these things at your command. Answer me, Lord, answer me, so these people will know that you, Lord, are God and that you are turning their hearts back again.

Consecrated anointing oil is important. Genesis 35:14 says, "Jacob set up a stone pillar at the place where God had talked with him, and he poured out a drink offering on it; he also poured oil on it." Satan has polluted whatever Yahweh uses. The unbelievers pour a drink, water, and blood offerings to Satan. They usually establish their altars with blood, and that makes them efficient. At the crucifixion of Christ on the cross as the ultimate sacrifice, we saw that the soldiers gave Him a drink, but He refused. The enemies pierced his side with the spear; then water and blood gushed out and poured on the ground. It was the highest altar. He did it all. Jesus said, "It is finished." That tells us that we no longer need a blood sacrifice. Now we use the anointing oil because our Lord commanded us to. The anointing oil symbolizes the power of the Holy Spirit, and sometimes water represents the word of God and also the Holy Spirit.

About sacrificial offerings, we read in 2 Samuel 24:18–25,

On that day Gad went to David and said to him, "Go up and build an altar to the Lord on the threshing floor of Araunah the Jebusite." So David went up, as the Lord had commanded through Gad. When Araunah looked and saw the king and his officials coming toward him, he went out and bowed down before the king with his face to the ground. Araunah said, "Why has my lord the king come to his servant?" "To buy your threshing floor," David answered, "so I can build an altar to the Lord, which the plague on the people may stop." Araunah said to David, "Let my lord the king take whatever he wishes and offer it up. Here are oxen for the burnt offering, and here are threshing sleds and ox yokes for the wood. Your Majesty, Araunah[d] gives all this to the king." Araunah also said to him, "May the Lord your God accept you." But the king replied to Araunah, "No, I insist on paying you for it. I will not sacrifice to the Lord my God burnt offerings that cost me nothing." So David bought the threshing floor and the oxen and paid fifty shekels[e] of silver for them. David built an altar to the Lord there and sacrificed burnt offerings and fellowship offerings. Then the Lord answered his prayer in behalf of the land, and the plague on Israel stopped.

King David understood what a sacrificial offering is. Araunah gave him the piece of land where he could build the altar and the animal to sacrifice free of charge, but David refused because it was free. His logic was if it doesn't cost, it's not a sacrifice. In verse 24, the king said, "I will not offer anything that will cause me nothing to the Lord my God." Here's what the *English-Greek Dictionary* has to say about the definition of the word *sacrifice*:

> Make an offering to a god; (God) sell at a loss; tolerate the loss of; surrender something for the sake of something more valuable; act of offering objects to divinity, thereby making them holy. The motivation for sacrifice is to perpetuate, intensify, or reestablish a connection between the human and the divine. It is often intended to gain the favor of the god or to placate divine wrath. The term has come to be applied correctly to blood sacrifice, which entails the death or destruction of the thing sacrificed. The sacrifice of fruits, flowers, or crops (bloodless sacrifice) is more often referred to as an offering.

Money can represent life because it's the sweat of the one who is offering it. As the devil has defiled the animal blood sacrifice, Jesus did it once and for all, so we need not provide any blood or drink offering. Sacrifice means that you are giving up something that will cost you or paying a high price that may be very painful, but in return, you will receive a greater reward than what you gave. It's a sacrifice because you are losing everything you gave, but spiritually speaking, you are gaining the upper hand on the matter presented to God. I hear you say, "Oh, Christ has made the sacrifice for us, and we need not sacrifice any longer," and you are right—if you don't want to go deeper by engaging your enemy supernaturally through a higher level of strategic intercession. Raising certain types of prayer altars takes the battle to a different realm. Some principles govern the supernatural and the cosmological realms. Here's the policy set forth not under the law but prelaw or before the law. Genesis 8:20–22 says,

> Then Noah built an altar to the LORD and, taking some of all the clean animals and clean birds, he sacrificed burnt offerings on it. The LORD smelled the pleasing aroma and said in his heart: "Never again will I curse the ground because of humans, even though every inclination of the human heart is evil from childhood. And never again will I destroy all living creatures, as I have done. As long as the earth endures, seedtime and harvest, cold and heat, summer and winter, day and night will never cease."

Engaging the Spiritual Forces through Altars
Anoint the ground. Anoint the building or the object you want to liberate. Sanctify it and repossess it. Sometimes if there is a community that has violence, you must anoint the grounds and then cast out the spirit of wickedness in high places.

You may be anointing some sensitive locations. Target an area for the reason of taking it. It could be a city, a community, a neighborhood, a house, or a family. Declare it for Christ. We must also realize that there are demonic forces that are known to be territorial spirits and strongholds in that area. It may be shrines, ghettoes, temples, playgrounds, government facilities, or business areas and so forth. One must be sagacious and tactical. You are God's secret service agent, his air force and Navy SEAL. Here are some strategies to use, but always be in tune with the direction of the Holy Spirit. Bring a small bottle with anointing oil with you, and anoint your hands or the soles of your shoes before you enter that territory if you are suspicious. As you enter a building, touch the walls. If you can't reach the walls, you will activate the oil under the soles of your shoes without any aggressiveness in the natural. Detonate your nuclear weapon of mass destruction against the territorial spirits and the strongholds as the Holy Spirit reveals to you. When you are touching the walls or using the oil, be very attentive. Nobody is supposed to know what you are doing. To exemplify these tactics, I went to visit a throne priest (a voodoo man) while the ritual was in motion. The priest or witchcraft practitioner happened to be in the same reconciliation council with me. I wanted to reach him with the gospel and destroy his powers. I don't know why I did this. It was dangerous. (*Caution*! I don't advise anyone to do this unless the Holy Spirit leads him or her.) I went to visit him while he was performing his rituals. When he saw me, he motioned to me to come. At that time, I had already anointed my hands and feet. I shook his hand. He offered me some of the food and meat, but I declined it. He was on a mission to win me, and I was on special assignment to invade him and his household. God had saved his family through other Christians, but we were still waiting for his appointment with God.

Attack on A Pastor Friend

It was 1993. I was a freshman in the Pastoral College in Accra after the conversion of Okumo the chief priest of Dipo Custom. I was in my dorm one evening, and our School Body President sent his Vice to call me. He didn't tell me that it was urgent, but the volume of his voice indicated that they needed me for an emergency, so I ran after him. There lay a friend, fellow pastor, and classmate unconscious. He was dying, gasping for air, and was falling off his top bunk. His body was stiff. I asked them to bring him to the bottom bunk. While praying for him, I saw a multitude of voodoo men chasing the pastor in the jungle. They all had rods, spears, and swords and were all beating him. He was helpless. The angel of the Lord appeared and scattered them as I prayed. He then lifted the man of God. As soon as he lifted him, the brother was freed and immediately became conscious.

I asked him what had happened when he went on Easter vacation a week before in Togo. He told us that he'd gone to convert a voodoo priest. He said the man gave his life to Christ, but he didn't have the chance to break the altars, shrines, and idols. He planned to do it when he returned to the village because the semester of the Pastoral College was over and he had no time to do it. He was from Togo. I told him that the man had changed his mind and that was why they wanted to kill him. Those are urgent "one-hundred-hour operations of spiritual Desert Storm," so you don't leave anything to chance. He witnessed to the voodoo priest and converted him because he was motivated by my story of how Okumo was converted.

He didn't ask how I did it. He became a good friend of mine and prayer partner after his deliverance. Please don't make the same mistake by raising certain types of strategic altars or engaging in certain strategic warfare just because you are reading this book or other books. You need guidance from the Holy Spirit and people who are already on the field. The greatest wise man said, "Wisdom is the principal thing. Therefore get wisdom: and with all thy getting get understanding" (Proverbs 4:7).

Anoint stones or a small object as a point of contact, drop them off on the ground where no one sees you, and then leave. Wherever you are, you may activate those points of contact in prayer warfare. Prayer walks are mostly famous for these acts. You may anoint some particular streets where you want to see a change. It must not be a one-time operation but continue until you see the desired result.

There is no distance in prayer. As you stand on the grounds, wherever you are in the world, you can still connect to any part of the world by anointing the grounds you stand on and entering into the supernatural realm through the power of the Holy Spirit.

Adopt a street. Drop a pin in a neighborhood that experiences violence, Satanism, nightclubs, and so on. Drop an anointed pin, or, if possible, nail it to a tree or the ground at the junction of that street or the neighborhood. America's military air supremacy around the world has given us an advantage over our enemies. It is these specific tactics that the prayer warriors also adopt. Spiritual air superiority is vital for our survival. The only solution to the racial violence and the police shootings, the hunting of black males, the anger and frustration, and the fear is the fervent and effectual prayer of the righteous.

Revelatory and prophetic prayer is the revelatory ministry that enables you to hear and see what heaven is saying concerning the situation. You can only enforce the will of God on earth if you deploy Him to take over the battle on the earth realm as He shows to you in the realm of the spirit. John Knox says, "God can do nothing except somebody prays." We prophetically declare what must be enforced, what God is doing, or destroy the operations of the enemy in the city.

Confess the Word with Revelation until it becomes Rhema
Rhema is the life that proceeds out of the word of God through Holy Spirit revelation. Religious confession of the word of God without a revelation makes it a little difficult. Many people confess the word without revelation. Recently, around 2013, while I was praying for a lady, I felt a struggle in the spirit. She was resisting the prayer. I saw in the realm of the spirit cancer descending from the tallest tree in the area toward her. I am not saying that the tree produced cancer, but the Lord was showing me the distance or how far away that disease was. No medical instrument could detect that or any satanic spell. The disease was still accelerating its progress to access her body, so when I saw that, I cast it out and it left. Unfortunately, two weeks later, this couple called me and wanted to meet with me to discuss an issue. As usual, I went, but to my surprise, she was furious with me. She asked, "Why did you cast out cancer from me? I confess the word of God every day, and also my doctor recently told me that every test they did was good."

I cautioned her, "I have not prophesied nor informed you that you have it. I just cast it out because I saw it coming, and it's not my business to discuss it."

She was still angry and said to me, "I think you have a demon and are not operating under the Holy Spirit."

I didn't want to continue the conversation, so I asked if we could pray and end the meeting. I was deeply hurt when she said I was not operating under the Holy Spirit. The moment I told them, "Let's pray," I felt the spirit of the cancer flew speedily into her again. I could do nothing about it. Later I tried calling them, but they ignored my calls.

Six months later, she called. I was excited to connect with them finally, but this time, the speech was different. She was in tears; her voice was shaking, and fear seized her tone. She was in agony and was apologizing for having accused me, having said that I was operating with a demonic spirit and not the Holy Spirit. She asked me to pray for her and to forgive her. I did pray and forgave her, but she specifically told me again, "I want genuine forgiveness and prayer from your heart."

She said that a few weeks after the accusation, her doctor, whom she believed more than the Holy Spirit, pronounced her a cancer patient, and she'd been in the battle ever since. It broke me, and I tried to visit her four times, but it never happened. Four times, I was on my way to their house, but something happened and they told me to come another time. God never allowed me to visit her. I did pray with them on the phone, and also during our forty-day fasting and prayer, we held her in our prayer, but the Holy Spirit showed me that she would die. No, I didn't want her to die, but it happened. She rejected the day of visitation. Jesus said, "Anyone who speaks a word against the Son of Man will receive forgiveness, but anyone who speaks against the Holy Spirit will not be forgiven, either in this age or in the age to come" (Matthew 12:32).

The sin against the Holy Spirit is when He uses somebody and then people ascribe the glory to demons. God has forgiven her because of His abundance grace, but she did not give access to her heart concerning the operation of the Holy Spirit. I wrote this story to warn people who think that confessing the word of God is enough and they don't need fervent prayer or the revelatory ministry or that the gift of the discerning of spirits is dangerous. Speaking the word from the head and mouth alone has no power; it's simply a religious practice. You must connect to the realm of the Spirit whenever you pray. Your heart, soul, and spirit must be in tune. See what you confess, and confess what you see. As you pray this way, the Lord will open your eyes to see what is going on in the invisible world. Things that we don't see are stronger than what we see. Jesus said, "The Spirit gives life; the flesh counts for nothing. The words I have spoken to you— they are full of the Spirit and life" (John 6:63). Don't just pray and confess. Pray passionately and fervently. "The prayer of a righteous person is powerful and effectual. Elijah was a human being, even as we are. He prayed earnestly that it would not rain, and it did not rain on the land for three and a half years" (James 5:16b–17).

Prayer Walk

The definition of prayer-walking is "praying on-site with insight. It is simply praying in the very places that we expect God to bring forth His answers," according to C. Peter Wagner in *Praying with Power.*

Engaging the demonic forces through altars, as mentioned earlier, requires a prayer walk. I encourage you to get some friends together and start this assignment today. Don't wait.

Spiritual Preparation

Fast and pray. A vigil is very powerful. I recommend 24-7 prayer chains. Allow the Holy Spirit to guide you in how many days and the type of prayer you will engage in. Confess any unconfessed sin in your life. Forgive those who offend you. Repent of any sin against one another, including your spouse or spiritual authority. Do not give the enemy an advantage to accuse you and then torment you thereby.

Prayer Cover

As you pray with a partner, cover one another. For example, if you are supposed to be the one praying tomorrow, your partner should fast and pray for you today. The one covering you will shut down any attack that the enemy will set in advance against you.

CHAPTER 17

WHAT ARE SPIRITUAL GATES?

And How Can We Invade Them?

Before we answer the question about spiritual gates, let's first see what the physical barriers are. In our world, there are doors and windows, but I want to deal with gates in this respect. It is an entrance or way out.

Dealing with Personal Gates

Everyone has gates in his or her personal life. These gates represent the five senses, namely seeing, feeling, hearing, smelling, touching. The eyes see. The ears hear. The mouth tastes. The nose smells. The hand touches. All of the activities mentioned here enters into one's soul. The sexual organs are also a critical access to the mind. They open greater doors for satanic covenants. Worldly or wild music are all controlled by the spirit of lust and violence. In the same way, praise music also elevates your inner person, and inspirational worship cools down your soul and then prepares the spirit to ascend to the presence of God.

Gates of the City and Nations

Gates provide protection. Biblically, the gates and gateways of the eastern cities had and still have an important part not only in the defense but in the public ceremony of the place. They sometimes take gates to represent the area or the city itself. Genesis 22:17 says, "Blessing, I will bless you and multiplying I will multiply your descendants as the stars of the heaven and as the sand which is on the seashore, and your descendants shall possess the 'gate' of their enemies." They use them for particular purposes, which I mention here:

1. Places of public resort—Genesis 19:1 says, "The two angels arrived at Sodom in the evening, and Lot was sitting in the gateway of the city. When he saw them, he got up to meet them and bowed down with his face to the ground."

2. Places for public deliberation, administration of justice, city hall, or of the audience for kings and rulers or ambassadors or the place where the city officials meet and make decisions concerning the city. In a simple definition in modern terms, a gate is the business boardroom. Deuteronomy 16:18 says, "You shall appoint judges and officers in all your gates, which the Lord your God gives you, according to your tribes, they shall judge the people with just judgment."

3. Public markets—in 2 Kings 7:1, it says, "Elisha replied, 'Hear the word of the Lord. It is what the Lord says: About this time tomorrow, a seah of the finest flour will sell for a shekel and two seahs of barley for a shekel at the gate of Samaria." In the cities of the unbelievers, the open spaces near the entrances were used as places for sacrifice. Acts 14:13 says, "The priest of Zeus, whose temple was just outside the city, brought bulls and wreaths to the city gates because he and the crowd wanted to offer sacrifices to them" (Paul and Barnabas). In 2 Kings 23:8, we read, "Josiah brought all the priests from the towns of Judah and desecrated the high places, from Geba to Beersheba, where the priests had burned incense. He broke down the gateway at the entrance of the Gate of Joshua, the city governor, which was on the left of the town gate."

The Significance of Gates
They are regarded therefore as the position of high importance. The gates of the cities were guarded to a high degree and closed at nightfall. Deuteronomy 3:5 says, "All these cities were fortified with high walls and with gates and bars, and there were also a great many unwalled villages." Joshua 2:5 tells us, "At dark, when it was time to close the city gate, they left. I don't know which way they went. Go after them quickly. You may catch up with them." Psalm 107:18 says, "They loathed all food and drew near the gates of death."

Every intercessor needs to understand the importance of spiritual gates and how to use them. According to the previous scriptures, we discovered that entrances are necessary for spiritual warfare if we want to take our communities, cities, and nations back to our God. Jericho had high walls and large gates. For the Israelites to take possession of the Promised Land, they needed to conquer Jericho. According to Nehemiah, the walls and the gates signified strength and protection of the city of Jerusalem, and whenever they were broken down, it brought shame and disgrace to that nation or city. After he had received a report from Jerusalem, it troubled him. He sought God's presence for the walls and the gates to be rebuilt. Nehemiah 1:3 says, "They said to me, 'Those who survived the exile and are back in the province are in great trouble and disgrace. The wall of Jerusalem is broken down, and its gates have been burned with fire." Nehemiah 3:3 says, "The sons of Hassenaah rebuilt the Fish Gate. They laid its beams and put its doors and bolts and bars in place."

Paul the Apostle said, "For the things which are seen are temporal; the things which are not seen are eternal." (2 Corinthians 4:18 KJB 2000) I paraphrased. "The invisible things are stronger than the visible things," so are the spiritual gates. If intercessors want to have ongoing spiritual warfare, then it must be done strategically by knowing how to spot the right target and hit it at once. There is no time to fail in our goal if we have the right information. To investigate those areas, we need spiritual mapping, refer to chapter 11. The three areas mentioned earlier are to be considered significant in spiritual warfare. The first is the areas of public worship, like mosques, temples, and even churches. Many shrines, temples, mosques, and even some churches raise altars that activate the presence of evil spirits or Satan's angels, known as territorial spirits. These territorial spirits fight the people, the progress of the city, and the word of God in the lives of the citizens. They invoke spirits by burning incense and candles and offering blood sacrifices.

The second is places for public deliberation, like the place of the administration of justice, the audience for kings and rulers or ambassadors, city halls, and more. These places are where they decide major issues concerning the nations. The demonic forces mainly influence, invoke, and preside over the conferences. In the elite countries, they activate the evil spirits in secret. But in Africa, it is part of the day-to-day practice of the unbelieving traditional rulers. They pour libations and call the gods and ancestors to guide them. Some high positions are occupied by satanic influential personalities who make laws that defy God's. This is why it is expedient to pray for every election. If gates are the modern-day boardrooms, then the decisions taken there have enough power to put the land in bondage or freedom.

The third is public markets and businesses. In Africa, it's easy to see those practices in the past and present in the cities and the countryside. They might not have a visible gate, but spiritually, those gates are their public meeting places. They don't just sacrifice the blood of animals anywhere; it has to be in the designated spot. These three areas are where the powers of spiritual darkness hold their conferences and make critical decisions about the land and the people. These same places are where they enter covenants with the devil and raise altars through sacrifices.

A Prophetic Word Destroyed the Gates
The town where the Lord sent me is called Agbom; the meaning of that is "gates." Another city is known as Asitey. They were both

physical and spiritual strongholds for that state just as Jericho was to the Promised Land. But thank God for the blood of Jesus. In 1993, after the conversion of Okumo the high priest of Dipo, the elders of Okumo opened a prophetic door for me to see the king. That king was fearful, and for him to call you to his house, you had to be shaken already to your shoes. Prayer conquers the power of darkness and brings the will of God to pass. Nene Terpkernor Adipa II prophetically pronounced what would become a victory for the kingdom of our God in his city. The messengers of Okumo told Prophetess Comfort Darley and me that their chiefs and spiritual elders had ordered them to bring us with them. Their names were Nene Adjimeh and Nene Asa. These are the grandmasters of the Dipo custom. They also told us that Nene Terpkernor Adipa II wanted to see us. We told them the kingdom of God had nothing to do with the kingdom of darkness, and for that reason, we would not go. We would visit the king; he was our ruler. When we went to see the king, he told us, "I, myself wanted to be baptized so if Okumo gave his life to Christ, who am I to judge?" He added, "I will call you when I am ready." He gave us money and called for a taxi to take us home.

I never had a dream of possessing the gate, Agbom. The Lord brought me to that city in 2001. It was just around the same time the king died. The Presbyterian church refused to officiate the funeral service because of the rituals that they performed at the burial, and they were right. The elders and the family came to me, begging me to officiate the funeral ceremony. It was on a Friday after our prayer and fasting; I wanted to rest in my room. The Lord revealed to me the chief linguist and the elders of the city were coming to see me. He said, "Whatever they ask, do it for them." I was still in the room thinking about the vision when they came. So I agreed and did what they requested. They asked me to officiate the king's funeral service and the vigil. The vigil turned into a revival and salvation night. It was an opportunity for me to tell the elders, family, and the entire city the king's prophecy, which he voiced: "When he needs me for his salvation, he will call me." He did not call when he was alive, but now he did for his family and the city to be saved. That night, I preached about the curses of sacrificing to Satan, and the benefit of the sacrifice of Christ on the cross. Apparently, salvation came to his family and the entire community. Our weekly all-night, which we hold consistently at the public square, broke the gates of brass and cut the bars of iron of the city in pieces. God had opened the heart gates of the people and the city of the king of glory to come in (Psalm 24). His wife, sons, and daughters and the entire family along with many people in the community joined us. The elders always call me when they need prayers or advice.

The Gates of Death
According to Psalm 107:16, 18, "For he breaks down gates of bronze and cuts through bars of iron ... They loathed all food and drew near the gates of death." These were deadly barriers that Israel had to deal with before possessing their possession. Many people are spiritually dead. Until the intercessors take the battle to the gates of the enemy, multitudes will continue their eternity in hell. We have the power to break the gates of bronze and the bars of iron.

The Angel and the Gates
When they kept Peter in prison, the angel went in to deliver him from the jail cell but first had to deal with the gates that kept Peter in bondage. Acts 12:10 says, "They passed the first and second guards and came to the iron gate leading to the city. It opened for them by itself, and they went through it. When they had walked the length of one street, suddenly the angel left him." Joshua 2:5 says, "At dusk, when it was time to close the city gate, they left. I don't know which way they went. Go after them quickly. You may catch up with them." This scripture implies the gates were also to shut up those inside, so they couldn't go out and to prevent those outside from coming in. There were watchmen or security set to guard, open, and close the gates. Those people vowed to arrest the spies because their lives were in jeopardy. How about Satan? He had spiritual forces or territorial spirits that he assigned to each city gate and individuals as well.

Intercessors do not need to be gentle about these. It has to be spiritual warfare. The devil uses the gates as a jail to keep many in custody in the invisible realm. We have to break those gates open with the power of God. Every gate has a lock, and before you can enter, you need a key. Teaching more about the subject concerning keys now is imperative.

CHAPTER 18

THE KEYS OF THE KINGDOM

Keys Signify Authority and Power

One of the most important terms in our daily lives is **key.** You will be locked out if you don't have a house key. You might need your car key in order to access and start your car. You need a key or badge to enter your job. If you cannot open the doors of your job, it could be that there's a problem that needs to be fixed or you are no longer an employee there. At an induction into an office, they give a golden key to individual officers of the government. The key suspended on a gold chain around the neck on their ceremonial uniform symbolizes their authority. Those in the higher ranks of the city present keys to citizens as an honor. Biblically, keys were a symbol of power. When one received keys from a person in authority, it signified the entrusting of that person with an outstanding charge. Jesus Christ, our Master, entrusted Peter with authority and power to open the gates of the kingdom and to preach the gospel on earth.

The Greek noun for *key* is *kleis,* and the verb for *key* is *kleo.* They use both of these terms in Greek literature. In classical Greek, *key* described keys as well as a bar, catch, or bolt. It also carried the idea of authority (the ability to open something). Here's the scripture reference concerning the Greek word *kleis* (cf. Judges 3:25, 1 Chronicles 9:27, and Isaiah. 22:22).

A general summary for the word *key* in the scripture is "a symbol of authority." In Judges 3:25 and other instances, "key" has a literal meaning, yet some other scriptures place a symbolical spiritual significance on it (see Isaiah 22:22, Matthew 16:19, and Revelation 1:18, 3:7, 9:1, and 20:1).

Matthew 16:19 says, "I will give you the keys of the kingdom of heaven; whatever you bind on earth will be bound in heaven, and whatever you loose on earth will be loosed in heaven."

To understand this deeper, *key* represents knowledge of Jesus Christ.

Five Types of Keys Christ Gave to the Church

1. The Key of the Kingdom of Heaven

The key to the kingdom represents the knowledge of Jesus Christ. The Pharisees and the Scribes had a knowledge of who Christ was, but they refused to accept Him and they also hindered the people who wanted to know. Jesus knew, and He rebuked them. Matthew 23:13 says, "But woe to you, scribes and Pharisees, hypocrites, because you shut off the kingdom of heaven from people; for you do not enter in yourselves, nor do you allow those who are entering to go in." Jesus gave the keys of the Kingdom to Peter after His resurrection from the dead to enhance the Father's business.

The Revelation that Gave Peter the Keys of the Kingdom

The people at Jesus's time did not know who He was. They were confused. Some thought he was one of the old prophets. Even some of Jesus's disciples did not know Him intimately. He asked them, "Who do you say I am?" Matthew 16:15–16 says, "He said to them, 'But who do you think that I am?' Simon Peter answered, 'You are the Christ, the Son of the living God.'"

After the Holy Spirit through Peter unveiled who Jesus was, that He was the Christ according to Matthew 16:16, it was a kingdom revelation that moved Jesus Christ to delegate His authority of the keys of the kingdom to Peter, but first He must be glorified through His death and resurrection. The Holy Spirit must come, and then the apostles must be endowed with power from on high.

After he receives power, Peter can then use his keys Jesus promised him in verse 19 "I will give you the keys of the kingdom ..." Acts 2:14 says, "Then Peter stood up with the Eleven, raised his voice and addressed the crowd: 'Fellow Jews and all of you who live in Jerusalem, let me explain this to you; listen carefully to what I say ...'" Peter spoke with authority and boldness such as had never been seen among the priests, scribes, or Pharisees. It was incredible, so God opened the heart gates of the people to establish His kingdom in them. It began with a question. Acts 2:36–41 says,

> Therefore let all Israel be assured of this: God has made this Jesus, whom you crucified, both Lord and Messiah. When the people heard this, they were cut to the heart and said to Peter and the other apostles, "Brothers, what shall we do?" Peter replied, "Repent and be baptized, every one of you, in the name of Jesus Christ for the forgiveness of your sins. And you will receive the gift of the Holy Spirit. The promise is for you and your children and for all who are far off—for all whom the Lord our God will call." Those who accepted his message were baptized, and about three thousand were added to their number that day.

Praise God for the intercession of the apostles and the disciples in the upper room, praying until the Holy Spirit came to accomplish the workload Jesus left for them. Can you see the power of the keys through the invasion of the Holy Spirit? Let's observe the life of Peter the disciple of Jesus without the Holy Spirit.

Peter denied Jesus three times. John 18:17, 25–27 says,

Then the servant girl who kept the door said to Peter, "You are not also one of this Man's disciples, are you?" He said, "I am not." ... Now Simon Peter stood and warmed himself. Therefore they said to him, "You are not also one of His disciples, are you?" He denied it and said, "I am not!" ... One of the servants of the high priest, a relative of him whose ear Peter cut off, said, "Did I not see you in the garden with Him?" Peter then denied again, and immediately a rooster crowed.

The Apostle Peter after He Received Power (The Key of the Kingdom)

He preached, and instantly, three thousand souls gave their lives to Christ. At his second preaching, five thousand did, and at the third teaching, seven thousand were saved. Look at the fulfillment of the prophetic numbers. At the time of Moses in the wilderness, three thousand men perished at once, and now Peter recovered those souls at just one preaching. Jesus fed five thousand men and seven thousand souls, but those people were just following for the food and the miracles. At Peter's preaching, those people willingly gave themselves to be baptized and to be saved. No wonder Jesus said to His disciples, "Greater works will you do." John 14:12 says, "I tell you the truth, anyone who believes in me will do the same works I have done, and even greater works, because I am going to be with the Father." Why did Jesus say those who believed in Him would do greater works because He was going to the Father? He said it was expedient for Him to go away. Otherwise, the Holy Spirit would not come and then we would not receive power (the keys of the kingdom) and that would allow the devil to continue his wickedness to humanity forever.

2. The Keys of the Kingdom in Our Personal Lives

As Adam lost the key or authority to the devil, God Himself couldn't access the human heart since then. It is explained in the Lord's Prayer. How can God have access to your heart? Jesus said, "I stand at the door of your heart and knock. If anyone hears my voice and opens it, I will come in with my Father and eat with Him ..." He also said,

"He who has ears, let him listen to what the Spirit is saying. It means that until you allow Him in, the Holy Spirit will not come. You must be willing and make yourself available; then He can speak to you. He can't teach you, and He cannot change you. In many occasions people would opt their desire to be educated in the things of God. I do asked if they are willing to learn with passion. Learning happens when the student empties his or her heart and comes with an open mind—when the person accepts the fact that he or she doesn't know and wants to know. To clarify this point, I am saying that you have the keys to your life because God created you in His image. You are not a robot. He gave you willpower, and you can decide to yield to Him or not.

3. The Key to Death and the Gates of Hell
The following are three types;

Identifying the gates of hell.

- **It is the strategies of the enemy to secretly find ways to fight you.**
- **Attrition** – It is an action or process of gradually reducing the strength or the effectiveness of someone or something through a sustained attack or pressure. The synonyms are; wearing down, wearing away, weakening, debilitation, enfeebling, sapping, attenuation, gradual loss. I hope by now you have identied the areas in your life or marriage, ministry, business, and so forth of what and where the devil had declared a constant battle in your life, one after another to sap your strength and wear you down in order to destroy you. This was exact tactics used to destroy Samson.
- **Devices or weapons could be deformation of your character.** Blackmailing and attacking your image by using people closer to you.
- **Disappointments and confusions.**

The Valley of Darkness and Shadows of Death

King David lived half of his life in fear and trembling in the wilderness. He said, yes though I walk through the (darkness) valley of the shadow of death but fear no evil. There are sometimes in the life of everyone when you find yourself in this strange and terrible situations. You may not even know how you got there but it's a set up of the enemy. It is called the gates of hell. But revelations will reveal secret plans of the enemy then authoritative prayer will break it open.

The gates of Bronze and Bars of Iron

Psalm 107:14, 16, 18, 20 says,

> He brought them out of darkness, and the shadow of death, and broke their chains in pieces ... for he has broken gates of bronze and cut the bars of iron in two ... Their soul abhorred all manner of food and drew near the gates of death. He sent His word and healed them, and delivered them from their destruction.

Jesus, during His three days in hell, took the keys of death and the gates of hell and came to His disciples. He gave them the Great Commission to preach the gospel in power by the demonstration of the Holy Spirit.

Matthew 28:18 says, **"Then Jesus came to them and said, 'All authority in heaven and on earth has been given to me.'"** Look at the phrase "Then Jesus came to them." From where was He coming? It was after His *resurrection*, so He came from hell or Hades. According to Peter, Jesus was not resting when He died but rather went to accomplish His fight with the devil, who had the power over death and the gates of hell. He took the keys from him. The first Adam gave the keys away, but the second Adam brought the keys back. Let's examine the scripture 1 Peter 3:18–19: "For Christ also suffered once for sins, the righteous for the unrighteous, to bring you to God. He was put to death in the body but made alive in the Spirit. After being made alive, he went and made a proclamation (preached) to the imprisoned spirits."

"When the second Adam brought the keys, He said, '... All authority in heaven and on earth has been given to me. Go ye, therefore ...'" (Matthew 28:18).

Now we have the "keys of death and the gates of hell."

It was a **delegated authority** to cast out the spirit of death and infirmity. To enforce this violent spiritual act, we need to do effective, fervent prayer of intercession. As I have said in the other chapters about raising the dead, when praying for the sick who are near to death, we need to deal with two spirits. Through the gift of discerning, you will know which spirit is at work. I have experienced a lot of situations in certain circumstances when the spirit of death needed to be cast out immediately because one might recover from sickness after medical treatment but later die. The point I am trying to make here is it is not the disease that kills but the spirit of death. I must clarify that we need a higher level of anointing to deal with such situations. We must also remember that Jesus did not send us to raise every dead person because the righteous will sleep when He accomplishes His job on earth. There were several situations in the 1990s where I prayed for the dead, and they rose, but many wanted to go back. There was one lady who died three times, and I raised her three times, but she needed to go so I allowed her to.

There was also a voodoo priest who converted to Christ, and he died suddenly in the middle of the service. Typically this happened during the sermon. I would pray and then he would come back to life. This thing started affecting me to the point that even when someone was falling asleep during service, I would get scared as if the person was also dying. I had to search and find out what was happening with this man. The Holy Spirit revealed the truth, and I asked him. He feared to leave the voodoo practices because he was the head of the

Samuel T. Padmore

family. Traditionally, every family head willingly—or unwillingly in Africa—was compelled to authorize the practice of rituals that evoked the spirits of the ancestors and the gods that protected the families. He wanted to serve God, but at the same time, he was scared he would die. I told him he had two choices. He could deny the devil and be saved or submit to the fear and die. He eventually died, and at this point, I did not bother myself with raising him up because he made a choice, but after his death, all his sons gave their lives to Christ.

4. The Key of David
Revelation 3:7 says, "To the angel of the church in Philadelphia write: These are the words of him who is holy and true, who holds the key of David. What he opens no one can shut, and what he shuts no one can open."

Here's what Emeka Nwankpa said concerning this scripture, "This speaks of one who possesses ultimate authority beyond any man. No one can undo anything the Lord has done or repair or reverse anything he has undone."

Now that we know that we have the authority, we are to take the battle to the gates of the enemy, invade, and detonate our atomic power and authority to destroy the kingdom of darkness which is waging war against the church. The key of David is the master key that can open any spiritual door of any jail to bring deliverance to the captive. The believer needs to reposition himself to activate a higher level of anointing to break open the prison doors and loose those in bandage and captivity.

In Luke 4:18–19, Jesus said,

> The Spirit of the Lord is on me because he has anointed me to proclaim good news to the poor. He has sent me to proclaim (preach deliverance) freedom for the prisoners (captives) and

recovery of sight to the blind, to set the oppressed free, to proclaim the year of the Lord's favor.

Isaiah 45:1–3 says,

This is what the Lord says to his anointed, to Cyrus, whose right hand I take hold of to subdue nations before him and to strip kings of their armor, to open doors before him so that gates will not be shut: I will go before you and will level the mountains; I will break down gates of bronze and cut through bars of iron. I will give you hidden treasures, riches stored in secret places so that you may know that I am the Lord, the God of Israel, who summons you by name.

Corporate anointing of intercessors invades the kingdom of darkness;
It causes the robust and high walls with their gates to fall instantly. Joshua and his troop marched around the walls of Jericho seven times, and they fell. The apostles interceded with a loud voice, and doors were opened, foundations shocked, and chains broken. Can you imagine—the angels freed all the prisoners, but none ran away? Paul said to the warden, according to Acts 16:28. "We are all here. Do not hurt yourself." Apostle Peter in Acts 12 saw the angel of the Lord open his gates and break his chains. By the power of corporate intercession, the prison doors and the iron gate opened of their own accord because the church interceded for them. Here's how Brother Luke observed it later in Acts 12:5. "Peter was therefore kept in prison, but constant prayer was made to God for him by the church"

The key of David is the master key to unlock any door or gate.
It is the authority of the lion of the tribe of Judah. It's the power of strategic prayer. Walking in the constant attitude of intercession activates unexpected victories over the kingdom of darkness and unleashes liberty on a nation, city, community, business, church, or individual.

5. The Key of Knowledge

Jesus said that the Pharisees had taken the key of awareness of the kingdom. Let's observe Luke 11:52: "Woe to you experts in the law, because you have taken away the key to knowledge. You yourselves have not entered, and you have hindered those who were entering." The devil's expertise is in operating through the darkness because that's where his power manipulates and enslaves people. He always tries to keep people in bondage. As long as they don't have any knowledge about their freedom, he holds them in captivity. It was the devil's primary purpose to eliminate Jesus Christ because He was revealing his deeds and opening the spiritual eyes of the people by His teachings. Here's what Jesus has to tell the people in John 8:12. When Jesus spoke again to the people, he said, "I am the light of the world. Whoever follows me will never walk in darkness, but will have the light of life."

The Pharisees and the scribes had the key to the kingdom, which is knowledge of the truth, but they refused to teach the people and they were not ready to enter. The lack of knowledge is the state of thick darkness. No wonder the Holy Spirit gave the apostle revelation concerning this ruler of darkness. Ephesians 6:12 says, "For we wrestle not against flesh and blood, but against principalities, against powers, against the rulers of the darkness of this world, against spiritual wickedness in high places" (NASV). Unfortunately, many Christians are not even making an attempt to learn the word of God.

They intentionally plan not to participate in Bible study or the school of the word on Sundays in their churches. They would rather occupy themselves or sleep. What good is it to be gorgeous in the flesh and be spiritually blind? You and your wealth are walking in darkness that brings curses and death to you and your offspring. The Lord taught me that the demons control many areas of people's lives, but Satan himself is the one who controls most Christians with the spirit of lukewarmness. They have no desire for the word of God or prayer. Matthew 11:15–17 says,

He who has ears to hear, let him hear. But to what shall I compare this generation? It is like children sitting in the marketplaces, who call out to the other kids, and say, "We played the flute for you, and you did not dance; we sang a dirge, and you did not mourn."

CHAPTER 19

CONCEPTS OF THE COMBAT (PART 2)

When we study the most common scripture, which almost every believer knows, we seem to overlook one part of that verse. It says "for the weapons of our warfare are not carnal but mighty in God for pulling down strongholds" (2 Corinthians 10:3–5). Verse 6 says, "If your obedience is fulfilled, we are prepared to punish every disobedience." Why does God wait until we fulfill our obedience before we can deal with the devil? You need to understand one important rule here. The name of our enemy is the accuser of the brethren. He is always accusing us to God and blaming God to us. He accuses God to us when we are going through some situations and it seems like God is not answering our prayers, and He also accuses us to God if we sin.

He was cast out from heaven because of pride. He and his cohorts are legalistic and operate under the rule of law. There are two reasons to keep believers ignorant. It was this that provoked God to announce to King Solomon, "If my people, who are called by my name, will humble themselves and pray and seek my face and turn from their wicked ways, then I will hear from heaven, and I will forgive their sin and will heal their land." If my children, who are surnamed after me, will submit and humble themselves and will not be arrogant and stubborn, then I will deal with their situation.

The text we are dealing with says that if you fulfill your obedience, then you will be ready to punish the enemy that will fight you. Demons will only obey people who understand authority. Brother James asserted, "Submit therefore to God. Resist the devil and he will flee from you. Draw near to God, and He will draw near to you. Cleanse your hands, you sinners, and purify your hearts, you double-minded" (James 4:7). In observing this verse, you will realize that the Lord was not making a suggestion; rather, it's a command to submit yourself to God and people in authority over you. Otherwise, forget about resisting the devil because he will not flee. He will say to you, "Jesus, I know, and, Paul, I know, but who are you?" It's tough for some people to humble themselves and take orders instead of doing what they want to do. They might even know that their decision is wrong, but they will not let go because it's not in their nature to submit. They will humble themselves when they need something from the man of God or even their parents but not because they want to. The centurion did it willingly. "For I am a man under authority, with soldiers under me. I tell this one, 'Go,' and he goes; and that one, 'Come,' and he comes. I say to my servant, 'Do this,' and he does it" as cited in Matthew 8:9; Luke 7:8.

Demons will only obey you if you obey natural or spiritual authority. Your boss in your job, your parents, people who are older than you, and most importantly, your spiritual father and mother are those you need to submit to. Demons know Jesus and submit to Him, yet when you mention His name, they would rather attack you due to pride and arrogance. Never rise against your spiritual father or mother, it's a dangerous business the devil can enlist you in.

Satan's Power Over Christians Is When He Keeps Them I-G-N-O-R-A-N-T

The definition of ignorant is lacking knowledge or information. Hosea observed, "My people are destroyed for lack of knowledge: because thou hast rejected knowledge, I will also reject thee….. seeing thou hast forgotten the law of thy God, I will also forget thy children." (Hosea 4:6).

Ignorant is generational. You cannot give what you don't have. You cannot teach what you don't know. If you reject knowledge, you will create ignorance for your children's children and God will reject both you and your generations after you. Learn, study, read, and pray for your unborn. Your children would have to stand on your shoulders. So where you standing right now?

Satan keeps Christians ignorant for several reasons. The primary strategy against believers is to keep them untutored in his devices. Such schemes include ignorance of his identity and personality. Satan doesn't want you to understand that he's the accuser, the Old Serpent, the Dragon, the Adversary, the Antagonist, and so on or to know of his defeat in heaven, the garden of Gethsemane, on the cross, in hell, and in the grave. He doesn't want you to know that even though he won the battle in the garden of Eden, he lost it in the garden of Gethsemane. He doesn't want you to know his position or place is under the feet of believers. He doesn't want you to discover that his abode is under the soles of your feet.

Jesus said, "I beheld Satan like lightning falling from heaven. Behold, I give unto you power to tread on serpents (Serpentine spirits) and scorpions, and over all the power of the enemy; and nothing shall by any means hurt you" (Luke 10:18–19).

The devil and his hosts also want to keep believers unenlightened about their inheritance, which Christ bought with His precious blood according to Ephesians1:3–6.

Blessed be the God and Father of our Lord Jesus Christ, who has blessed us with every spiritual blessing in the heavenly places in Christ, just as He chose us in Him before the foundation of the world, that we should be holy and without blame before Him in love, having predestined us to adoption as sons by Jesus Christ to Himself, according to the good pleasure of His will, to the praise of the glory of His grace, by which He made us accepted in the Beloved.

The Identity of the Believer
Verse 5 says that you are a son or a daughter to God the Father through our Lord Jesus Christ. You must know who you are and to whom you belong.

The Place of the Believer
Verse 3 aroused a question in my heart for you. Where were you during your Kairos or season of your blessing? You were (a) in Christ Jesus or (b) in the heavenly realm.

The Position or Authority of the Believer
Verses 19 to 21 read,

And what is the exceeding greatness of His power toward us who believe, according to the working of His mighty power which He worked in Christ when He raised Him from the dead and seated Him at His right hand in the heavenly places, far above all principality and power and might and dominion, and every name that is named, not only in this age but also in that which is to come.

There are four super words in this scripture. The apostle was praying for the new Ephesian Christians and consequentially for us who believe. He wants us to know the power available to us and still working in us. If we are uninformed, we will walk and talk in fear and defeat. Let's take a look at those terms Paul the Apostle used— *dunamis, energeia, ischus,* and *kratos.*

To understand these four power-packed words, let's treat each separately.

God's power to us who believe is translated *dunamis.* To show the weight of this word, the apostle Paul used two superlative words. The *exceeding greatness* of His power or "the exceeding power" is the Greek word *hyperballo,* which in English is "hyperbole," to throw beyond the target or goal. This power is beyond us and at the same time is in us. It is a mystery, and until the Holy Spirit opens the eyes of our hearts, we will be completely ignorant.

The word **greatness** in Greek is **megathos**, and it means huge, vast. So now you have those words, **hyperballo** and **megathos** connecting to **dunamis**. This verse can be read thus, "and what is the **hyperballo megathos**, of His (**dunamis**) exceeding greatness of his power toward us who believe ..."

Now let's throw a little light on the word *dunamis.* According to *The Greek-English Lexicon of the New Testament,* the *duna-* signifies "being able," and it refers to the "immanent or inborn" power we received the moment we were born again. John 1:12 says, "But as many as received Him, to them gave He Power ..." *Dunamis*'s English equivalents are *dynamic, dynamite,* and *dynamo.* These words are always associated with atomic or nuclear power, which is connected to an explosion. Are you still with me? This dynamite power is working through you and available to you who believe, so you can now use it in spiritual warfare.

As for **"Dunamis"** in Revelation 1:16, the glory or the brightness of the face of the Son of God was the **"strength"** of the Sun, which according to Dr. Mike Bagwell, depicts **"nuclear power."** Revelation 1:16 says, "And He (Jesus) had in His right hand seven stars: and out of His mouth went a sharp two-edged sword: and His countenance was as the sun shineth in his strength, dunamis."

Malachi 4:2 shows us that Jesus Christ is the *sun* of righteousness. Jesus is atomic, and the nuclear power is residing in you, waiting for you to detonate it. Do you know how happy the world would be if Russia and North Korea would forfeit their weapons of indignation and Iran would back off from building theirs? The secret is that you are a walking nuclear power plant of mass destruction of the kingdom of darkness. The enemy fears that you will know your identity, what you have, and also your knowledge of detonating it. It is no coincidence that the apostle did not stop praying for the church of Ephesus to understand who they were and what they had. Ephesians 1:16–19 says,

I do not cease to give thanks for you, making mention of you in my prayers: that the God of our Lord Jesus Christ, the Father of glory, may give you the spirit of wisdom and revelation in the knowledge of Him, the eyes of your understanding being enlightened; that you may know what is the hope of His calling, what are the riches of the glory of His inheritance in the saints, and what is the exceeding greatness of His power toward us who believe, according to the working of His mighty power.

I do not have the time to expand the rest of the terms, but I will do my best to go straight to the point. The second word the apostle used in verse 19 is *energeia*. It is a noun, while *energeo* is a verb. The verse reads thus, "... according to the working 'energeia' of His mighty power ..."

The Greek word *energeia* is the root of the English *energy*. It is the spiritual energy or work of God exerted in the believer the moment he or she gives him- or herself to Christ. If that was the work God did in the spiritual realm in hell during the resurrection of Jesus Christ, then the same work was done for us before He resurrected us from the dead and trespasses according to Ephesians 2:4–6, which says,

But God, who is rich in mercy, because of His great love with which He loved us, even when we were dead in trespasses, made us alive together with Christ (by grace you have been saved), and raised us up together, and made us sit together in the heavenly places in Christ Jesus.

The third word to treat in the text is *ischus,* the mighty power. The Greek term *ischus* is translated **"mighty."** I hear you asking, "How do you pronounce that?" It is "is-khoos." *Echo* is the root word for *ischus* and signifies "to hold on" or "to possess." I like the way Dr. Mike Bagwell explains it; it is God's "holding on" power. He said, "God is holding me." Wow, that sounds great, as the apostle Peter asserted, "the power of God keeps us." In 1 Peter 1:5, we read, "Who are kept by the power of God through faith unto salvation ready to be revealed in the last time."

God is not only holding you with that mighty power, but you also possess the same power within you or at hand as a militant to set the world free.

The fourth word is *kratos* (spelled "krat'-os"). According to *The Strong's Exhuastive Concordance*, *kratos* is defined as **"dominion, strength, power; a mighty deed."** Its root meaning is "to perfect, complete," and Thayer observed, it is "properly, dominion, exerted power." The verb *krateo* denotes "to seize, to arrest, to imprison, with force."

As Christians, we are God's law enforcement agents who have a warrant for the detention of Satan and his hosts. To seize his power and imprison his demons in the seas is the authority we possess. We have authority to bind and cast out demons and resist the devil, and he will flee. We have to make it known to him that we are aware of his devices and he is no more in charge.

The Victory of the Believer

The moment the disciples were able to release power over Satan and his demons according to Luke 10:17, "The seventy-two returned with joy and said, 'Lord, even the demons submit to us in your name.'" Immediately Jesus saw victory and mission accomplishment. Read the next verses (18–19):

> He (Jesus) replied, "I saw Satan fall like lightning from heaven. I have given you authority to trample on snakes and scorpions and to overcome all the power of the enemy; nothing will harm you. However, do not rejoice that the spirits submit to you, but rejoice that your names are written in heaven.

Now Jesus delegated authority to the disciples to overcome *all* power of the enemy. Watch out. Did you see something powerful in verses 18 and 19? There are two things I want to elaborate on: First, "Satan fell," which means he is no longer standing. The wrestler needs to stand and have his balance in order to fight, but Satan lost his ground. He is no more in charge if only you could see with the eyes of Jesus. I pray that the eye of your understanding receives illumination to behold as Jesus saw the Devil falling. Second is all the power of the enemy, the serpentine spirits, and the scorpions. The first agent that was used to introduce sin into the world stealthily and capture the authority from Adam for Satan was the serpent or snake. That serpentine spirit is the old spirit of deception and camouflage, an occult spirit. The last power of the enemy that the Lord will destroy, according to Revelation, is a scorpion. We have power over any serpentine spirit and the torment of scorpions.

Pray this prayer:

> I command every serpentine spirit and scorpion to be dethroned from my life right now, and I release the nuclear arsenal into my life and abort the devices of the enemy that reside in my body or family in Jesus's name. Amen and amen.

The Glorious State of the Believer
Ignorance is the spirit of darkness and bondage. The apostle dealt
with ignorance at different levels. He mentioned the veil in the temple
under the law.

> But their minds were made dull, for to this day the same
> veil remains when the old covenant is read. It has not been
> removed because only in Christ is it taken away. Even to
> this day when Moses is read, a veil covers their hearts. (2
> Corinthians 3:14–15)

The veil here represents a lack of knowledge of the Son, who is the
express image of God the Father. The veil is darkness. The veil is
a religious spirit. The veil is spiritual blindness. As the Holy Spirit
ignited His light upon your heart, He will illuminate the eyes of your
heart, and then He will take the veil away. Now watch what is about
to happen. He said because of the removal of the mask, you are now
changing from glory to glory into the image of the Son of God. Read
2 Corinthians 3:16–18:

> Nevertheless when it shall turn to the Lord, the veil shall be
> taken away. Now the Lord is that Spirit: and where the Spirit
> of the Lord is, there is liberty. But we all, with open face
> beholding as in a glass the glory of the Lord, are changed into
> the same image from glory to glory, even as by the Spirit of
> the Lord.

CHAPTER 20

CONCEPTS OF THE COMBAT (PART 3)

Before you engage the enemy, you need to check yourself. Do you remember 2 Corinthians 10:6? "And having in readiness to revenge all disobedience, when your obedience is fulfilled." We cannot do active warfare until we fulfill scripture. We are expected to be obedient to those to whom it's due. We must respect those who deserve it and humble ourselves to those who have natural or spiritual authority over us.

Take a notepad and do reality checks in your life before you begin. Jesus said, "The prince of this world is coming, (but) he has nothing to me." (John 14:30) Any property of the enemy will be his grounds to accuse you. Here's an ideal scenario. A man had a fantastic house, and a gorgeous man walked up to him and offered to buy the house. The owner said, "I am not selling the house." The rich man offered a higher amount, but still the owner refused. The rich man continued to increase the price and even told the owner that he would buy it at any cost. Finally, he grudgingly agreed to sell it but on one condition. "I will only have a small spot on the door where I will keep a nail." The rich man quickly agreed that it was not a problem. They closed the deal, signed the papers, and exchanged money. The new owner took possession. Three months later, the former owner, who still owned the nail on the door came and suspended a dead dog on the door. That was his possession, and he chose to do whatever he pleased with it. What do you think will happen to the new landlord? He has to evacuate the building without any refund of his money. Many Christians have allowed the enemy a spot in their lives to put in a nail when they converted to Christ. There was no complete surrender. One foot is in the world, and the other foot is in the church. Ephesians 4:27 says, "And do not give the devil a foothold." Look, the devil knows the law and he has no mercy. He is legalistic and understands spiritual authority. How can you have his nail and still rebuke him? Here is a reality check.

Disobedience to Natural or Spiritual Authority
Everyone was once a child before graduating into adulthood. You were a child in something from the beginning. Do you remember when you were growing up and you had parents? Yes, you were also a child when you became a freshman in college. How about being a Christian? Somebody won you to Christ. Someone discipled or mentored and fathered or mothered you. According to Ephesians 6:1–3, the apostle Paul observed,

> Children, obey your parents in the Lord, for this is right. Honor your father and mother—which is the first commandment with a promise—so that it may go well with you and that you may enjoy long life on the earth. Fathers, do not exasperate your children; instead, bring them up in the training and instruction of the Lord.

The Old and New Testament commanded us to honor our parents. It does not apply only to children and their natural parents but all of the above. Here's what the apostle has to say to the Ephesian church. After he had pointed out their identity, position, wealth, power, weapons, and armor and all the mysteries from Ephesians chapters 1 through

5, he concluded with chapter 6, saying that the church cannot survive all these battle if they do not align themselves with the principles of spiritual authority. It is easy to disrespect those in spiritual power over you, but it's a disaster to receive the reward. Someone asserted it is beautiful and sweet to walk in the hand of God, but woe to those who fall into the hand of God. He will crush them.

Confess Any Known Sin

There are sins of omission, commission, forgetfulness, willfulness, ingratitude, and presumptuousness.

Sins of omission are things you were supposed to do but refused to do. Brother John summarized it this way: Whoever knows what is right and does not do it is sin. **Sins of commission** are things that you were not supposed to do but you did it anyway. Willful sins are sins that you intentionally commit even though you knows they do not glorify God. Paul the apostle observed,

> Because that which may be known of God is manifest in them; for God hath shewed it unto them. For the invisible things of him from the creation of the world are clearly seen, being understood by the things that are made, even his eternal power and Godhead; so that they are without excuse. (Romans 1:19–20)

Sins of ingratitude—we are living in the ingratitude generation. When they need something from you, they will address you as the most wonderful person and they will show their best behavior. The moment they get what they want, they will walk over you. They are never appreciative. They do the same to God. Isaiah said it best, (Isaiah 1:2) "The wickedness of Judah hear, O heavens, and give ear, O earth; for the Lord has spoken: 'Children have I reared and brought up, but they have rebelled against me. The ox knows its owner, and the donkey its master's crib, but Israel does not know, my people do not understand" (Isaiah 1:2–3, Romans 1:21 ESV). The Psalmist also explicitly asserted, "If I regard iniquity in my heart, the Lord will not hear me" (Psalm 66:18).

The general epistle of apostle John also admonishes, "If we say that we have no sin, we deceive ourselves, and the truth is not in us. If we confess our sins, he is faithful and just to forgive us our sins, and to cleanse us from all unrighteousness. If we say that we have not sinned, we make him a liar, and his word is not in us" (1 John 1:8–9).

Forgive—Let It Go and Let God Take Over

Here's Jesus's number-one principle to a prayer of faith that could move mountains but mostly does not even shake a needle because of the sin of an unforgiving spirit. Jesus asserted, "And when you stand to pray if you hold anything against anyone, forgive them so that your Father in heaven may forgive you your sins" (Mark 11:25).

Fear and Doubt

Fear and doubt are the power of the enemy. Jesus warned us in Mark 11:22–24.

> "Have faith in God," Jesus answered. "Truly I tell you, if anyone says to this mountain, 'Go, throw yourself into the sea,' and does not doubt in their heart but believes that what they say will happen, it will be done for them. Therefore I tell you, whatever you ask for in prayer, believe that you have received it, and it will be yours.

Faith is the shield or the door that protects. In the absence of faith, there are fear and doubt, which open the door for evil agendas to be carried out without check or restriction. Fear has a torment, so please close your door before you start the fight.

Pride and Selfishness

Pride goes before a fall. Be warned about the three Gs—gold, glory, and girls. These are the trap the enemy usually sets for Christian leaders, musicians, and those who are gifted. As God begins to manifest His power through them, they receive the praise of the people and soon forget that it was God who granted and decorated them with His favor. Michael execrated and expelled Lucifer from heaven because of the sin of pride. "Pride goes before destruction, a haughty spirit before a fall" (Proverb 16:18).

PART IV
THE KROBO STATE
INVADED (AFRICA)

CHAPTER 21

THE POWER OF GOD OVER THE MUNICIPALITY

The District Chief Executive

After he won the Minucipal Chief Executive of Lower Manya-Krobo E/R Ghana election in 2001, they swore Mr. Andrews Teye into office. I was passing by in front of the Minucipality the next day. I did not know what had happened. I overheard somebody talking about the swearing in to office of the new MCE. Instantly, I became very concerned and wanted to do something profound. I felt a burden on my heart, so I went to the office of the MCE. His secretary informed him of my visit. Like many of the indigenous people, he had never met me but had heard about Rev. Padmore, who baptized Okumo, the Dipo chief priest. He wanted me in. I went after he escorted some dignitaries who were with him out. Everyone who hears from God or wants to hear from Him needs to pay close attention to the following statement. Here's what I call the voice of wisdom. "Prompt in action after you hear His command is the power of obedience. Delayed obedience is disobedience. The moment God speaks, His power is ready for action, and the host of heaven is deployed to back you up. If you obey, a miracle will follow you. If you choose to do it later, you are bound to fail."

After the DCE had received me into his office, he asked if he could be of help. I told him, "I am here to help you. I heard that you were installed yesterday as the new MCE. Congratulations. Do you mind if I pray for you?" I asked. He agreed. After the prayer, I met Brother Yohannes (John), who is a strong believer, and he happened to be the personal secret service personnel for him. I told him my plan, and he encouraged me to make it known to the MCE. You might be wondering why I prayed again for somebody whom the Roman Catholic priest installed.

Here's the assignment. For many years, the Krobo State had suffered enormous attacks from the kingdom of darkness. Since the democratic government had reinstituted the District Assembly in the late 1980s, there had never been a DCE who had stayed over two years in office, let alone the full term of four years. The first DCE was from my family. Mr. Samuel Teye Appertey was so close to President Jerry John Rawlings. Despite their relationship, he couldn't survive the attack. It happened that suddenly he was removed from office. Since then, no one else had ever accomplished a full term of office. Their accusation letters to the presidents were almost the same from the same group of people. They never wanted to see any progress. It was a simultaneous attack from generation to generation. It was the spirit of the lame and the blind who said David could not come into the city of the Jebusites. In 2 Samuel 5:8, it says, "On the day of the attack, David said to his troops, "I hate those 'lame' and 'blind' Jebusites. Whoever attacks them should strike by going into the city through the water tunnel." That is the origin of the saying, "The blind and the lame may not enter the house."

I asked the new DCE if he wanted to be reinducted with a special prayer. We needed to destroy the power that controlled the seat he was occupying and bring deliverance to the land. Mr. Andrews Teye agreed. Every public leader needs personal intercessors as well as men and women of God. After my discussion with Brother Yohannes (John), his security guard, I asked if he wanted strategic intercessors to pray with him on a weekly basis. Mr. Andrews Teye was so happy at the idea. He made a difference in his term of office. He became the first DCE to complete his period of four years from 2001 to 2005. Since then, the period of four years has become the standard for his successors. Prayer works if we do it with passion and as to the Lord.

Intercessors Are History Makers
If God wants to change the future of a nation, He works with intercessors. If God intends to change a life, He sends a person. Breaking the stronghold over the Minucipality would only come from intercessory prayer. I organized another prayer ceremony. This time, it was an effective, fervent prayer service, which brought prayer warriors together. I was the general secretary of the Manya-Krobo District Council of Churches (MKDCC). All churches and pastors got together and celebrated prayer in the Minucipality. It was to the glory of God. James 5:16b-17 says, "The effective, fervent prayer of a righteous man avails much. Elijah was a man with a nature like ours, and he prayed earnestly that it would not rain, and it did not rain on the land for three years and six months. And he prayed again, and the heaven gave rain, and the earth produced its fruit." Elijah was a man of passion as we are, but we are not prayerful like he was. Here's how the Holy Spirit testified about him in just two words: "He prayed." What is He going to say about you?

"For though we live in the world, we do not wage war as the world does. The weapons we fight with are not the weapons of the world. On the contrary, they have divine power to demolish strongholds" (2 Corinthians 10:3–4 NIV).

With prayer and fasting, the anointing took over in his office. Mr. Andrews Teye's seat was sanctified and we dethroned the strongman who controlled the district. I also discussed it with the pastors of the Council of Churches, and we organized a prayer celebration in front of the city hall and the court. It was extraordinary, and the entire city was full of joy. After that, I formed a pastoral intercessory team of six. The district chief executive and his personal secret service agent were part of it, making our team eight in total. Two of the pastors dropped out because they did not like the DCE political party. They accused me of organizing prayer for him. One thing I believe is pastors must not tie themselves to a political party. We must focus on the personality and what God wants to do with that individual to bring change to the people. Mr. Andrews never asked if I or any of my friends of the intercessory network belonged to his party or a different party. He just desperately needed a prayer to change the land, period! When you are in desperation, do you care who the first responders or rescuers are? No, you just need help. You do not even ask if your doctor is gay or an unbeliever. Your only prayer will be that God will guide him or her and grant him or her wisdom. He must not be the one who will kill you; otherwise, you are left with no choice of who will be present in the emergency room.

The Five Landmarks of the Krobo State Represent Parts of the Gates of the City

The Kingdom Intercessors Network team included Pastor Francis Cande, late Pastor Alfred A. Sai, Pastor Honest Eklica Etse, Brother John (Yohannes), and the late DCE, Mr. Andrews Teye. Our midweek night of prayer in five different locations allowed us to rotate and reach the critical areas in the land. They included the Lassi Stadium at Odumase (the capital city) where they organize major yearly thanksgiving celebrations for the entire state and Methodist School Park at Agbom (Gates). Gates keep everything within protected or hold hostages. They also prevent the outsiders from entering. This city was like the town of Jericho, which protected Canaan. We also met at St. Matthew's Roman Catholic School Park at Agomanya. This park hosts major interschool sports competitions and many other activities. It is adjacent to the district assembly. We met at Aklomuase School Park and finally at MAKROSEC (Manya-Krobo Senior Secondary School Park). After a year, we centralized our meeting at St. Matthew's Roman Catholic School Park. We met continuously for the period of four years throughout his term of office from 2001 to 2005. He never missed a prayer meeting. Mr. Andrews Teye was so faithful, despite his busy schedule and frequent travels. He brought every problem that seemed difficult to handle in the administration to God, and He answered all the requests. The DCE was generous.

Abraham interceded until Lot, and his family were saved. Genesis 18:17 (NIV) says, "Then the Lord said, 'Shall I hide from Abraham what I am about to do?'" Samuel interceded for King Saul and the nation of Israel. Jeremiah wished his eyes were like fountains full of water; he would have cried for the daughters of Zion. They were the watchmen over the cities. Ana and Simeon prayed until Christ the Savior was born. This man, Mr. Andrews Teye, became the first person in the history of the Manya-Krobo State who fully completed his four-year term.

Although the same demons that fought his predecessors fought him, they did not prevail. They fought him not only to then-president J. A. Kufour's office but also in the media. Several attempts to remove him from the office did not succeed. The battle was so bad that a lady who worked in his office once told me that she wanted to accuse the man of rape. I asked her, "How will you do it?"

She said to me, "It's easy. Since he always leaves the office late, I will wait, and when all visitors leave the room, I will shut the doors and then shout that he is raping me."

I told her that this was a wicked idea and God would not hold her guiltless since the man's hands were clean. The Holy Spirit prompted her to inform me in order to abort her evil plan.

The president rejected the accusations from both his party and the opposition party. One day, the battle was fierce to the point that his party members came to the District Assembly to attack me. They realized that I was the problem, making their evil plans void. What did I do? Was I a politician? Was I part of any party? No. So why? It was because I had a passion for my city and was praying against the strongman, corruption, and their evil intents. They said it was the prayers that we had been praying. The prayer had been destroying their plans, so they had to get rid of me. We kept the prayer network secret. I did not know about any attack set against me. The Lord knows the hearts of all people and how deceitful they are. Jeremiah the prophet observed, "The heart is deceitful above all things, And desperately wicked; who can know it?" (Jeremiah 17:9). I was the Chaplain for the period of four years. Before the commencement of their daily activities, I would meet the DCE and his staff in the City Hall every day for Morning Devotion.

Obedience to the Holy Spirit Protects the Warrior
Obeying the Holy Spirit protects and saves the intercessor. It is imperative that the intercessor know that he or she cannot do spiritual warfare his own way. One needs to be attentive and listen to the direction and guidance of the commander in chief, the Holy Spirit. Move when He moves, and stop when He stops. Don't do it because you are familiar with the assignment. Ask His direction at every moment. The cloud above the tabernacle was not static.

Numbers 9:20–22 says,

> If sometimes the cloud remained a few days over the tabernacle, according to the command of the Lord they remained camped. Then according to the leadership of the Lord they set out. If sometimes the cloud remained from evening until morning, when the cloud was lifted in the morning, they would move out; or if it stayed in the daytime and at night, whenever the cloud was lifted, they would set out. Whether it was two days or a month or a year that the cloud lingered over the tabernacle, staying above it, the sons

of Israel remained camped and did not set out; but when it was lifted, they did set out ..."

In the week the enemies planned to attack me, I did not know about it. The Holy Spirit did not reveal it to me. But the Lord prevented me from going to the morning devotion that week. He just didn't allow me to go. Being a man of integrity, it was necessary for me to be there, but I couldn't honor the responsibility that week. The District Chief Executive and the Coordinating Director expected me, but I chose to obey God. I was told the following week when I returned to the City Hall about the failed attack. The one who told me asked me, "Where were you? Do you know about what happened?" I didn't. All attempts to remove the DCE from the office, as usual, had failed. Prayer works. Let's pray until prayer prays us. The incredible power of strategic prayers has amazing results. It brings deliverance to the people and the cities, but it needs selfless, committed, and passionate people to carry out this God-given assignment.

The Disobedient Prophet
When you hear the Spirit whispering or you hear the still, small voice or any form of His communication with you, you need to obey, and that will save you. There's an enemy who looks like a lion, and his purpose is to steal, kill, and destroy you. Here's what happened to the disobedient prophet. First 1 Kings 13:24–26, we read,

Now when he had gone, a lion met him on the way and killed him, and his body was thrown on the road, with the donkey standing beside it; the lion also was standing beside the body. And behold, men passed by and saw the body thrown on the road, and the lion is standing beside the body; so they came and told it in the city where the old prophet lived. Now when the prophet who brought him back from the way heard it, he said, "It is the man of God, who disobeyed the command of the Lord; therefore the Lord has given him to the lion, which has torn him and killed him, according to the word of the Lord which He spoke to him."

If you are young in your calling, you must be careful. Some old prophets who are not on fire anymore will be jealous over you. They will try to give you wrong advice. Please, seek clarification from the Lord. Everyone needs a mentor, so don't try to guide yourself. It's dangerous out there. Jesus sent His disciples two by two.

Hearing the Voice of God Comes with Responsibility
Hearing and listening to the voice of God is not enough. The desire of many people who want to hear from God increases each day. I heard over and again from people asking for prayer because they wanted to hear from God. There's nothing wrong with that. It's the will of the shepherd that all his sheep will hear his voice. When you hear his voice and know His will, you have to obey immediately and not delay. Delayed obedience is disobedience. Many people want to listen to the voice of God. My question to you is, are you willing to obey and take immediate action? Hearing His voice comes with responsibilities, because when God speaks, one must follow. You might want to do your will because yours makes sense to you, but the Holy Spirit wants you to do something else, even if doesn't make sense. He always uses the foolish things of this world to confound the wise.

Obeying the voice of God will save your life. The young prophet died because he refused to obey the voice of the Lord and instead followed the voice of a man. The old prophet, out of jealousy, cunningly created a loophole for him to disobey God even though he knew the consequences. If the young prophet had refused to turn back to the old prophet and eat his food, he would have passed a long time before the lion who tore his flesh into pieces would have met him. Intercessors must hear and promptly obey the voice of the Lord. Sometimes the Holy Spirit will prompt you to pray, say something, or act; it might be that He wants to save someone in danger somewhere. Your instant obedience could save somebody's life.

The enemy can use a human agent to trap you or get you sick. They will offer you food or a gift after God has used you, but the Holy Spirit will tell you not to eat. You only need to obey. It is important to all church leaders and even every Christian, especially those who are challenged in their homes or community by those who don't believe. Be on guard and watch out, the enemy is roaring like a lion, looking for someone to devour.

The Battle of the Election of a Presiding Member (Except by Prayer)
Several times, the election was held, but no one got the vote. They scheduled another vote. The DCE invited me to be present. He told me that the then-president J. A. Kufour vowed that he would choose somebody if the Krobo State couldn't find one. They cast their vote for three consecutive times that day. It was tough, and everything looked hopeless. The DCE and District Administrator asked me to pray before they took the final vote. The Holy Spirit led me to read Psalm 123:1–4 (NIV):

I lift up my eyes to you, to you who sit enthroned in heaven. As the eyes of slaves look to the hand of their master, as the eyes of a female slave look to the hand of her mistress, so our eyes look to the Lord our God, till he shows us his mercy. Have mercy on us, Lord, have mercy on us, for we have endured no end of contempt. We have endured no end of ridicule from the arrogant, of contempt from the proud.

After reading this, I prayed and bound the territorial spirit and the strongman that had bewitched the State for so long. Suddenly, the Lord showed me that victory had come. He also told me the number of votes that Mrs. Regina Apotsi would secure and that she would be the winner. I told them that success had come. Lo and behold, it came to pass. It brought great joy to the city.

Richard Foster asserted, "We are working with God to determine the future. Certain things will happen if we pray rightly." John 5:17 (NIV) says, "But He answered them, 'My Father is working until now, and I am working.'"

Tune in to the Supernatural Realm

In his defense, Jesus said to them, "My Father is always at his work to this very day, and I too am working." I like the way the King James Version put it, "My father work hitherto, and I worked." It means that Jesus was in a constant relationship with His father. Whatever He saw the Father doing, that was what He did. Whatever He heard from the Father, that was what He said. When soldiers are disconnected from their commander, their enemies will destroy them. They will lose their source of information, supplies, and directions. To invade the territories the enemy has taken, we need to get connected and intensify our relationship with God in the secret place of the prayer closet. That's where our power lies. The secret place is the place of power.

The Audible and Other Peculiar Voices of God

Jack Deere observed, "God speaks to us through supernatural means; distinct voice only to you, inner audible voice, and the voice of angels. He also speaks through nature, such as dreams, visions, trance, sentence fragments, single words, impressions, and human messengers." God speaks through our thoughts as well. When we come to His presence in a complete submission, He takes over your thoughts and drops a word to your heart. How can you hear from God? Refer to chapter 4, page 32 under the topic, **"Wait on the Lord."**

The Incredible Voice of God

I do hear audible and remarkably distinct voices most of the time, but these two instances I want to talk about were amazing. This particular voice came because of a precious soul. It was 2003, and one of my spiritual daughters who was committed in her spiritual life was backsliding. I love Vanessa dearly, so I went to visit her. She was not home, and nobody knew where she had gone. I prayed for the Lord to bring her to me. On my way back to visit some other members, I heard a loud and clear voice. It was the very sweet voice of the one I was looking for across the street in a saloon. It was Vanessa's voice. She called me, "Pastor!" I stopped and looked around, and then I saw a saloon where I thought the voice came from. I went in. Lo and behold, Vanessa was in there. With great astonishment, she screamed just as I heard it. "Pastor! How did you know that I was here?"

I said, "You just called me."

She said, "No, I didn't call you."

Indeed, they had closed the door so there was no way she could have seen me. Then I remembered that it was an audible voice. I told her, "Well, you can't hide because God knows where you are and He's looking for you."

She was euphoric that God knew her and where she was. It revived her spiritual life. She became active again in the Lord. Dear reader, God knows you and where you are right now. Don't hide from Him, and if you think your battle is too much to bear, give it to Him for He cares for you.

Be ready for your audible voice. God is about to speak to you in a crystal-clear tone. Just keep waiting, but don't make the hearing of his voice the only priority. Focus on seeking His presence at all times, and He will speak to you.

The Heart of an Adversary Audibly Heard
During a Friday prayer and fasting meeting with my intercessors, some neighbors had conspired evil. While I was praying for the people, I heard a familiar voice. I paused and asked if anybody had heard what I had heard. It was the loud and clear voice of my neighbor. When I lifted up my head, there he was, passing. After the prayer meeting I asked about what he was saying. He denied it vehemently; the Holy Spirit then alerted me that it was an audible voice, but it was an evil plan they set. They were wondering who

came from their group to inform me of their wicked intentions. His confederacy had a shock at the fact that I knew their secret plan, and they eventually failed.

The Lord will not hide anything from His servants. The confidentiality of the Lord belongs to those who are closer to Him. This scripture is paraphrased. I just want to use these particular two audible voices for the sake of the subject at hand. You must understand that God can use anyone's voice to speak to you, depending on what He wants to communicate. He can even use animals or nature.

> When the donkey saw the angel of the Lord, she lay down under Balaam. And Balaam's anger was kindled, and he struck the donkey with his staff. Then the Lord opened the mouth of the donkey, and she said to Balaam, "What have I done to you, that you have struck me these three times?" And Balaam said to the donkey, "Because you have made a fool of me. I wish I had a sword in my hand, for then I would kill you." And the donkey said to Balaam, "Am I not your donkey, on which you have ridden all your life long to this day? Is it my habit to treat you this way?" And he said, "No." Then the Lord opened the eyes of Balaam, and he saw the angel of the Lord standing in the way, with his drawn sword in his hand. And he bowed down and fell on his face. (Numbers 22:27-31, English Standard Version)

It Happened to Elisha
After he had revealed the secret plots of the king of Syria, he asked if any of his army officers or cabinet members had breached their trust by betraying the plans they had in secret. But one said, "There's a prophet in Israel who knew what the King planned in his bedroom." When the King of Syria heard it, he sent his servants to slay Elisha. Before the messenger got there, the Lord spoke to him. In 2 Kings 6:11-12, 15-17, we read,

This enraged the king of Aram. He summoned his officers and demanded of them, "Tell me! Which of us is on the side of the king of Israel?" None of us, my lord the king," said one of his officers, "but Elisha, the prophet who is in Israel, tells the king of Israel the very words you speak in your bedroom."

Intercessors have no surprise from the devil. God consistently reveals the evil plans of the adversary of our country. It makes intercessory prayer very active and productive. It brings great deliverance to people, families, communities, cities, nations, and the world as a whole. If you are praying without seeing into the realm of the spirit to know what is going on, you will be treading on dangerous ground. You want to know what the devil is doing and what strategy God wants you to use. Otherwise, you will be like Saddam Hussein; as someone observed, "When Saddam Hussein fires his scud missiles, he will run to his TV and tune in to CNN to see if his bullets hit the target." If you can see or hear, it makes the warfare much easier and more victorious. You will become a prudent strategist operating with higher intelligence.

Chapter 22

The Holy Spirit Stormed the Reconciliation Council

God's Innovations to Rescue the Perishing

It was the year 2000 when the Manya-Krobo in the Eastern Region of Ghana was going through a paramount kingship battle. The reconciliation council was established to settle the disputes between the two royal families fighting against each other. One royal family wanted to dethrone the newly installed king because they thought that their brothers had used chicanery against them for far too long. The members of the reconciliation council comprised the most qualified, wise, highly educated, wealthiest, and respected businessmen, as well as renowned men of God from the Presbyterian Church, the Roman Catholic priest or chancellor, and Sr. Pastors of the United Christian Church and Action Praise Ministries International. I was also the general secretary of the Manya-Krobo District Council of Churches (MKDCC). The representatives of the traditional rulers were sent by the then acting president of the state of Manya-Krobo, Nene Angmortey Zogli II.

We had several separate private meetings with both royal families and the traditional rulers. There was a defining moment in the final session with the Azu royal family. They presented videos and much other documentation to our council. They also explained the reason why they couldn't give in for any more reconciliation. All the pastors, the distinguished men, and the members of the committee spoke, trying to convince them to agree to a peace process. It looked utterly hopeless; it looked like our board had failed in its mission when one of the men from the Azu royal family took the stage. He spoke defiantly and declared that both royal families were going to drink blood. He also said that there would be a bloodbath in the land, and those who had duplicity in them would bear the consequences. As he was talking, I saw that there was no hope for our endeavor to bring peace, but suddenly the Holy Spirit told me to speak. Naturally speaking, there's nothing to show that my speech would save our effort. I was the least among all present. The Holy Spirit dropped a word to my spirit and asked me to speak it. It was prophetic. "The earth shook, and the heavens also dropped at His presence ..." (Psalm 68:8).

I asked permission to speak, and they all granted me an audience. The Holy Spirit found an opportunity, as He often used the apostle Paul strategically when he was given a chance to address his opposition. He looked for their words and beliefs and then used them to entangle them. Acts 17:22–23 says,

> Then Paul stood up before the council of the Areopagus and delivered this address: "Citizens of Athens, I note that in every aspect you are scrupulously religious. As I walked about looking at your shrines, I even discovered an altar inscribed, 'To an Unknown God.' Now, what you are worshiping in ignorance I intend to make known to you."

I congratulated them on all their efforts and the presentations. "We will all drink *blood* as you said, but we will drink the *blood of Jesus Christ*," I told them and then reached out to my back pocket for my little Gideon's Pocket Bible and opened to Ephesians 2:13–16 (NIV).

But now in Christ Jesus, you who once were far away have been brought near by the blood of Christ. For he is our peace, who has made the two groups one and has destroyed the barrier, the dividing wall of hostility, by setting aside in his flesh the law with its commands and regulations. His purpose was to create in himself one new humanity out of the two, thus making peace, and in one body to reconcile both of them to God through the cross, by which he put to death their hostility.

I said, "It was the blood that brought us peace, breaking the wall of separation, slaying the enmity that is between you. That's why we can't drink any human blood but the blood that washed us. According to your documentation and speeches, which history also bears you witness, your brother the (Sackitey Family) has double-crossed you for too long. Azu and Sackitey were princes to the first paramount chief Nene Sackitey I. It was at that time that the missionaries came with the gospel. King Nene Sackitey I, gave his second prince Matey Azu to go with the German Missionaries (Basle Mission) to train for the work of God. It has marked the first temple built just close to the shrine. After Azu had completed his training as a first presbyter, he was brought back to serve his state. He did it faithfully, and all his posterity followed his blueprint.

"So the Azu family, being the chosen generation, royal priesthood, holy nation, a peculiar people, to offer the sacrifice of praise to the Living God, according to 1 Peter 2:9. Why then do you want to alter the divine plan and the sacrifice your fathers had covenanted with God? Your patriarchs vowed, 'I and my family, we shall serve the Lord.' They laid those foundations for you. My advice is that you do not disappoint them. Go back and seek for God's purpose. It was that calling which has distinguished your family from the rest of the royal families.

"According to your documentation, you have tried in several instances to install a king, but when you do, he will die or go blind in the process and never have the chance to rule. Why do you want to fight against God and your father who committed his family to the service of the Lord? It is my prayer that you obey the voice of the Lord." And I declared, "Peace be still!" As I was speaking, the entire room was silent to the point that if an ant had been passing by, you would have heard its footstep. The Holy Spirit took absolute control, and I finished with the supernatural power of prayer, which has invaded the kingdom of darkness.

The head of the Azu family said they had nothing to argue but would submit to God's will. They wanted peace to prevail and opted for the reconciliation to continue. This honorable man later became my friend. He was the head of KLM and then became the president of Ghana Airways during its crisis.

I didn't know that what I did then brought great honor to our council, but one remarkable instant was when the entire team of our board respected me. Some of the members of our team told me later, "Everybody respected you because of the wisdom you executed." I told them it was the Holy Spirit at work and that we should ascribe all glory and honor to Him alone. Jude 1:24–25 (NIV) says, "To him who can keep you from stumbling and to present you before his glorious presence without fault and with great joy—to the only God our Savior be glory, majesty, power and authority, through Jesus Christ our Lord, before all ages, now and forevermore! Amen."

Exposition of the Word Drop
I want to expose a deeper revelation here in this scripture in the above story. Psalm 68:8 says, "The earth shook, the heavens also dropped at the presence of God: even Sinai itself moved at the presence of God, the God of Israel."

The Hebrew word **naw-taf is translated as "drop."** Cited in Psalm 68:8, according to Strong's Exhaustive Concordance number (5197). Thus the word **"naw-taf"** is defined in the primitive root, "to ooze, i.e., distil gradually; by implication, (to bubble up,) to fall in drops; figuratively, to speak by inspiration—drop (-ping), prophesy." It is a process of receiving a prophetic word from the Lord. When you receive a word, it bubbles up, it takes time to build up. It's a gradual process, like distilling water. Sometimes you will have to ask God for clarity to be able to share. Or it's like raindrops from heaven.

So after the Holy Spirit released His word through me, the hearts of the royal family were shocked, and they had no choice but to submit. It is imperative that every Christian allow the movement of the Holy Spirit in every aspect of life. More important, when we feel that we have no control over a situation, He must be the One who makes the final decision. Every intercessor and church leader must be careful not to allow the flesh to dictate to him or her or circumstances to define his or her faith. Our God is still speaking.

The next chapter will show you how God raised the dead and brought revival to the city. Miracles are the announcement that Jesus still saves. They open the hearts of the unbelievers, and they glorify God.

CHAPTER 23

RAISING THE DEAD PROMOTED THE GOSPEL OF THE KINGDOM

Miracles Bring Joy to the City and Open the Heart Gates for Christ

Miracles are the keys to open the doors of cities wherever we need to preach the gospel. The apostolic and prophetic faith detonate the nuclear bomb against the principalities and powers that might have bewitched the town for a long time.

Before you read this, note that healing and raising the dead are the work of the Holy Spirit to glorify Jesus Christ, but He wants to use you to manifest His presence. It's not your power, and for that reason, no one can manipulate anything to bring about whatever he or she wants to satisfy his ego. I believe that Jesus saw the disabled person at the beautiful gate of the synagogue but did not heal him. He reserved that miracle for the apostles Peter and John (Acts 3:1–6). Sometimes people try to compel men or women of God to perform miracles. Don't be forced, or you will be compelled to use occult powers. It is dangerous. It is God's desire to use you and His children to perform miracles, and if that happens, it's because He is announcing that His kingdom of heaven has come to the earth to invade the kingdom of darkness. Because the kingdom of God comes with power, we must

Samuel T. Padmore

walk in power. All miracles mentioned in this book are to show how God wins the battle over the enemy that has bewitched the people from one generation to the next. I humble myself for whatever God uses me to do, yet I want you to know that there are some miracles left for you to perform as you read this book, so go and do likewise. Greater works than this shall ye do. May your heart blaze with fire to the point that you cannot hold it anymore but release power as Jeremiah did.

Raising the Dead Was an Entrance into the City
Between 1989 and 2004, the Lord raised several dead through His servant. To Him be the glory. I deserve nothing. I want to talk a little about the last three. In 2001, I finally moved to a town known as Agbom ("the Gate"). That city was a spiritual stronghold in the Krobo State. It used to be a very dangerous place, but glory to God for His goodness. Before the 1980s, one could not pass through that city after 6:00 p.m. The believers started to pray, and then the Lord began to reign over the stronghold of the city. The Lord moved me to this town in 2001 where I began to host all-night deliverance services at the community gathering ground. It was an open place where the community held their public celebrations and ceremonies. That was the altar for the city.

Once upon a time, on one Sunday morning during our Sunday school of the Word of God, (Bible Study) on the book of Mark 16:15–20, as I was teaching about the authority of the believer, one brother asked if we could go and pray for his aunt to excecise that power. I said yes. After the service, we all went to his house across the street. This woman was lying down with stroke. She couldn't talk or move any part of her body. She was just there, awaiting death. That house had one of the strongest thrones of the gods that controlled the city of Agbom. I spoke the word of faith and told her she would rise if she believed, but I was not sure if she was able to hear because of her condition.

While we were praying, I began to declare, **"Rise and walk! Rise and walk!"**

The Holy Spirit said to me, **"Open your eyes."**

The woman rose up from the bed and began running. That was it. Her miracle came, and it brought revival in the city. Her cousin Auntie Koryo, who was famous in the town, began to tell people about our all-night prayer vigil. We invaded the region with the secret prayer of intercession, and eventually, we took over the entire city.

My Angel Helped Me

After some months when this lady made up her mind to be baptized, she began to have an attack with a severe headache. During the service, we prayed for her, but it was getting worse. After the service, we went to the Volta River at Kpong for the baptism. The pain was getting out of hand, but I knew where the attack was coming from and what the Lord wanted to do. After the baptism, we went home; the lady was afraid to go to her house. She told me that she would sleep in the church. When I was leaving, the Holy Spirit said to me, "Don't go away. Stay with her." So I returned and was praying while she was sleeping. I asked the guys to help me carry her to my house, but on the way, the Holy Spirit said, **"No, not to your house."** We **brought her back to the church. My people left, but I was still there praying. Suddenly, something happened. The lady died.** I began to pray intensively. My Intercessory Team were not far from us; they heard me, and all of them came to join me in prayer. It was at the center of the city. Immediately, the place filled with all the people of the community and bystanders. They came there not to pray but to watch us with contempt. I was telling God in my spirit, "If you don't raise this lady, I cannot preach in this city again." I was looking at the mountain beyond the city where I would run to and hide from the shame, because when I came to build the church, the witches in the town specifically told me that no one could build a church there. But I obeyed the Lord and planted His ministry right in the center of the city. So I believed God would visit this lady. Otherwise, we would make God a liar, yet He cannot lie. Meanwhile, the family who hated this woman began to meet and plan for what they would do to me.

Suddenly a man who looked like me but was taller broke through the crowd of people surrounding us. I was holding the anointing oil, and he addressed me with a voice of urgency. He said, "Pour the oil into my hand!" I did, and he rubbed her face with the oil. The lady opened her eyes and woke up. Amen. Suddenly, the man disappeared. I asked everyone if they knew him and saw when he left. Nobody knew him or where he went. But after that, I began to meet him in the realm of the spirit. He always visits me when I am in danger. He is my angel. You have your angel too whom God sent to help you in the time of need. This angel will only assist you if you are doing the work of the Father.

God Raised Another Dead Lady to Life
Spiritual warfare still going on unabated, but God was invading the kingdom of darkness at Agbom, the same city where my angel helped me. In the year 2003, one of my leaders, Alfred, told me about his dying friend. He said that the lady was helpful to him. The woman was very sick to the point of death. The family neglected her and laid her at the spot where they usually put the dead; nobody attended to her anymore. One day, Brother Alfred went to visit her, but his heart broke from what he heard the dying lady crying and telling her only four-year-old daughter. "I am dying, and there's no one to care for you, but the Lord will take care of you." I was hurt when I heard that. I never had the opportunity to know her when she was healthy but only at her deathbed.

I went in with my prayer partner, Brother Francis Azah. When we went in, she was at her last breath. She was not talking or making any movement. While we were praying the power of the Holy Spirit was so great. His presence was so strong that unwisely and by faith presumption, Brother Francis held the lady and was lifting her up.

But the woman died in his hands. I told him to lay her down. Now the battle had just begun. She was halfway alive and hadn't given up the ghost yet when we walked in. But because they neglected her, no one accompanied us to her bed. Now there was a big question there to answer. What if we walked out and they walked in and found her dead? What would happen to us? The family would deal with us, and they would also call the police. I was not worried much about the police or whatever they would do to us. My greatest fear was the disgrace that would come upon me, the name of the Lord, and upon our church. Don't forget that the city was a satanic stronghold, and they hated pastors. They would do anything to prove that the Christians had failed, just to discredit us. It was the same community where the Lord raised the other lady.

After Brother Francis had laid her down, lifeless and breathless, I was looking at the shame and frustration this might bring upon my ministry and the name of Christ in the unbelieving community, when they had specifically told me that no one could establish a church in that place. The apostolic faith had to move into action. The Holy Spirit took over supernaturally. Power began to flow, life was realeased at the mention of the name of Jesus Christ of Nazareth, as I cast out that spirit of death and spoke the resurrection power of Christ into her. I called her to come back to life. She opened her eyes and then sat up. I called a family members and told them to give her food. We left. After she had eaten, that was the end of the sickness or the death story. She didn't know what had happened to her. Nobody was there, only Brother Teye Francis and I. Amen. Glory to God in the highest. This sister became so beautiful. Jesus Christ did it again. Amen. As I am writing right now, I can recall her sitting in our church just once the first time. Her house was near to our church. She didn't plan to come to church; she was passing by, and the Holy Spirit showed her to me. He told me that was the lady I had raised to life. Suddenly the Lord touched her, and she came and sat at our service. If I met her right now, I would not even recognize her.

The Breathless Baby Came Back To Life

It was around 2:00 a.m., and I heard the urgent knocking on my door. When I woke up, my whole body was shaking. I came out; there stood two of our members, Auntie Koryo and her daughter, holding the beautiful granddaughter, who was breathless, and they were crying. As I stretched my hand, praying for the baby, suddenly, I started to feel a soft hand holding my finger pointed at the dead child. She was playing with my finger. Praise God! Jesus did it again! It was the third sign and wonder this lady, Auntie Koryo, witnessed. It happened in the same community. She saw the healing of her best friend from a stroke in less than five minutes of prayer. She also observed the resurrection of her best friend and then her granddaughter. This woman was a strong Catholic and had great influence in the city and on the market. So the Lord wanted to use her to witness. Now she saw it with her own eyes; she started testifying, and the majority of the people in the city yielded to Christ. We invaded and took the city for Christ. We accomplished all this through the secret power of prayer. As Pastor Thomas put it, "What is gained by prayer must be maintained by prayer."

The Prophetic Created a Six-Month Baby within Two Weeks

My spiritual son Kenny introduced me to his friend Pastor Blyber Bello in Paterson, New Jersey. My wife and I were invited to preach on August 13, 2016. After the sermon, as I was praying for the people, because of the limited time, I was rushing to end the ministration so we could return to Worcester, Massachusetts, but the Holy Spirit had an agenda. He showed me a woman at the back of the pews. I struggled in my spirit for about five minutes before saying anything to the woman because I was not sure how she would receive this message. I called her. "Lady, you are pregnant and you are going to have a baby but there is a problem which needs to be dealt with." It took quite some time to speak to her, but she did not believe, so I prayed for her. After a month, Pastor Blyber and my son Kenney called me. "Breaking news! Do you remember the woman you prophesied to that she would have a baby?" one of them asked. I said I did. "She did not believe when you spoke because she's forty-seven years old and her son is nineteen years of age, but two weeks after the prophecy, she had a sharp and unbearable pain in her belly. She went to the hospital, and the doctor said she was six months pregnant. Wow, she had the baby shower on this past Saturday, October 15, 2016, and is due around November 17, 2016."

The Pastor said, "This woman now loves God more than ever before, and many people began to come to the church, giving their lives to Christ. The prophecy brought the hidden things to manifestation or it created a six-month baby in two weeks. Wow! Amazingly, our God reigns!" I was glad to hold the baby two weeks after the baby was born.

Dear reader, you have the same power that raised Christ from the dead. It's flowing inside of you. It is the transcendent and immanent power of God. It is beyond you and yet flowing to you and through you. Jesus said, "He that thirsts … out of his belly shall flow wells of living waters." (John 7:37–38). The Holy Spirit has equipped every Christian with the power from on high to do greater works. The world is waiting for you to allow yourself to be ruptured by the transcendent and immanent power of His presence. Mark 16:15–18 (NIV) says,

He said to them, "Go into all the world and preach the gospel to all creation. Whoever believes and is baptized will be saved, but whoever does not believe will be condemned. And these signs will accompany those who believe: In my name they will drive out demons; they will speak in new tongues; the believers will pick up snakes with their hands; and when they drink deadly poison, it will not hurt them at all; they will place their hands on sick people, and they will get well.

Intercessors Must Be Able to Rebuke and Cast Out

The Greek word for "rebuke" is *epiplésso*. The definition is "to strike at, to rebuke" (with words). The Greek word for "cast out" is *ekballo* (ek-bal'-lo). The definition is "to cast out, drive out, to send out with the notion of violence."

Christians have been authorized to rebuke and cast out the devil and bind the demons. It's by applying excessive force that we drive them away from the people, families, communities, cities, states, and nations they hold in captivity or are tormenting.

As led by the Holy Spirit, when praying for the sick, rebuke and cast out the territorial spirit of death. The Holy Spirit revealed some secrets to me. Most of the time, it is not a sickness that kills people; it is the spirit of death or the agents of death. On certain occasions, you will see an individual who was sick and then received a cure but suddenly dies with just a little headache. Everyone wonder why that person died although he or she recovered? It was because the agent of death or the territorial spirit that was controlling the situation had not been cast out. It still had its grip on the person. Whenever you sense the presence of such a spirit during a prayer for any sick person, bind, rebuke, and cast it out before praying for healing. After it is gone, then you can activate life into the individual. Sometimes you might feel odd casting out the spirit of death if the person's loved ones are present, but you must not allow any intimidation by others who are there. It's your job to get the person out of the gates of bronze, cut the bars of iron asunder, and destroy the power of the grave. Whenever you start casting out such invaders, ignorant religious people become alarmed and do not feel comfortable. They feel disrespected by you praying in such a way for them, but that's your job. Sometimes, if the person is in the hospital, some nurses don't want to allow that kind of prayer.

Psalm 107:16, 18–20 says,

> For He has broken the gates of bronze and cut the bars of iron in two ... Their soul abhorred all manner of food, And they drew near to the gates of death. Then they cried out to

the Lord in their trouble, And He saved them out of their distresses. He sent His word and healed them, And delivered them from their destructions.

Demons Can Use Nurses and Health Workers

I moved to a community for ministry purposes between 1999 and 2000. The brother I met there was exquisite. As I was winning him for Christ, he got an attack, which was life threatening. While at Atua Government Hospital in the Manya-Krobo, I visited him and prayed for him. There was a nurse who wasn't happy because of my presence. She did not want me to pray for the brother. I prayed and left, but the next day, I went to pray again. This time, she attacked me, but I refused to leave because the Holy Spirit showed me that the man would die if I did not deliver him. I prayed until I saw him rescued, and the moment I left the hospital, they discharged him. The demons almost used the nurse to kill him. As an intercessor, you must see what is happening in the realm of the spirit.

The Devil Used Another Nurse to Block Healing

In the same year, 2000, a friend of mine who was a church elder and also worked at the bank told me to visit and pray for his sister who was also a nurse at St. Matthew's Hospital at Agomanya. The doctors gave me permission to meet her. She had had a stroke and could not walk. When I taught her the gospel, she believed that God would heal her. As I started praying, commanding her to walk in Jesus's name, she got up and started walking back and forth. Suddenly a nurse walked in, and she shouted at us, "What do you think you are doing?" She did this with anger, as if she never wanted this lady to walk again. The woman was scared. She sat on the bed and was not able to get up again. I couldn't challenge the nurse because I had no authority there. Thus Satan used the evil nurse to block her coworker's healing. Jesus couldn't do many miracles in His home town because of unbelieve. We must bind these territorial spirits while praying for people. Otherwise, they will interject.

Samuel T. Padmore

Activating Life

John 11:25 says, "Jesus said unto her, 'I am the resurrection, and the life: he that believeth in me, though he were dead, yet shall he live." Speak life to the dead person, dead situation, or lifeless city and nation, and they will come back to life. John 6:63 says, "It is the spirit that gives life, the flesh profits nothing: the words that I speak unto you, they are a spirit, and they are life."

The Holy Spirit breathes life into the word, and the word manifests life in the lifeless image. Genesis 2:7 says, "And the LORD God formed man of the dust of the ground, and breathed into his nostrils the breath of life and man became a living soul." Here's the revelation in this verse. Genesis 1:26 says, "And God said, Let us make man in our image, after our likeness: and let them have dominion over the fish of the sea, and over the fowl of the air, and over the cattle, and over all the earth, and over every creeping thing that creepeth upon the earth."

I remembered the newborn baby of Brother Jesse admitted to Boston Children's Hospital. They told me, and I went with our intercessors, but only two people were allowed to enter the room at a time. I went in with Brother Jesse. He said that the doctor had given his child only two hours to live. While I was praying, Brother Jesse felt the entire room was shaking, and indeed, God restored life the same hour. The child is now over eight years old, glorifying God. When we activate the life of Christ to a lifeless situation, life will sprout.

The Image of God

When God formed the image from the dust, it was just a lifeless creative art. It was the incomplete work of God. His image was not the clay that He formed from the dust. It was not something that looked like an idol image. It was not something that depicted a human model. God breathed His image into a man, and he became a living soul. Thus the image of God was His Spirit, which gave life to humanity.

208

Observe Jesus Christ's statement in John 6:63: "It is (He) the Spirit that gives life." Here Jesus Christ was speaking concerning life in the Spirit as well as the flesh. When we possess the image of God, we inherit the power that creates. Hence God called the things that were not as though they were. Let there be, and there was. It is the same power that a believer possess through which he or she can call the dead to life as Jesus Christ did to Lazarus. John 11:43 says, "When He had said these things, He cried out with a loud voice, "Lazarus, come forth." The transcendence and inherent power of God flow through you. Ephesians 1:19 says, "And what is the exceeding greatness of his power to us-ward who believe, according to the working of his mighty power."

Romans 8:11 says, "But if the Spirit of him that raised up Jesus from the dead dwell in you, he that raised up Christ from the dead shall also quicken your mortal bodies by his Spirit that dwells in you."

When a person is healed or resurrected to life, the person him- or herself becomes a believer. The community around gets saved, and many who hear about it give their lives to God. Yes, it is the purpose of our intercession that God will use His people to perform signs and wonders for His glory to announce to the unbeliever that Jesus Christ saves. You are the image of God so exhibit that spirit of intercession to draw men to His Kingdom.

The Revelation Knowledge

Before we can use the word potently for compelling results, we need to catch the spirit of the revelation knowledge of Christ as we read the logos of God. At the age of innocence, Adam was a spiritual man who had constant fellowship with God. Their communication and relationship were in depth and rich. They related Spirit to spirit. Adam clearly understood God, but when Adam lost the battle in the garden of Eden, then the Lord said, "My Spirit will not contend with humans forever, for they are mortal; their days will be a hundred and twenty years" (Genesis 6:3 NIV).

The image of God, which was the Spirit of God, left Adam. Though he was alive physically, he was dead spiritually. That death affected the human race. Adam was cut off from the source of life and the light of the Holy Spirit that shone upon his mind so he could see what God saw and hear and understand what God said was disconnected because God is light, according to 1 John 1:5). "This then is the message which we have heard of him, and declare unto you, that God is light, and in him is no darkness at all." The man began to live in the darkness. When one becomes born again, the Holy Spirit breathes life into him and shines His light upon his spirit. Then the spirit, which is the eyes of his spiritual mind, begins to see clearly and the understanding is illuminated. That's why the songs that didn't make sense to you do after your encounter with the Lord. You now enjoy the scriptures you used to read and never understood are now becoming clearer. That means your mind has eyes and can see. If it can see, then it will make meaning out of the word of God. That is the illumination of the Holy Spirit and Apostle Paul called it, revelation mind.

Let me explain it in another way. Imagine you have been thinking about seeing a brother. At the parking lot, somebody waved to you and you waved, but after the person had left, you came to your senses and remembered that that was the brother you wanted to meet. You looked at him but didn't see him because your mind did not make a connection with your eyes. Seeing happens when the mind and the eyes connect toward the same object. Then you can look and see at the same time. The mind begins to make meaning out of what the eye sees, not what it looks at. When your spirit and your mind are connected, then the eyes of your mind will be enlightened. There will be an illumination that causes understanding of the things of the Spirit. When the Spirit throws light upon the word you are reading, that is what the Apostle Paul called revelation knowledge.

This revelation brings out a fresh and the living word by the Spirit, this is called Rhema. It is this word that brings life and transformation to one's life or situation. The written word is known as logos and that is the Bible we reads.

The Transcendent and Immanent Power of God

God's immanence and transcendence relate to His relationship with the created world. They do not refer to His specific actions, but to His relationship with the world. According to the *World Book Dictionary*, the definition of immanence is, "the pervading presence of God in His creation," and the definition of the transcendence of God is "To be above and independent of the physical universe." The two attributes are opposite but complementary and need to be kept in the proper balance to understand God. He is both superior to and absent from His creation and yet very present and active within the universe.

We see the immanence of God in His presence and activity within nature, with humans, and in history. There are numerous references to God's immanence in Scripture. We observe His actions within nature according to Psalm 65:9–13 (NIV), which says,

You care for the land and water it; you enrich it abundantly. The streams of God are filled with water to provide the people with grain, for so you have ordained it. You drench its furrows and level its ridges; you soften it with showers and bless its crops. You crown the year with your bounty, and your carts overflow with abundance. The grasslands of the desert overflow; the hills are clothed with gladness. The meadows are covered with flocks, and the valleys are mantled with grain; they shout for joy and sing.

God's presence with man is noted in Job 33:4: "The Spirit of God has made me; the breath of the Almighty gives me life." And His activity in history is recorded in Isaiah 63:11: "Then his people recalled the days of old, the days of Moses and his people—where is he who brought them through the sea, with the shepherd of his flock? Where is he who set his Holy Spirit among them?" These are but a few of the examples of God's immanence in the world.

Two of the attributes that exemplify God's immanence are His omnipotence and His omnipresence. He has an all-pervading presence and power within the world. The *transcendence* power of God is across or above us. It's beyond our reach, but the immanence power lives within us. To exemplify these terms for your understanding, the **transcendence** and the **immanence power** of God can be liken as the following; "**The Transcendent Power** is like the **High Tension of the electricity.** The **Immanent Power** is like the **Local Electrical Wires** that connects power to your home" although you couldn't reach the high tension due to it's danger, the local wirings are able to transmit power to your home for your usage. That's exactly how the transcendent and the immanent power operates. The same power that raised Christ from the dead still flows through us. That's what the apostle Paul cited in Ephesians 1:19 and 3:20–21 (NIV): "Now to him who can do immeasurably more than all we ask or imagine, according to his power that is at work within us, to him be glory in the church and Christ Jesus throughout all generations, forever and ever! Amen."

My early ministry of healing dealt mostly with emergency situations because in Africa, people believe in prayer more than the hospital— and their faith works. It all about presenting Jesus Christ as the Savior and Life-giver. You can release power that is flowing in you.

CHAPTER 24

FIRE FELL

The Kings and the priests saw fire fall from heaven.
The open doors to send the gospel to the traditional rulers. Their invitations for private deliverance, salvation and protection. People who don't understand your vision will criticize you. So do not be discouraged. The Ngmayem Thanksgiving Planning Committee wanted the Council of Churches to join them. So I, being the general secretary, was a representative on the planning committee. I was going for their hearts. It was an opportunity to pray and preach to all the traditional rulers, including the voodoo priests and the unbelievers on that day. When I came to give a report to our council, one pastor I thought was a friend accused me before the general assembly. I did not say a word because I knew what the Lord was about to do.

The thanksgiving celebration in the year 2000 was a success. The people of Manya-Krobo have a thanksgiving celebration they call the Ngmayem Festival. Those who planned and officiated the ceremony were the fetish or voodoo priests and the traditional rulers. The church had nothing to do with it for many years because it was considered idol worship. The body of Christ had separated herself from the traditional rulers and the pagans for a long time. In 2000, the new paramount chief, Nene Sackitey II, and the traditional council wanted to find a way to raise funds. The king organized all groups and religious leaders, which included the church and the faith-based groups.

I was appointed a general secretary of the Manya-Krobo District Council of Churches. The idea of meeting with the traditional rulers was not a good one to some of the pastors. Some of us saw an effectual door and extra-ordinary opportunity so we encouraged the invitation. I was elected by our council to be the representative on the Ngmayem Thanksgiving Planning Committee. The committee comprised traditional rulers, business representatives, and many other groups in the land. As they were looking for ways to involve us, I was looking for an opportunity to deliver our message of the cross. Our Council of Churches embarked upon the idea.

The celebration takes a week. Every tribe takes a turn. The Friday of October is a grand celebration, which demands all Krobos to participate. Now as the church was asked to be a part, we could not take part in the Friday activities because it was paganism. We chose Sunday for thanksgiving.

On the thanksgiving Sunday, no church worshipped in its sanctuary. All the churches met at Lassi Stadium at Odumase. The service included seven pastors to offer intercessional prayers. All the traditional rulers, the fetish or voodoo priests, people of the land, and the government officials were present. As the pastors were praying one after the other, my spirit was provoked within me, blazing my heart with fire. Finally, I could not take it any longer. I was burning and uncomfortable because the prayers of other pastors sounded pious and ceremonious, not to offend but to please. I was the last to pray. The Holy Spirit began to speak to me. He said, **"Pray as I pray."**

I asked Him, "How do You pray?"

He said, **"With boldness. Say whatever I will put into your mouth and do not be afraid."** I was the youngest among the pastors.

It was now my turn. I felt the presence of the Holy Spirit robust and ready to do battle. When I took the microphone, it was as if everything was shaking in the stadium. I broke and cast out all the gods and the demonic powers present. I prayed for deliverance over all the traditional rulers and the fetish priests; I also dethroned the power that controlled the throne of the paramount chief, the king of the entire land. Jeremiah 1:9–10 was the focus, to throw down, destroy, build, and plant. I call this type of prayer, (PPP), which means, the **power of preaching in prayer.** As I was praying, I saw heaven open and fire was falling like rain with hailstones everywhere in the stadium. Everyone felt it. When I finished, the chairman of our Council of Churches, Rev. Fr. Paul Lawer, took the microphone, and this was what he said, **"Fire fell."**

When he said that, I responded in my spirit, "The Lord has opened your eyes."

This type of prayer, you execute it when there is a situation that needs to be solved, but you don't have control over it or nobody will listen. You would rather request their audience for prayer. When you get that opportunity, hit it hard and once because you might never have it again by the leadership of the Holy Spirit.

The Traditional Rulers Confirmed That Fire Fell
After the ceremony, all the pastors went to greet the kings. When I shook the Paramount Chief's hand, he told me, "Small boy danger." All the other kings did too. From that day, the Holy Spirit opened doors for me to visit the traditional rulers. Other pastors are still taking advantage of the opportunity. The Kings told me they had problems and needed help from the pastors. But the pastors considered them evil, so they had separated from them. Most of these kings began to invite me to their homes. I began to do secret

deliverance for them. One of the kings told me that he had a church that he went to in secret for spiritual backup and God's protection. I started ministering to the then acting president of the Manya-Krobo State, Nene Angmortey Zogli II, who used to be a regional court judge before becoming a king. He eventually gave his life to Christ. Sometimes, the Holy Spirit would tell me to visit him. When I get there, he would ask me, "How do you know that I am going through terrible situations and need prayer?" My visits paid off. He denounced the pagan traditional kingship and resigned. Nene Zogli then called for the church to enthrone him as a Christian king. It was a beautiful ceremony celebrated at the UCC Auditorium. God won the land at last.

There was one King whom I always asked God to forgive me whenever I remembered him. I never knew he needed me, but every time he met me, he would ask me to visit him. I did not take his invitation seriously because I thought he was jesting. He was a father of one of my schoolmates. It was later when I came to the United States that I heard he was having a big situation at the time. It was painful that I did not attend to him, and I don't know how I could have missed that opportunity. I believed that God would use someone to minister to him. I regret and ask God for forgiveness.

All these doors the Lord opened because of obedience to the Holy Spirit, and He allowed the Fire to Fall. I commission you to practice the PPP, the power of preaching in prayer, whenever an unusual opportunity shows up. Preach (pray) in season and out of season.

CHAPTER 25

INTERCESSORS ARE
SPIRITUAL WARRIORS

The transitions of the seasons of intercession was that in the Old Testament, the watchmen watched over the nation from the high tower. The prophets watched over the lands on the spiritual high tower through prayer. Their radar was the gift of discernment, an audible voice, visions, and dreams. In the twenty-first century, the continents and nations use powerful radar or even satellites. The United States uses the most sophisticated radar to spy on its enemies in its lands and strikes them before the enemy realizes what is going on. How about the twenty-first-century intercessors? Our process has not changed but has been upgraded to a higher standard. God has added to what we had from the Old Testament, praying with understanding as well as praying in the Spirit and in tongues. As we enter to intercessory prayer, all the host of heaven joins with us. Here's what happens.

The Holy Spirit intercedes with groaning, which one cannot utter, and He also helps our infirmities if only we pray in the "will of God." Romans 8:26–27 says,

> In the same way the Spirit also helps our weakness; for we do not know how to pray as we should, but the Spirit Himself

intercedes for us with groanings too deep for words; and He who searches the hearts knows what the mind of the Spirit is, because He intercedes for the saints according to the will of God.

Jesus Christ became our Chief Intercessor. "Who is he that condemns? Christ Jesus, who died, more than that, who was raised to life is at the right hand of God and is also interceding for us" (Romans 8:34).

The enemy's scheme is to keep us in bondage and weak. He wants us to walk in defeat and condemnation, but watch out; he lost the battle. Christ, who is supposed to condemn us, is the One who died for us, and more than that, He is even praying for us. If we have the Holy Ghost interceding and Jesus Christ our Lord is doing the same for us, why can't we do even more? Intercession is necessary for our walk with God in this turbulent sea. We have support from heaven. We have the courage and boldness to rise to our highest tower to watch out for our families, churches, communities, cities, states, and nations at large. We don't have to blame the politicians. If we Christians do our part, they will fear God. We talk more than we pray for our leaders and those in authority.

Is It a Necessity for Every Christian to pray in the Spirit and in Tongues?
Jude 1:20 (NIV) says, "But you, dear friends, by building yourselves up in your most holy faith and praying in the Holy Spirit." Praying in the Spirit is not praying in tongues. It is a prayer that originates from the deepest part of the heart as King David observed it, the deep calls to the deep. (Psalm 42:7) Many people pray from their heads. Such prayers are not effective. It is just like people who pray for show. Either praying in tongues or understanding, there must be a connection between your mind and the Spirit. You must fully resign from the flesh and concentrate on God and pray with the Word.

Praying in Tongues

When an intercessor is praying in his understanding, he cannot edify the Spirit, but unfortunately, it might open the door for more attacks. Did you ask why? There was an instance where an intercessor was praying for God to give her a husband. She wanted God's purpose for her life. Some of the women in her church who had husbands or fiancés started talking about her. When she sought counsel from me, I advised her to change her way of praying. Especially for sensitive and personal matters, she should pray like Hannah. Then she changed her style and began to pray like Hannah prayed. It worked, and later she received the baptism of the Holy Spirit and the evidence of speaking in tongues. She bypassed the human radar of limitation and accusations. She began to pray more in the Spirit. Every Christian, especially the intercessors, needs to avoid humans' and Satan's radars to switch to the tongues when necessary.

Did the Early Church Pray in Tongues?

Yes, at the inception of the New Testament Church, the Holy Spirit came upon the disciples. They stayed in fasting and prayer until the promise of the Father was fulfilled. Acts 1:4–6 (NIV) says,

On one occasion, while He was eating with them, He gave them this command: "Do not leave Jerusalem but wait for the gift My Father promised, which you have heard Me speak about. For John baptized with water, but in a few days you will be baptized with the Holy Spirit.

In chapter 2, we saw how they received that baptism. Acts 2:1–4 says,

When the day of Pentecost came, they were all together in one place. Suddenly a sound like the blowing of a violent wind came from heaven and filled the whole house where they were sitting. They saw what seemed to be tongues of fire that separated and came to rest on each of them. All of them were filled with the Holy Spirit and began to speak in other tongues as the Spirit enabled them.

They were filled again in chapter 4 verse 31. "After they prayed, the place where they were meeting was shaken. And they were all filled with the Holy Spirit and spoke the word of God boldly."

Frank Damazio asserted, "The New Testament church prayed spontaneously by, in, and through the Holy Spirit. The beginning of the Christian life is marked by the indwelling spirit crying out to God, 'Abba' Father." Here's what the apostle Paul by the guardians of the Holy Spirit wrote in Galatians 4:6 NIV, "Because you are his sons, God sent the spirit of his son into our hearts, the spirit who calls out, "Abba, Father." On all occasions, the scriptures encourage the believer to pray "in the spirit" and "by the spirit." This injunction applies to every kind of praying, especially intercessory prayers.

Ephesians 6:18 (NIV) says, "And pray in the Spirit on all occasions with all kinds of prayers and requests. With this in mind, be alert and always keep on praying for all the Lord's people."

When we are weak and do not know how to pray or what to say, the Spirit Himself takes over and prays for us. He quickens us like a recharged battery. Romans 8:26–27 (NIV) says,

> In the same way, the Spirit helps us in our weakness. We do not know what we ought to pray for, but the Spirit Himself intercedes for us through wordless groans. And he who searches our hearts knows the mind of the Spirit because the Spirit intercedes for God's people by the will of God.

If you don't have experience, you will take everything for granted. They told him, "This is what Hezekiah says: This day is a day of distress and rebuke and disgrace, as when children come to the moment of birth and there is no strength to deliver them" (2 Kings 19:3).

There were many instances where I faced situations but had no strength to deal with them. Suddenly, I receive divine help by praying in the Spirit. In 1992, I was sick to death for three days— no food, no water, no walking, and no talking—but after the third day, I was taken up into the heavenly sanctuary where the Lord and His angels were at the table. An angel brought me to the table and gave me the Communion. Just as I ate the bread and drank the wine and the Lord restored my strength, I woke up praying in the tongues. As I was praying in tongues, the Holy Spirit filled me with power and sweating, and immediately He healed me without any medication.

Bishop T. D. Jakes, in his book *Release Your Anointing*, asserted, "Praying in the Spirit is the frequency that Satan cannot pick up." There are varieties of channels for different purposes. The bishop used the CBS radio for his illustrations. CBS radio is an exclusive channel used to communicate with the police for any emergency assistance. No one else can monitor the conversation because of the frequency. The Bible made it clear that Satan is the "prince of the power of the air" (Ephesians 2:2). It frustrates him when we speak in tongues. He cannot pick up our transmissions because we are on a different frequency. And his squelch cannot tune in. It becomes static to him. We tune in to the unknown language with the Father in our prayers. The Scripture says that when we pray in the Spirit, we speak mysteries to God, who understands the mind of the Spirit. Romans 8:26–27 says,

Intercessors Are Secret Invaders of the Kingdom of Darkness
We have kept our movement and plans secret as intercessors. We are the prime target to the enemy, as he is to us. So we are not proud but humble. We don't announce our presence when we invade the predominantly satanic territories, but when finished, they know that we came there. Our movement is like the US Navy SEALs who killed Osama bin Laden. The United States' had a one-hundred-hour war in Iraq, referred to as Desert Storm. They finished the first mission

of the war before the Iraqi soldiers knew what had happened. Judges 18:9 says,

> They answered, "Come on, let's attack them! We have seen the land, and it is very good. Aren't you going to do something? Don't hesitate to go there and take it over. When you get there, you will find an unsuspecting people and a spacious land that God has put into your hands, a land that lacks nothing whatever.

Sometimes the enemy we are dealing with is unsuspecting. If so, we do a one-hundred-hour war, and we will accomplish our task before they realize it. On some occasions, we are compelled to face the battle at its worst moment. Whatever the condition might be, we attack in season and out of season because we know that Our Redeemer lives. Our Commander in Chief goes before us, just as Sabine Baring-Gould wrote in his popular hymn in 1865, which was composed by Arthur Sullivan in 1871.

"Onward, Christian Soldiers, Marching as to War"

> With the cross of Jesus going on before

> Christ, the royal master, leads against the foe
> forward into battle see His banners go

> Onward, Christian soldiers, marching as to war
> with the cross of Jesus going on before …

The Christian life is warfare, and so we must be fully equipped to carry out the King's business in haste because we have only one chance to hit the target.

PART V
PRAYING TO RESCUE THE NATIONS

CHAPTER 26

A CALL TO PRAY FOR THE NATIONS

Interceding for Your Family and Community; Pray for America, Jerusalem, and the Persecuted Church; National Repentance and Reconciliation for the United States; the Call to Pray for America and Jerusalem.

After September 11, 2001, America became desperate for prayer like never before. Our Council of Churches and Krobo Pentecostal Fellowship regularly prayed for America, Jerusalem, China, and all the 10/40 windows of the Islamic countries while in Ghana. When I came to America, I asked the Lord, "Why did you not bring me here when there was peace but in this difficult time?"

He answered me, "America did not need you then, but this is the season she needs you the most. I am bringing America to her knees, then she will seek for Me. I am dealing with them due to their sin, and I want you to intercede so that I will not destroy her."

I remembered a magazine my pastor friend Rev. Francis brought to our class. It was 1996 when we were in the Pastoral College in Ghana. Billy Graham said, "If God does not punish America, then God owes

Sodom and Gomorrah on the judgment day." What America is doing today is worse than what they did then.

After this confirmation for my call to intercede for this great nation, I joined the Christian Intercessor's Network in Milford, Massachusetts. The Christian churches in the city and the neighboring counties organized prayer meetings. At that time, I was worshipping at Family Worship Center working with my great friends Pastors Peter and Soreness Lopez. From 2005 until 2010, being the pastor for the intercessory ministry and missions, I was the only African among the Spanish and white churches there.

There I met Sister Mary, who organized the "Call 7/7/07" in an open field of Uxbridge, Massachusetts, to pray for America. During the prayer, everyone felt the Southwind blowing softly, and the prophetic word came that God was visiting the land. Since then, the Lord visited America with restoration from the great financial depression. Before this prayer gathering, Pastor Linda Clark heard about me and wanted to meet with me. She came to our church in Milford, Massachusetts, and she invited me to the "Call 7/7/07." After Uxbridge, we went to Haven Hill, Massachusetts, to a church, Somebody Cares Ministry. We went to Dorchester, Boston, and other places to pray for America. Pastor Linda is a leader of APN and the Boston Prayer Network in New England. Around 2009, Sister Down Cosby started another prayer network in Worcester, Massachusetts, and I was part of it. We met at the public library. In those days, one felt the spiritual atmosphere was a very thick, dark cloud over the city. Our prayers had consumed the darkness. After that, God raised the Know Worcester, Citywide Prayer Network, and City Prayer Concert through Rev. Len Cowan and Rev. Lou Soiles. As we are trying to incorporate other churches, I am still the only African among the white intercessors. What is happening here? God is birthing a mission to reach the black, Latino, and other communities to connect to this citywide prayer network. Today, the city is filled with many prayer networks and churches.

As led, I have started the United Prayer Network, working together with the Citywide Prayer Network across the nation. This prayer network is bringing diversities of cultures together to pray. Our vision PUSH—Pray until Something Happens—has become a very robust system, and we will not rest until God avenges Himself upon His enemies and causes an awakening in this dark age. Join us to fight the good fight.

The World Is Crying for Help

The world is crying for help like Egypt did to Moses. Did you hear it? We have a job to do. Exodus 8:8 says, "Pharaoh summoned Moses and Aaron, **'Pray to the Lord to take the frogs away from my people and me, and I will let your people go to offer sacrifices to the Lord.'"**

Even though we are praying for our cities, we will need to expand the horizon of our prayers. As the Lord spoke to me in 2014 about the church declaring spiritual war on ISIS, Boko Haram, Al-Qaeda, and the enemies of the church, the question came to me pointedly, "Where will our cities and churches be in the ocean of the wickedness of ISIS if they strike in the homeland? We have the power to intercept their strategies now before it is too late." It is a call to all intercessors and every believer to pray for our cities as well as our nations. America is the only active hindrance to the extremist agenda. If we don't pray for the United States, the Christian world is heading to the worst persecution. We are in the end time prophecies. Queen Gorgo in the movie (*The 300: Rise of an Empire*) made an action remark and moved to fulfill it. When she saw that the enemies were overcoming their troops, she said, "I am not here as a witness." She took her husband's sword and killed many Persian warriors. I don't think we believers want to be witnesses what the enemy is doing to our people. How do we invade the territories of the enemy, who is slaughtering and crucifying men, raping women, and burying children and youths alive? America, Israel, Iraq, Syria, Nigeria, the United Kingdom, and many other countries are crying "Pray for me," just as Egypt cried to Moses, "Pray to the Lord ... for me."

Urgent Global Call to Prayer

The Lord spoke to me several times in November and December 2014 to call for urgent nationwide prayer against this evil engulfing the world at this crucial hour. I heard in my spirit while writing this that somebody was doubting and saying, "How can our prayer stop these evils?" Here's what Prophet Amos said the other day, "Surely the Sovereign Lord does nothing without revealing his plan to his servants the prophets" (Amos 3:7). God will do nothing except His people pray. Herod killed James at the inception of the church as the first martyr. At that time, the church was not praying for him when King Herod arrested him. They were not familiar with the prevailing prayer that breaks through the gates of jail and liberates the preachers. Take a moment and observe the next action when they took Peter, and detained him, ready to be beheaded. The church refused to stay quiet and to become witnesses to Peter's death. They did something different this time. The law of insanity says you cannot continue doing the same thing over and over again and expect different results, according to Albert Einstein. Here's what the church did differently.

The Power of Prayer in Action

So Peter was kept in prison, but the church was earnestly praying to God for him. The night before Herod was to bring him to trial, Peter was sleeping between two soldiers, bound with two chains, and sentries stood guard at the entrance. Suddenly an angel of the Lord appeared, and a light shone in the cell. He struck Peter on the side and woke him up. "Quick, get up!" he said, and the chains fell off Peter's wrists. Then the angel said to him, "Put on your clothes and sandals." And Peter did so. "Wrap your cloak around you and follow me," the angel told him. Peter followed him out of prison, but he had no idea that what the angel was doing was happening; he thought he saw a vision. They passed the first and second guards and came to the iron gate leading to the city. It opened for them by itself, and they went through it. When they had walked the length of one street, suddenly the angel left him. (Acts 12:5–10)

Let's observe this phrase again in verse 5 after they kept Peter in Prison. **"But the church was earnestly praying to God for him."** But it is in contrast to what is happening. It seems like there's no hope, but we will pray. Fear grips us, but we will not give up. They were taken by surprise by Stephen and James's death but no more. That would not happen to Peter. Peter was the one who had the keys of the kingdom. The leader of the apostolic movement. No gates of hell can prevail against him. They took a stand and did something different. The church earnestly prayed unto God for Peter and what happened? The Lord sent His angel to rescue him. Why didn't the Lord send the same deliverance to James? It was because either the church gave up or they didn't know what to do. Oh, believers, is it time to limit ourselves to logistical prayers for our personal needs or only for our churches and cities? No, it is time for a national and global prayer intercession. Is the church sleeping today as the disciples did when our Lord needed their prayers like never in His life? "And He came to the disciples and found them sleeping, and said to Peter, 'So you men could not keep watch with Me for one hour?'" (Matthew 26:40). How excruciating would it be to see people whom you trust, those you lean on, sleeping in the worst moment of your life?

There are a thousand and one reasons why we are called to raise the Ensign of Prayer Warfare. According to John Ankerberg's TV show, there is Sharia law in fifty-seven countries, including Britain and the United States (New Jersey and Texas are implementing it in the courts). Iran has threatened nuclear war. Undercover terrorist cells are brooding in the United States, waiting to strike at the same time in the main cities, and the plan is to eradicate Christians and Jews from the world. Syria, Iraq, and all the countries that are being demoralized are the reasons to pray like never before. Dr. Morris Cerullo asserted, "The world sits on a powder keg, ready to explode and rain down destruction! Is there an answer?"

The only answer we have is intercession. If the prophet Jeremiah were here today, he would say this, "Oh that my head were waters and my eyes a fountain of tears. That I might weep day and night for the slain of the daughter of my people!" (Jeremiah 9:1). Are there Jeremiahs today, the weeping prophets? Will you be one? God is looking for people who will lift up the **"ensign."** What is the ensign? The Greek is *nasas*, **meaning "a standard, ensign, signal, sign," and in late Hebrew, it is *id*, meaning "flag," as a rallying point.**

King David observed, "But you have raised a banner for those who fear you—a rallying point in the face of attack" (Psalm 60:4).

Do you remember "The Star-Spangled Banner"? How did the Founding Fathers know they won the battle against the British? It was because after all hope was gone, they saw the flag was still flying in the air. I love this because of the victory it depicts.

The flag is the rallying point; the spiritual meaning is the call to prayer.

Those who have been facing a threat and those who already lost their loved ones in Syria and Iraq are entangled with unusual situations and may never have a clue of how to escape. The world is looking on but does not know what to do. Millions of people around the world are perplexed and heartbroken but have no answers and Christians are on the radar of eradication. We Christians must rise and do something about these seemingly impossible situations incited by the devil. He has released demonic spirits of wickedness in high places into the world. Look, do not blame those whom the devil is using. It's not their will to destroy another human, but when the enemy demonizes or possesses someone, then that person is not in charge of his or her life. It is just like when a person is under the influence of drugs, he or she will finish whatever he or she is authorized to do and afterward come to his or her senses and then begin to cry. Create a mental picture and just imagine right now if the leaders of this terrorism should have an encounter with Jesus Christ; what do you think will be their reaction? The political leaders have no answer to this crisis. The UN and NATO can't do anything to thwart the fiendish plan set against us.

The answer is spiritual warfare and intercessory prayer. We need to cry and set up the ensign prayer rallying points throughout the cities and across the nations of the world. How do we invade these defiant human destroyers in the name of religion? The ensign is the stopping point. We must engage this urgent situation with the highest level of spiritual warfare. It is a global intercession of all Christians. In the history of some of the tribal wars in Ghana back in the day, one king asked his opponent, **"Who are your warriors?"**

The candidate replied, "All the circumcised males."

Imagine the devil asking Jesus Christ this question today. "Jesus, who are your warriors?"

He would answer, "Every blood-washed, Holy-Ghost-filled person and the believers of the cross of Calvary."

So you need to respond to this question today. Are you part of the army of the cross of Christ? If you answer yes, then you are automatically enlisted. You don't need to be an old widow, widower, pastor, or church leader to be an intercessor. You don't need to be poor or lose your job, marriage, or have a problem before you accept the call for intercession. We need help and don't care where the help is coming from or who is bringing the remedy. We just need prayer. Somebody, please, we need your prayers. My heart is hot within me as I am writing right now. Can you see what I am seeing? Can you feel what God is feeling, and can you hear the cry of the nations? They are beheading Christian men, and Christian women are becoming sex slaves to people who hate them. Children and youth are being buried alive. I pray that as you read this book, you may be filled with the

Spirit of intercessory prayer. Never have your peace without praying. Raise a group, adopt a street and neighborhood, and drop a prayer and anointed pin. Do you remember what the disciples of Jesus Christ did when He desperately needed their prayers? They were sleeping; although they promised Him to die with Him, they couldn't watch and pray for just one hour. Is the church still sleeping today? Or are the churches too busy building their cathedrals or busy looking for their wealth and have no time? I know every church prays and every believer prays too, but this time around, the prayer bulletins must change. Here's what Jesus said in Matthew 26:38–45:

> Then He said to them, "My soul is deeply grieved, to the point of death; remain here and keep watch with Me." And He went a little beyond them, and fell on His face and prayed, saying, "My Father, if it is possible, let this cup pass from Me; yet not as I will, but as You will." And He came to the disciples and found them sleeping, and said to Peter, "So, you men could not keep watch with Me for one hour?" … "Keep watching and praying that you may not enter into temptation; the spirit is willing, but the flesh is weak." He went away again a second time and prayed, saying, "My Father, if this cannot pass away unless I drink it, Your will be done." … Again He came and found them sleeping, for their eyes were heavy. And He left them again, and went away and prayed a third time, saying the same thing once more. Then He came to the disciples and said to them, "Are you still sleeping and resting? Behold, the hour is at hand and the Son of Man is being betrayed into the hands of sinners …"

I invite you to observe the verses 41–43 and 45. Three times, Jesus came to the disciples to see if they were praying, but He found them sleeping and resting. Finding them asleep and resting? It's remarkable in such a situation, permeated by suffering and surrounded by great danger. Peter received a special command to watch—which means don't sleep but pray and make sure your brethren are praying too.

Why should they so soon fall asleep? Did the church see the danger engulfing us? The Hamas, Jihadists, or terrorists made a statement that if they finished destroying the Saturdays, they would turn to the Sundays. Do you understand this statement? They are saying that if they finish killing the Jews, they will continue with the Christians. Jesus said, "Pray that your flight may not be in the winter," which means that although we are living in the end times and the prophecies are unfolding before our own eyes, we still need prayer so that our enemies cannot have the upper hand over us. According to 2 Samuel 24:14, "David said to Gad, I am in deep distress. Let us fall into the hands of the LORD, for His mercy is great, but do not let me fall into human hands."

A Syrian business partner of one of my members visited me, and while we were talking, he told me that he just came from Ghana. He said Ghana was peaceful, magnificent for business, and religion was very dynamic. He continued with a surprising observation he had while he was there. He said, "I saw the Islamic communities and how peaceful they are, but I am afraid for Ghana in some few years to come. These people are always calm in the initial state, but after they take root, and gain financial and intellectual control, and move into strategic positions, they will strike. In actuality, that was what happened in Syria. My family were wealthy and successful business people. Just one day, my father's shepherd, who was a Muslim, attacked us and told us to evacuate the house without taking a single item or else we would lose our lives that day. We ran for our lives, and he took over our wealth. A very rich doctor who helped the entire village also had a similar situation, but he chose to stay and save the people's lives. In turn, he lost his family and wealth." As he was telling his story, tears were running down his cheecks.

The only antidote to this helpless situation is prayer. If you think you are too busy to pray, then I have a question for you. Where were you when the September 11 strikes occurred, and what did you do during the breaking news? What I am seeing will be worse than September 11 if we don't pray intensively.

The Prayers of the Saints
An essential commodity in the kingdom today is prayer. The will of the Father of all lives is that no one will perish but that they will all know His Son and have eternal life "as it is in heaven." What is going on in heaven right now? The angel of the Lord is waiting to present the prayers of the saints.

> Another angel came and stood at the altar, holding a golden censer; and much incense was given to him so that he might add it to the prayers of all the saints on the golden altar which was before the throne. And the smoke of the incense, with the prayers of the saints, went up before God out of the angel's hand. Then the angel took the censer and filled it with the fire of the altar, and threw it to the earth, and there followed peals of thunder and sounds and flashes of lightning and an earthquake. (Revelation 8:3–5 NKJV)

In my observation, I realized that the angel of the Lord was waiting on the Christians to offer enough prayer. The apostles and the early church offered their prayers. The church fathers, the theologians, the church of the medieval period, and the reformers throughout history are waiting for our prayers to fill up the golden censer before the angel offers it with the incense. It is going to be a great judgment upon the wicked. Our prayers have power greater than the nuclear weapons of North Korea, Russia, and Iran put together. Why are we waiting as if we have no power? We are not cowards; we are not weak, not defeated, but more than the conquerors. Let's detonate our weapon of mass destruction. We have the power to intercept every authority and warhead thrown against us.

"For the weapons of our warfare are not carnal, but mighty through God to the pulling down of strongholds."

We are commanded to pray for the kingdom of God to come to the earth. The hearts of humanity, including those who are killing us, must be opened up to the kingdom of God. The kingdom is the Christ ruling in the heart the believer. Satan is the one influencing those who are killing us. He is operating through the strongman who controls the demons of wickedness in high places. We cannot stop them naturally except we detonate the nuclear power of prayer. They must repent and give their lives to Christ, and if they refuse to, then pray the legislative and judgmental prayers. Let's pray, and heaven will release His angels to unleash the prayers of the saints. God has not yet answered some of the prayers because they are waiting for us to activate them in this era of the last days. You may try to ignore this call to pray and continue with your business, but where will you be if nobody prays for God's intervention and if the enemy strikes in the area where you live?

The Viciousness of the Russian President
What do you think about the constant practice of hacking by the Russians? President Vladimir Putin has a plan to destroy the United States, and he is looking for the secret information. Once he gets it, the damage will be irreversible. The enemy cannot obliterate until he creates division. Now America is more divided than at any time in history. The cause is racism and politics. The threat we are facing is serious so we need to avoid the blame game, but stopping the mouth of the lion is our goal and the motivation of the sellers of the United States.

It is time to pray David's prayer against Ahithophel, who was advising Absalon with strategies to kill David. Do not forsake to pray mafia prayers as the need intensifies. As for the US politicians, pray for the visitation of the Holy Spirit.

The Only Weapon to Thwart the Plan of the Enemy
Intercessory prayer is the only weapon we are given to thwart the devil's plan. Be consistent, and you will see the promise fulfilled. "If

my people, which are called by my name, shall humble themselves, and pray, and seek my face, and turn from their wicked ways; then will I hear from heaven, and will forgive their sin, and will heal their land" (2 Chronicles 7:14 KJV).

Take a critical look at what the preceding verse is saying, "If my people ..." God will not do anything on earth until we give Him permission. And you ask why? It's because He gave humans dominion over the earth, and so He's not in charge of this planet. If we don't invite Him to take over, He will not come. That's why even though He promised the coming of the Messiah, Anna and Simeon and many other intercessors could not depart from the temple until they saw the Messiah. Brethren, catch something here. Our beloved physician Luke mentioned that Anna was an eighty-four-year-old when she saw the Lord's Christ.

> And there was a prophetess, Anna, the daughter of Phanuel, of the tribe of Asher. She was advanced in years and had lived with her husband seven years after her marriage, and then as a widow to the age of eighty-four. She never left the temple, serving night and day with Fasting and Prayers. At that very moment, she came up and began giving thanks to God, and continued to speak of Him to all those who were looking for the redemption of Jerusalem. (Luke 2:36–38)

Now join me in this calculation. Anna married seven years and became a widow. She saw Christ in the temple when she was eighty-four years of age. So 84 − 7 = 77. According to Saint Augustine, seventy-seven is the last limit of sin because it is the product of 11 and the number 7 is the number of perfection. According to our beloved physician, the generation from Adam to Christ was 77. (See Luke 3:23–38.) If this was the reason why Anna became a widow within seven years of her marriage, then Christ came to answer her prayer at the end of 77 years in pain, sin, sorrow, and also console her and the Lord's Israel. Prayer is inevitable and must not be the last thing to do when we are faced with life's hardest challenges. In the kingdom economy, prayer is priceless and the first commodity in the time of need. We must burden ourselves with the heartbeat of God that if pestilence strike and you call, I will answer. "If my people who are called by my name ..."

We see pestilences today in the form of the Ebola pandemic, the rise of the haters of Jesus Christ and His church, and the rise of ISIS. What are we waiting for to start praying? Are you waiting for American politicians to save you? You want them to stop the Russian, North Korean, and Iranian nuclear threat? Look, they are divided. They cannot compromise. Do you know why? I hear you say *no*! I will tell you why. According to our beloved physician Luke in 11:17, "Any kingdom divided against itself will be ruined, and a house divided against itself will fall."

Do you see why America is finding it difficult? The secret is that the ISIS, the Jihadists, and Iran are all operating under strong spiritual leaders who are continually raising altars of confusion among the American politicians. The devil has gotten four loopholes and is bombarding us to weaken and to create division. What are they? Well, if I mention them, will you accept them? Will you do something about it? Okay, I know you are ready for it so here they are: separation of religion and state, political parties, racial profiling, and same-sex marriage. The state prophet said it best the other day in Daniel 11:32 (NIV), "But the people that do know their God shall be strong, and do exploits." American politicians and the unbelievers said they don't need God. Yes, the devil knows the defense of Israel is God and likewise America's protection cannot be outside God Almighty. Second, the political parties will not agree on the issues that will save the nation but only work for their interest. How about the genetic profile? You be the judge. They both saw that America is falling, but the only hand holding her is that of the intercessors. That is the hope we have. You will read the full vision that there is still hope for America in a later chapter.

Unity of the Church in Prayer Is Inevitable
Unity in the body of Christ is invariable. Let's answer Christ's prayer that they may be one as we are one.

My prayer is not for them alone. I also pray for those who will believe in me through their message, that all of them may be one, Father, just as you are to me and I am in you. May they also be in us so that the world may believe that you have sent Me. I have given them the glory that you gave me, that they may be one as we are one.

If the church is united, Christ will release His glory upon us, and this will speak to the world that Jesus is Lord. What will happen in the world of our enemies today if the church consistently comes together and raises our voice as it occurred in Acts 4:23–24?

And being let go, they went to their companions and reported all that the chief priests and elders had said to them. So when they heard that, they raised their voice to God with one accord and said: "Lord, You are God, who made heaven and earth and the sea, and all that is in them …"

They cried out to God, and He shook the place and empowered them, and no one could join them with any evil intentions. Thus, the church triumphed and turned the city upside down.

Prayer Brings Prophecies to Fulfilment
God promised Abraham that his children should serve in a foreign country for 400 years. After that, they would cry out for help and He would send them a Savior. If you observe the scripture carefully, you will realize it is amazing. At the end of the 400 years, the Israelites were still in Egypt because no one was interceding. But by 430 years, there were more intercessors in the land praying for their deliverance. These prayers moved God to come down and assess the situation. Now the intensity of their prayers placed a high demand, so He sent Moses to their rescue. "So God heard their groaning; and God

remembered His covenant with Abraham, Isaac, and Jacob. God saw the sons of Israel, and God took notice of them" (Exodus 2:24–25).

During Israel's seventy years in captivity, no one was praying until Daniel began to read the prophecy of Jeremiah and started to pray and fast. Immediately God brought deliverance.

> In the first year of his reign, I, Daniel, observed in the books the number of the years which was revealed as the word of the Lord to Jeremiah the prophet for the completion of the desolations of Jerusalem, namely, seventy years. So I gave my attention to the Lord God to seek Him by prayer and supplications, with fasting, sackcloth, and ashes. I prayed to the Lord my God and confessed and said, "Alas, O Lord, the great and awesome God, who keeps His covenant and lovingkindness for those who love Him and keep His commandments." (Daniel 9:2–4)

Isaiah prophesied over 700 years and Malachi proclaimed 400 years earlier that the Messiah would be born to deliver His people from their sin but not until Anna and Simeon made the temple their dwelling and interceded for the Savior to be born. Imagine how Simeon would have been praying when the Holy Spirit told him that He was not dying until his eyes beheld the hope and Savior of Israel.

> And it had been revealed to him by the Holy Spirit that he would not see death before he had seen the Lord's Christ. And he came in the Spirit into the temple; and when the parents brought in the child Jesus, to carry out for Him the custom of the Law, then he took Him into his arms, and blessed God, and said … And there was a prophetess, Anna, the daughter of Phanuel, of the tribe of Asher. She was advanced in years and had lived with her husband seven years after her marriage, and then as a widow to the age of eighty-four. She never left the temple, serving night and day with fastings and

> prayers. At that very moment, she came up and began giving thanks to God, and continued to speak of Him to all those who were looking for the redemption of Jerusalem. (Luke 2: 26–38)

In the like manner, God will not fulfill certain things until we believers begin to pray beyond the walls of our churches and our individual needs. Jeremiah prophesied to his people to seek the good of the city and the country in which the Lord will bring them. "Also, seek the peace and prosperity of the city to which I have carried you into exile. Pray to the Lord for it, because if it prospers, you too will prosper" (Jeremiah 29:7). Many churches and believers are accustomed to a logistic prayer as John Hull and Tim Elmore asserted in their book *Pivotal Praying*. They used three military terms to illustrate different types of prayer. Logistical prayer focuses on one's personal needs. Tactical Prayer focuses on helping others, but it's still from a temporal perspective. It does not capture God's heart and purpose for the world. Many Christians prays only logistical prayers. Some pastors and prophets focal point are emphasized only on tactical prayers which are the cynosures of the needs of the people. Many Intercessors also focuses on their communities and cities. It hurts me and I asks, "who will pray for the nation/s?" Strategic prayer focuses on God's ultimate objective for the world. It is a prayer from an eternal perspective. It captures God's heart and purposes. God is calling intercessors to pray for the world harvest. Will you be part of this movement?

Repentance for the Nations
America, being the beacon of the nations, has deviated from the principles of the founders. There were many satanic plans to bring America down and to crush her kingdom. The devil knew that the United States derived her power from God and the unity of the church and state. Schools taught moral behavioral transformation, and the nation was at peace. It made her foundations and walls firmer and stronger. **"In God we trust"** means that United States' strength is of

God. Here are some relevant quotes from the founders of our great nation and the only backbone for the Jews and Christian nations in the world.

The following quotes are taken from "God and the Bible in the U.S. History by Pastor Steven Andrews.

George Washington, the first US president and the father of the United States, said, "While we are zealously performing the duties of good citizens and soldiers, we certainly ought not to be inattentive to the higher duties of religion. To the distinguished character of Patriot, it should be our highest glory to add the more distinguished character of Christian" (*The Writings of Washington*, 342–343).

John Adams, the second US president and a signer of the Declaration of Independence said, "Suppose a nation in some distant Region should take the Bible for their only law Book, and every member should regulate his conduct by the precepts there exhibited! Every member would be obliged in conscience, to temperance, frugality, and industry; to justice, kindness, and charity towards his fellow men; and to piety, love, and reverence toward Almighty God … What a Eutopia, what a Paradise would this region be" (Diary and Autobiography of John Adams, Vol. III, 9).

"The general principles, on which the Fathers achieved independence, were the only Principles in which that beautiful Assembly of young Gentlemen could Unite, and these Principles only could be intended by them in their address, or by me in my answer. And what were these general Principles? I answer, the general Principles of Christianity, in which all these Sects were United: And the general Principles of English and American Liberty, in which all those young Men United, and which had United all Parties in America, in Majorities sufficient to assert and maintain her Independence. Now I will avow, that I then believe, and now believe, that those general Principles of Christianity, are as eternal and immutable, as the Existence and Attributes of God;

and that those Principles of Liberty, are as unalterable as human Nature and our terrestrial, mundane System" (John Adams, excerpt from a letter to Thomas Jefferson, on June 28, 1813).

"The second day of July 1776, will be the most memorable epoch in the history of America. I am apt to believe that it will be celebrated by succeeding generations as the great anniversary Festival. It ought to be commemorated, as the Day of Deliverance, by solemn acts of devotion to God Almighty. It ought to be solemnized with pomp and parade, with shows, games, sports, guns, bells, bonfires, and illuminations, from one end of this continent to the other, from this time forward forever" (John Adams, in a letter to his wife, Abigail, on July 3, 1776).

Thomas Jefferson, the third US president and drafter and signer of the Declaration of Independence wrote, "God who gave us life gave us liberty. And can the liberties of a nation be thought secure when we have removed their only firm basis, a conviction in the minds of the people that these liberties are of the Gift of God? That they are not to be violated but with His wrath? Indeed, I tremble for my country when I reflect that God is just; that His justice cannot sleep forever; That a revolution of the wheel of fortune, a change of situation, is among possible events; that it may become probable by Supernatural influence! The Almighty has no attribute which can take side with us in that event" (*Notes on the State of Virginia*, Query XVIII, 237).

"I am a real Christian—that is to say, a disciple of the doctrines of Jesus Christ" (*The Writings of Thomas Jefferson*, 385).
(Congress printed a Bible for America and said)

"The United States in Congress assembled … recommend this edition of the Bible to the inhabitants of the United States … a neat edition of the Holy Scriptures for the use of schools."
– *United States Congress 1782*

Congress passed this resolution:

"The Congress of the United States recommends and approves the Holy Bible for use in all schools."
– *United States Congress 1782*

By Law the United States Congress adds to US coinage: "In God We Trust"
– *United States Congress 1864*

John Hancock, the first signer of the Declaration of Independence, said, "Resistance to tyranny becomes the Christian and social duty of each individual ... Continue steadfast and, with a proper sense of your dependence on God, nobly defend those rights which heaven gave, and no man ought to take from us" (*History of the United States of America*, Vol. II, 229).

Benjamin Franklin, a signer of the Declaration of Independence and the United States Constitution, wrote, "Here is my Creed. I believe in one God, the Creator of the Universe. That He governs it by His Providence. That He ought to be worshiped. That the most acceptable service we render to him is in doing good to his other children. That the soul of man is immortal, and will be treated with justice in another life respecting its conduct in this. These I take to be the fundamental points in all sound religion, and I regard them as you do in whatever sect I meet with them. As to Jesus of Nazareth, my opinion of whom you particularly desire, I think the system of morals and his religion, as he left them to us, is the best the world ever saw or is likely to see" (from a letter to Ezra Stiles, president of Yale University, dated March 9, 1790).

The following quotes are from Ronald Reagan.

"If we ever forget that we are One Nation Under God, then we will be a nation gone under."

"Within the covers of the Bible are the answers for all the problems men face."

"We are never defeated unless we give up on God."

"The struggle now going on in the world will never be decided by bombs or rockets, by armies or military might. The real crisis we face today is the spiritual one; at root, it is a test of moral will and faith."

As we have studied the beliefs of the fathers, it has become crucial for any thoughtful person to see where our nation is heading. The devil has a long-term plan for destroying America, which is revealed in the quotations from President Ronald Reagan. "We are never defeated unless we give up on God" and "If we ever forget that we are One Nation Under God, then we will be a nation gone under."

The devil has achieved his goal for causing the United States to forget the God who made her the greatest nation on earth. They gave up on God. The grace and the sovereignty of the Almighty have sent many intercessors from other countries to help fight. So I have confidence that the adversary will soon lose the battle.

The Plan to Destroy the United States
Satan has devised some intents to destroy the United States—communism and socialism and his plan to separate the state and the church. He knew that if the church was not in the affairs of the government, the moral standard would fall. The communists over a hundred years ago planned this, and little by little, the tactics were implemented and enforced by groups and politicians. According to US history, almost twenty-four of the fifty-six men who signed the declaration of independence had theological degrees. What has happened to the United States now? The schools were forbidden to teach religious education and prayer, but teachers are allowed to teach witchcraft and immorality and other practices, which bring the anger of God. They are protesting to have nothing to do with God.

The Illuminati and the communists have planned to wipe out Christianity and the Jewish people. They have the same goal. The agenda is to set up one world government. There are thirteen family bloodlines that control this world of which three families dominated the rest and owned it. Most of the presidents are controlled by the secret cult of Satanism in the Illuminati initiations. It became clear why the Bible admonished us to pray for our national leaders and all those in authority.

The History of Gay and Lesbianism in the Ancient World

Anal sex between male and male and then female and female was viewed as an offering to the goddess Diana or Ashtaroth and Molock. Ashtaroth was the female goddess while Molock was the male god. They even burn their children as a sacrifice to Molock. These practices provoked the apostle Paul to write Romans 1:23–27 in the first century. Unfortunately, the belief and practice of homosexuality is an unyielding spirit that has overpowered America and the United Kingdom and ultimately covered the rest of the world. For this reason, people who speak against it are attacked spiritually and sometimes find themselves tempted to do the same thing because it is a sacrifice to the sun god. Some of the the people who quit goes back. He will make sure he silences whoever takes a stand against it.

The United States did not detect the secret agenda of the enemy. If God is for you, why do you reject Him? What evil has He done to you? The United States didn't keep the God that established us but rather rejected Him. All this did not start with this generation. It's just that the evil seed of hatred of God that they planted in the 1960s and 1970s in secret is now bearing fruit. It is our job to change the destiny of this great nation by the united voice of the church in prayer.

Pray for Jerusalem

God Himself is the warrior and an intercessor for the children of Israel. He will not rest until the plan of the enemy is disappointed. But God will not do anything on earth without a person. If He wants to do it by Himself, it will not take that long, but to work with a human, it has to take some time. We need the seer and the Shamar prophets in this kind of battle.

> For Zion's sake I will not keep silent, for Jerusalem's sake I will not remain quiet, till her righteousness shines out like the dawn, her salvation like a blazing torch ... I have posted watchmen on your walls, O Jerusalem; they will never be silent day or night. You who call on the Lord, give yourselves no rest and give him no rest till he establishes Jerusalem and makes her the praise of the earth. The Lord has sworn by his right hand and by his mighty arm: "Never again will I give your grain as food for your enemies, and never again will foreigners drink the new wine for which you have toiled." (Isaiah 62:1, 6–8)

We are seeing how hatred against Israel and Christianity has spread to the killing of millions of people around the world. As many Christians are praying, God is calling for resilience in His warriors against the spirit of wickedness. The world is sitting on a powder keg. The politicians are going all out to thwart the death toll, but the battle is beyond human imagination.

Pray on Purpose
They hate the Jews for the following reasons:

- They gave to the world the greatest book of deliverance and life (the Bible).
- Through them, the world received the Savior (Jesus Christ).
- They did not accept the Messiah.

God's number one prayer He commanded all Christians to pray is for the peace of Jerusalem. He said, "For Zion's sake will I not hold my peace, and for Jerusalem's sake I will not rest, until the righteousness thereof go forth as brightness, and the salvation thereof as a lamp that burneth….. [6] I have set watchmen upon thy walls, O Jerusalem, which shall never hold their peace day nor night: ye that make mention of the LORD, keep not silence,

[7] And give him no rest, till he establish, and till he make Jerusalem a praise in the earth." (Isaiah 62:1, 6-7) Let us stand with our brothers the Jewish people. Pray that they will all accept Jesus Christ as the only Messiah.

Repentance for America and Israel
The church must take it seriously and ask God for forgiveness on behalf of our countries. Many nations did what America is doing—neglecting the commandments of God and trying to please the majority who hate the Lord. America has to repent for wickedness against the slaves, racism, rejecting God, and much more.

Reconciliation
Racism divided America. Now it has affected the police and the African American men. There is not enough room in the prisons, so the devil wants to eradicate the African American men and especially the youth through shootings and drugs. They are walking in fear to the point that most of them do not have any hope for the future, so they either kill themselves or the police shoot them. Hatred is building up every day. It is time to come back to God and ask for forgiveness. Both parties have to know that there will be a judgment by the Almighty God.

Ambassadors of Reconciliation
According to Apostle Paul,

"And all of this is a gift from God, who brought us back to himself through Christ. And God has given us this task of reconciling people to him. For God was in Christ, reconciling the world to himself, no longer counting people's sins against them. And he gave us this wonderful message of reconciliation. So we are Christ's ambassadors; God is making his appeal through us. We speak for Christ when we plead, "Come back to God!" (1Corinthians 5:18-20. NLT)

God has given to the church the ministry of reconciliation to unite people to Him. There's a problem with the church right now. What is it? We see in America today how the police and the blacks are crushing each other each day. It is getting out of hand, and every effort is exhausted, but we never hear too much about what the church is doing concerning reconciliation. My intercessors continue to pray for God's intervention. Maybe we are thinking some great men and women of God should do it, but God is looking for the Gideons to rise and bring that ministry to the desperate nation.

CHAPTER 27

ASSIGNMENT IN AMERICA

My assignment in the Kroboland lasted from 1986 to 2005. My mother and all my nine siblings live in Accra. I couldn't forget our beautiful sister Rebecca who passed away. She was the first among the seven girls. My family tried to persuade me to join them in Accra, but I turned down their request several times. I rejected several opportunities because of the burden on my heart. I saw the same passion in my compatriot pastors of the Krobo state. Read more of what the Lord did in that state.

As soon as I finished my job, the Lord transitioned me to the United States. I asked Him in 2006, "Why did You bring me here now and not when America was peaceful?"

The Lord answered me, "America didn't need you then, but now she needs you to intercede for her."

Then I realized that it's not all about us; it's mostly about what the Lord wants to accomplish through us. Are you willing to surrender to His call to pray? You have an assignment that needs haste to achieve it. "And David told the high priest, 'The King's business required haste'" (1 Samuel 21:8). Have you felt that urgency yet?

Our call to intercede for the United States, Israel, and the rest of the world is urgent. If they destroy America, there's no hope for the Christian world except the Lord saves a remnant. Where are you called to intercede? It is a global call to prayer. As you read this book, I urge you therefore brethren to join a prayer team or intercessors network in your community or start one for your city and nation. Don't forget to connect with us for more guidance. We can all tune in together, but be not silent.

The second and third confirmation of the call to intercede for America came again in one month. On the Lord's Day, May 3, 2015, at 6:30 a.m., the Lord forbade the one who saw the vision to tell the details. The Lord took him, and as they were in the heavenly realm in the Spirit, the Lord was talking with him. He then asked the Lord. "Why did you bring us here to America?"

He replied, "The United States needs you." The conversation continued, but I can't narrate it here as the Lord forbade me to. The third revelation and confirmation came again in the month of May on the Lord's Day. It was between 6:30 and 7:00 a.m., on May 17, 2015. It was not a call to only the couple who saw it. It was a global call for all Christians around the world. Although everyone is praying, God wants to hear the unified voice of the intercessors. Please don't put this book down. Read on.

Chapter 28

There Is Still Hope for America

The Special Vision
"It is not expedient for me doubtless to glory. I will come to visions and revelations of the Lord.

[2]I knew a man in Christ above fourteen years ago, (whether in the body, I cannot tell; or whether out of the body, I cannot tell: God knoweth;) such an one caught up to the third heaven." 2 Corinthians 12:1-3)

I want to talk about a heavenly vision the Lord shown to His servant. Here's how he saw it. He narrated, "The Lord took me up into heaven and said, 'I am going to show you something.' We came into an atmosphere, and we stood in the air. The Lord said, "Keep watching," as I was looking, behold the cloud above us began to change. It was as the grassy sea. It also looked like a sea tide. It was more beautiful than anything I can describe. The cloud was blue and white. While I was looking, a woman appeared from the cloud, dressed in the colors I saw. She was gorgeous. The top of the dress the woman was wearing was white, but from the waist down, it was blue. I couldn't see any woman as extravagant as her. The Lord was holding me in the palm of

His hand. He then told me, "This lady is America. America is falling! America is falling! Go quickly and receive her into the palm of your hands so that she does not fall."

Oh my God! One can never compare movement in the realm of the Spirit to the chronos or time of this universe. No seconds can correlate to a second over there. What we call moments here in the earth realm are not the same there, as Prophet Isaiah asserted: "Before they call, I will answer; and while they are speaking, I will hear" (Isaiah 65:24). It means the seconds over there are what we call "before." Before you pray, he hears it. Before you think, He has answered it.

"In the vision, as soon as the Lord said to me, 'Receive her and don't let her fall.' I was already there waiting for her to land on my hand. After she had landed, I began to move fast. I saw a hill and thought, *I am going to drop her off on that hill.* The Lord said, 'Don't drop her off because if her feet touch the ground, America will fall. You must ascend higher to where I will show you.' She fell from the third heavens, from the presence of God, and we need to restore her to her former place.' We began to ascend from the first heaven into the third heaven. It was the most difficult ascension I had ever experienced. In the first atmospheric realm, the ascent was fast and easy, but on reaching the second atmospheric field, which is the second heaven. We couldn't go straight upward. First, we were ascending just as on a winding mountain road. I saw cloud covered a tall building and the top of the roof, and I wanted to enter and drop her off there, but I was forbidden. So I continued. As we reached the top of that building, I was about to land again, but the Lord said to me, 'Do not land. Continue to go up higher.' I beheld a second extravagant high-rise glass building. It was taller than any building on earth, and it reached into the other clouds, but I couldn't see the end of it. We were supposed to go beyond that height into the realm of the third heaven to the presence of God. It was difficult. The Spirit lifted us up and ascended with us to the third heaven. Thus she got to her destination at last. Let's confess this together; "There's still hope for America."

It is the end of the vision the Lord gave to me. The servant who saw this represents the intercessors in America. The Lord is calling all intercessors to hold America with their hands and the voice of unity, so she does not fall.

The Meaning of the Vision
The man who saw the vision represents the intercessors, and they are holding America in their hands. Otherwise, she will fall. The ascension from the first heaven was easy because many people are praying in that atmospheric realm. But the ascension through the second heaven was terrible because that domain needs the combined force of the intercessors. Different groups are doing separate intercessory prayers. It will make it difficult to win the spiritual battle in Satan's jurisdiction. The second heaven is where Satan is ruling. Now he has transferred that authority to the United States of America's atmospheric realm in the spirit. Satan is in charge of the nation but we won at last. Satan's power is broken and we have ascended into God's presence.

The vision came on May 17, 2015, and exactly on June 26, 2015, the Supreme Court judges legalized same-sex marriage, which millions of Americans celebrated, mocking Jesus Christ our Lord and Savior. God is saying, because of your prayers, He will restore America.

When God is speaking about America, it's about the entire Christian world and not only the United States of America. Whatever happens in the United States is imitated by the whole world. So if we save America, we save the world for Christ. God brought my wife and me for this purpose. It is the third confirmation of our assignment, but no one can do it alone. The Lord is calling you alongside to join the frontiers. The Bible says, David, after he served his generation, slept with his fathers.

God raised many men and women for the nation of Israel. He raised prophets, judges, and kings. He also raised men like Charles Wesley, John Wesley, John Knox, Charles Spurgeon, and Rees Howells in their generations for their nation.

On reaching the peak of the ministry of intercession in his life, his prevailing prayer changed World War II. At the point of his death, Rees Howells turned to his son, Samuel Howells. "Whatever you do, stand and maintain these intercessions." According to Richard Maton, Samuel became faithful to his commission as an effective intercessor. Samuel raised hundreds of intercessors who prayed whenever gospel liberty was threatened. They prayed for a global revival, beginning with China's revival. "Samuel's intercessory battles led him to bind the strong man during the Korean War to the Cuban Missile Crisis and from the Six-Day War to the fall of the Berlin Wall."

We have great men and women God is using to raise this and the next generation in America, Israel, and other parts of the world. God's generals of intercessors, like Cindy Jacobs, C. Peter Wagner, Bishop T. D. Jakes, Chuch D. Pierce, Linda Clark, Rev. Len Cowan, Rev. Lou Soile, Bill, and many more are on the move. Will you be part of the new movement?

Revival in the Shelters and the Streets among the Homeless
During the prayer walk with Straight Ahead Ministry and United Prayer Ensign Network in Worcester, Massachusetts, Brother Richard told me about a dream a homeless drug addict had. "The man slept, and he couldn't wake up for almost two days. What he saw was beyond explanation. The man saw heaven open suddenly, and they took him to a place. The voice that was speaking to him was like thunder and loud until he couldn't understand the words. The voice told him, the Lord was about to do something and he should be getting ready for it." I wrote it here just to encourage the Worcester Citywide Prayer Network, the United Prayer Ensign Network, and all the prayers that are going on in the various places.

God is about to do something on the street, and even the homeless and drug addicts will catch the revival fire first. Oh, our God still has people in the stones yet to be raised to praise Him. Get ready! Get ready! Get ready! Something is happening. If someone asks you, "What is the time right now?" what will you say? "It is the season of intercessory prayers."

The Three Heavens

The Hebrew word for *heavens* is *shamayim* and is pronounced "shä·mah'·yim." Its meaning in the plural form is "heights." "The heavens" occurred 420 times in the King James Version, eight times between Genesis 1:1 and Exodus 20:22. Refer to Genesis 1:1 and 2:1: "In the beginning, God created the heavens and the earth." The phrase "heavens and earth" means the entire universe. The Jewish tradition from a biblical standpoint indicates there are three "heavens." The first heaven is the earth's atmosphere. The second is outer space as far as it can stretch. The third heaven is the abode of the Almighty, the dwelling place of the Most High God.

The First Heaven

The first heaven is the firmament, Earth's atmospheric realm. This is the immediate sky where we see aircraft fly to and fro. It is the place where the "fowls of the heaven" are according to Genesis 2:19 and 7:3. It is the place where light and darkness were separated during creation, according to Genesis 1:14: "And God said, 'Let there be lights in the firmament of the heavens to divide the day from the night.'" The first heaven consists of the atmosphere and the clouds. Genesis 7:11 says, "In the six-hundredth year of Noah's life, in the second month, the seventeenth day of the month, the same day were all the fountains of the great deep broken up, and the windows of heaven were opened." "Windows" and "doors" of heaven represent the firmament and the atmospheric earth realm.

Second Heaven

Outer space, the starry heavens, is the second heaven. Daniel 12:3 says, "And they that be wise shall shine as the brightness of the firmament, and they that turn many to righteousness as the stars forever and ever." (See also Jeremiah 8:2 and Matthew 24:29.) The Hebrew word is *raqa* "expanse," i.e., the firmament or visible arch of the sky. "Raqia" is the starry heaven. It starts at where the earthly atmosphere ends. It is where the sun, moon, and stars are fixed in orbit. The prophet observed in Jeremiah 8:2, "They will be exposed to the sun and the moon and all the stars of the heavens which they have loved and served ..."

Satan and his hosts control the earth's atmospheric realm, which is the first heaven. They operate from the second heaven. The Holy Spirit unveiled this to Paul the apostle in Ephesians 2:1–2: "And you hath he quickened, who were dead in trespasses and sins; Wherein in time past ye walked according to the course of this world, according to the prince of the power of the air, the spirit that now worketh in the children of disobedience." This is the dangerous realm. Paul continued in his revelations concerning the satanic hierarchy in the heavenly places, which depicted the second heaven. He asserted, "For we wrestle not against flesh and blood, but against principalities, against powers, against the rulers of the darkness of this world, against spiritual wickedness in high places" (Ephesians 6:12). Don't be confused about the natural realms of the skies and clouds. Satan and his demons are not flesh and blood. They cannot operate in the earth realm without human or animal bodies because they are spiritual beings. He is the prince of the power of the air, and his higher-ranked demons dwell there. He is not everywhere at the same time, but he has territorial spirits who control territories and individuals in the earth realm. They feed him with information. In another vision, the servant of the Lord was taken to the 2nd heaven. In that realm there's no light at all. It's absolutely dark. You cannot see anything. There's no floor or ground to stand on. It is an atmosphere. I am forbidden to talk about what transpired there. Warning; it is injudicious or inadvisable to conduct a spiritual exercise or warfare over there if the Lord has not ask you to, because it's dangerous. The devil could fight everything around you. We always win if the Holy Spirit is in charge of the battle.

The reason why I tried to explain the three heavens and the activities of the devil is for you to understand the vision you just read. It's about the falling of America. America fell from the third heaven into the first heaven, but it did not crash into the earth. The Lord held her and kept her from falling, and she was being helped to ascend back into her former place in the third heaven. There is still the grace of God. The second heaven was difficult to break through during the ascension because it's Satan's jurisdiction. He controls the air and that atmosphere. It took God's grace to bring her there. The intercessors need to unite to pray until America takes her position in the third heaven where the founding fathers placed her and declared with power, "In God we trust. One nation under God."

I also want to unveil the attacks that pervade in the second heaven against the church. Whenever men and women of God are rising to the higher level of the supernatural, especially those who do spiritual warfare, they are faced with severe attacks and some of them crash. When you pray sometimes, you feel tired and want to give up because you feel that God is not answering your prayers. Others are attacked by the lukewarm spirit to weaken their prayer life. Sometimes the attacks are geared to your family. That sense comes directly from Satan himself. There is something important you need to know. Your persistence in faith and consistency in prayer will bring victory. The reason why Our Lord Jesus warned us not to doubt when praying but believe is due to these battles.

Some men and women of God and people who are experiencing the call of God in their lives also attract attacks. The devil uses deception through the angels of light. They look like God's holy angels, but they are not. They carry little lies to dilute the word of God with wrong interpretations of the word. They lead many away by their dreams of celestial beings. Unfortunately, they don't utilize the gift of discerning of spirits. A pastor went to a mountain alone for a forty-day fast and prayer. He was seeking for the power of God to perform miracles, but something went terribly wrong, which changed his life and ministry. The angel of light visited him, and now he is not normal. He is now proclaiming that he is God. Dreams and visions mislead most of the White Garment Churches, which are commonly known as Alla-dulah or occult churches in Africa. They receive messages from the angels of light. I learned this at the University of the Holy Spirit during my early years of calling into ministry. I can't detail it now, but I might try to write another book. It will teach about the levels of spiritual dimensions, which every prayer warrior needs to know about, especially those whom the Lord is calling into ministry and intercession. Satan operates directly from the second heaven. He gives orders to his principalities and powers.

Third Heaven
The third heaven is the abode, the secret place of the Most High God. It is the dwelling place of the Almighty. It is where the holy angels, living creatures, elders, and spirits of holy ones dwell. "But will God really dwell on earth with humans? The heavens, even the highest heavens, cannot contain you. How much less this temple I have built!" (2 Chronicles 6:18 NIV). The NIV called it "the heavens, the highest heavens," while the KJV says "the heaven of the heavens" in Psalm 115:16. No scientist has ever discovered this place, even with the most sophisticated equipment or with any human eye.

The Fall of America from the Third Heaven
The time to take our stand is now. More than ever before, we will face oppositions, but that must not deter us. Everywhere you are in the world; please join us by praying like never before. Just as God

revealed the falling of America, within the third week on June 27, 2015, the Supreme Court of the United States of America legalized same-sex marriage, even though the Constitution did not allow it. It isn't ISIS that will destroy America but those who have the power to twist the law. The secret I have learned over the years is that if the devil tries to destroy someone and cannot succeed, he will allow the person to kill himself. Have you ever seen people who were restricted by their doctors concerning particular food or behaviors but they still eat it or do it? As the devil couldn't succeed in destroying America, he set the leaders up. The politicians have the power to destroy their countries. They are fulfilling their job. You and I have a job to do too. Our assignment is to give God no rest and give ourselves no rest until He makes our Jerusalem a paradise on earth.

There's hope for America. There's hope for Jerusalem. There's hope for your country. There's still hope for the Christian world because God is coveting our prayers. Here's His plea: "If my people, who are called by my name, will humble themselves and pray and seek my face and turn from their wicked ways, then I will hear from heaven, and I will forgive their sin and will heal their land" (2 Chronicles 7:14).

CHAPTER 29

HE TEACH MY HANDS TO WAR AND MY FINGERS TO FIGHT

Psalm 18 and 144

Have you ever been in the four seasons and you still survived? If you have ever been chased, you will know how to jump over a wall. If you have ever been attacked, you will know how to run through a troop. If you have ever faced the enemy, that's when your hands can bend a bow of steel. Yes, He teaches my hands to war and my fingers to fight, and He made my enemy dust under my feet. Have you been known in hell? In certain types of spiritual warfare, no one can teach you better how to win the battle, but the Holy Spirit takes you through that process in order to teach your hands to war and your fingers to fight. There are battles to fight, fights to engage in, mountains to climb, strongholds to take, and cities to invade. Get ready and arm yourself. Until your spirit boils up with anger against the enemy, you cannot change the destiny of a nation.

King David didn't pray a pious prayer but rather an aggressive one. Your hands can never be trained to war in the palace. No, not in your comfort zone. You must come to a place of desperation for survival. King David knew what he was talking about concerning his struggles. The only mentor he had was seeking for his life to kill him. King Saul was jealous of him because of the songs of the women. King Saul killed his thousands and David his ten thousand. King David spent his life in the desert, and the worst part of it was when he wanted to take refuge in the country of Goliath during his state of exasperation. Don't forget that David was a wanted man of that city because it was the slaying of that giant that elevated him and trumpeted his fame. He had to run to it to take refuge. In 1 Samuel 21:10–11, we read, "Then David arose and fled that day from Saul, and went to Achish king of Gath. But the servants of Achish said to him, 'Is this not David the king of the land? Did they not sing of this one as they danced, saying, 'Saul has slain his thousands, And David his ten thousand'?"

And in 2 Samuel 22:29–30, it says, "For You are my lamp, O Lord; And the Lord illumines my darkness. For by You I can run upon a troop; By my God, I can leap over a wall. As for God, His way is blameless; The word of the Lord is tested; He is a shield to all who take refuge in Him …"

When systems and human efforts bring us fame and wealth, how do we need God? We will not pray with desperation but rather with piousness. We will think that we must just confess the word and it's enough. Huh, David saw it differently. He knew that the only way to engage the enemy was through prayer warfare. He experienced the deliverances of God through the seasons of consistency and intercessional wars. Here's how the king prayed.

Psalm 144:1–15 says,

> Blessed be the Lord my strength, which teacheth my hands to war, and my fingers to fight: My goodness, and my fortress; my high tower, and my deliverer; my shield, and he in whom I trust; who subdueth my people under me. Lord, what is a man, that thou takest knowledge of him! or the son of man, that thou makest account of him! Man is like to vanity: his days are as a shadow that passeth away. Bow thy heavens,

O Lord, and come down: touch the mountains, and they shall smoke. Cast forth lightning, and scatter them: shoot out thine arrows, and destroy them. Send thine hand from above; rid me, and deliver me out of great waters, from the hand of strange children; Whose mouth speaketh vanity and their right hand is a right hand of falsehood. I will sing a new song unto thee, O God: upon a psaltery and an instrument of ten strings will I sing praises unto thee. It is he that giveth salvation unto kings: who delivers David, his servant from the hurtful sword. Rid me, and deliver me from the hand of strange children, whose mouth speak vanity, and their right hand is a right hand of falsehood: That our sons may be as plants grown up in their youth; that our daughters may be as corner-stones, polished after the similitude of a palace: That our garners may be full, affording all manner of store: that our sheep may bring forth thousands and ten thousand in our streets: That our oxen may be strong to labour; that there be no breaking in, nor going out; that there be no complaining in our streets. Happy is that people, that is in such a case: yea, happy is that people, whose God is the Lord.

What Is Intercession?

According to *Strong's Exhaustive Concordance*, the Hebrew word for *intercession, paga* (pronounced "paw-gah") means "approach, attack, cut him down, entreat, intercede, kill, make supplication, meet, pleaded, spare, strike the mark, urge."

I want to illuminate the subject of intercession for you. According to this definition, intercession is to approach, plead, and make supplication. Here we have two levels of strategic prayer.

The first is to stand in the gap between people, city, nation, and God. The prophet Ezekiel asserted, "I looked for someone among them who would build up the wall and stand before me in the gap on behalf of the land so I would not have to destroy it, but I found no one" (Ezekiel 22:30). God was looking for an intercessor. Did you ask why? Couldn't He just save them? Why did He need someone to stand in the gap? Justice is one of the characteristics of God. He demands discipline or punishment of sin because He set a law and He cannot break it. Dr. Myles Monroe asserted, "God is sovereign until He speak." It means God cannot go against His word.

Moses was a great gap builder. He met with God; he pleaded their case even when God was ready to destroy that rebellious generation and raise a new people for Moses. But Moses stood in the gap. Exodus 32:10–11 says,

> "Now then let Me alone, that My anger may burn against them and that I may destroy them; and I will make of you a great nation." Then Moses entreated the Lord his God, and said, "O Lord, why does Your anger burn against Your people whom You have brought out from the land of Egypt with great power and with a mighty hand?"

The second part of intercession is spiritual warfare. A section of the definition of *paga* is to "attack, cut him down, kill, strike the mark." Here, this point calls for a deeper level and employing a higher intelligence and heavy-duty weapons.

Remember—as you attack, you are to cut the enemy down by striking against the target. You have only one chance, so you need to be strategic and accurate. In this part of the warfare, you will have to activate your spiritual radar to watch the activities of the enemy and then know what type of weapons you are to deploy. You must ask God to show you what is going on at the camp in the realm of the spirit as well as what He is doing or about to do.

Intercessory Prayer Opens the Gates of the Heart
An intercessor is the one called alongside to help. He or she is the one elected to help in the spiritual journey. It's a call, and we

must take it seriously, as the king's business requires haste. You don't do it because you want it but because there is a burden you cannot ignore. My wife is called alongside me on this journey of intercession. She's my backup. Every intercessor needs a covering and a backup just as Jesus sent the disciples two by two. In the particular warfare that we undertook, I paired our intercessors two by two. If we plan to fast and pray for twenty-one days, two people take turns. One partner will fast and pray to cover the primary person who is supposed do the warfare the next day to destroy any attack that the enemy will launch against him. This strategy works and brings a great result.

Psalm 24:3–10 (NIV) says,

> Who may ascend the mountain of the Lord? Who may stand in his holy place? The one who has clean hands and a pure heart, who does not trust in an idol or swear by a false god. They will receive a blessing from the Lord and vindication from God their Savior. Such is the generation of those who seek him, who seek your face, God of Jacob. Lift up your heads, you gates; be lifted up, you ancient doors, that the King of glory may come in. Who is this King of glory? The Lord is strong and mighty, the Lord mighty in battle. Lift up your heads, you gates; lift them up, you ancient doors, that the King of glory may come in. Who is he, this King of glory? The Lord Almighty—he is the King of glory.

"If we are to win the battle, we must win it in the air. Before the ground troop invades the territory of the enemy, the victory must be achieved in the invisible world" (from *Praying with Power* by C. Peter Wagner).

Our forty-day fasting and prayer in 2013 and 2015 was the season of invading the kingdom of darkness in America. It was a period of declaring the kingdom of light of His dear Son Jesus Christ on earth in the hearts of Americans.

Here's the prophetic word for the church.

> You will be like a burning torch to America.
> You will take your place in the land.
> You will become a kingdom soul harvester in the nations.
> America will be declared again, "One nation under God."
> No jihadist will take America.
> There is still hope for America by the hand of the intercessors.
> Signs and wonders will be performed again in this land.
> You will not have to worry about your personal needs. You will become an active warrior for the kingdom.
> The church is going worldwide, equipping a new generation of intercessors.
> Multitudes will come into the kingdom in times such as this and find their place to serve with everything they are only for the glory of God.
> There's going to be another great awakening taking over the kingdoms of America.
> Don't give up. Your time has come, and the Lord will openly reward you, Intercessor.
> Don't get tired until you will see His glory over the nations.
> America is about to catch fire, and there will be a revival on the streets again.
> The homeless and drug addicts will speak in tongues and prophesy because there will be a high visitation in the shelters.
> God loves and is awaiting the repentance of the gays and lesbians. They will catch fire too, and they will not walk according to the desires of the flesh but in the will of God.

The Gays and Lesbians Need Our Help

I don't personally condemn those who practice such things but rather pray for them. You ask, "Why?" The reason is that God has given me the grace to help and deliver those who want to be free. The truth is they fell into a trap, and now they cannot get out. It's a dark pit. The spirit in charge is unyielding. It is stubborn. Have you ever seen a drug addict who quickly gives up on such behavior? No. The same level of bondage and the strongman who controls them also have dominion over the gays and the lesbians. The new converts who just joined though look at it as fun. The old ones know that they cannot get out; yet, miserable, they only want to recruit more people. The blind leading the blind will fall into the nearest ditch. They see it as a war between the church and them, so they are doing everything in their power to win many. Our assignment is to pray them out of the power of darkness. The gays who we helped out of this kind of situation confessed that many people who has been in the movement for a long period of time are miserable and they want out but don't know how. He told his friends that they must really be desperate for their deliverance and freedom then they can be helped.

CHAPTER 30

THE WARRIOR'S PERSONAL BATTLE

Some of our warriors lost their lives in the war in Iraq. Some lost their legs; others lost their minds and their lives. Some lost their families because of the trauma they went through. It's difficult to reintegrate into a healthy life. Their lives are never the same, yet they were counted heroes. The heroes of faith never win without a fight.

The intercessor is a warrior. Every warrior is a prime enemy to his opponent. As someone observed, "If you call the deep, the deep will come." We are in the place where it doesn't matter if one is willing to call the deep or refrain from fighting the spiritual war. That does not keep the enemy from attacking you. When Germany fought against British in the World War II, the British Prime Minister Winston Churchill called the United States to join, but the United States wanted to remain neutral, and then Japan launched a surprise attack on the US naval base at Pearl Harbor, Hawaii, on December 7, 1941, which led the United States into the war. The enemy knows where to touch in your life that will directly or indirectly involve you in the fight. As an intercessor, men and women of God, the fact that you are a Christian means that you are at war and you have no reason to retreat. Our warfare is spiritual. The attack might be that people will be talking about you in the church. Maybe there will be an attack on your family, health, finances, ministry, job, or any other area. The reason is that the enemy wants to touch your heart and weaken you for defeat.

Who Is Sufficient for All These Things
Abraham, our father, couldn't stand it when he realized both he and his wife were old and the promises of God were still far away. He ran out of patience. He accepted the proposal of his wife and had a child with his maid, although he was a man of faith and righteousness was imputed to him because he believed and obeyed when God called him to leave his country.

Moses, the greatest and meekest man, performed signs and wonders. He released ten plagues of judgment upon the pharaoh and Egypt. He divided the Red Sea and brought water from the rock. He even met with God face-to-face every day, but when he faced his weakness, look at what he said to God: "I am not able to bear all these people alone because it is too heavy for me. And if thou deal thus with me, kill me, I pray thee, out of hand, if I have found favor in thy sight; and let me not see my wretchedness" (Numbers 11:14–15).

Here you have Elijah, the prophet of fire. He could bring fire down anytime he wanted. A very mighty man of God who would not see death, but he ran for his life and met with the spirit of suicide and succumbed to it. Here's his prayer to the God of Life after the spirit of fear sent from Jezebel got ahold of him. If Jezebel wanted to kill him, she would have sent the soldiers at once, but knowing the strength of Elijah, she strategically sent the messengers of fear to weaken the weary prophet, who had just finished his mountain-moving revival. Here's what transpired:

> Then Jezebel sent a messenger to Elijah, saying, "So may the gods do to me, and more also, if I do not make your life like the life of one of them by this time tomorrow." Then he was

afraid; he got up and fled for his life, and came to Beer-sheba, which belongs to Judah; he left his servant there. But he went a day's journey into the wilderness, and came and sat down under a solitary broom tree. He asked that he might die: "It is enough; now, O LORD, take away my life, for I am no better than my ancestors." (1 Kings 19:2–4)

John the Baptist began to testify about Jesus right from the womb and continued until his public ministry, but when his fragility showed up, he doubted and sent his disciples to ask Jesus if He was the Christ (Messiah) or if they should look forward to someone else.

I hear you saying, "Why did he do that?" The answer is we fight not against flesh and blood. Our enemy never comes against us when we are strong; he is always looking for our weakness. Then he strikes at once and repeatedly. The Amalekites always dealt with Israel's frailty because they knew that they could not face their strength. Look at what they did to David.

David, a giant slayer, a mighty warrior, found himself in the wilderness and caves because he fought an award-winning and generational battle. Remember Goliath was a champion from his youth. Just one song that the women sang after he had slain the giant was enough for his death. David was once King Saul's favorite, but the next moment, the perfect psalmist became the prime enemy. The devil was still not satisfied that he had kicked David out of his home—away from his wife and best friend, Jonathan.

David became great in the wilderness with six hundred mighty men whom he trained. They were worthless people. Society did not even care if they existed. One fateful day after a victory over the Philistines, their return was a disaster when they got closer to their camp. The women did not welcome them. Children were not crying or playing on the street. The camp was quiet. What was happening? The Amalekites had taken their wives and children and possessions and then burned the camp with fire. David and his men sat down and wept until there was no strength left in them. After the six hundred men of war had stopped crying, David was expecting a word of encouragement, but to his disappointment, they all picked up stones to kill David.

Has this ever happened to you? The people you trusted, those who knew your weakness and strength, rose against you. It could be your associate pastor, elders in the church, the financial committee, or the church members whom you suffered to help if you are a church leader. It could be your wife or husband connived with your children or stepchildren against you. Maybe someone you trained in your job began gossiping to your boss about you. It could also be that the health of your spouse started to deteriorate, and all your plans came to a standstill. It might even be your finances or that someone you trusted stole your favor or opportunity. Maybe your children were on the street instead of living the real dreams you had for them.

Don't forget; the enemy will always touch something dear to your heart to weaken you. Do not be taken by surprise. Remember that the warrior has wounds, fears, doubts, frustrations, disappointments, and weaknesses. The warrior even falls, and no one tries to help him.

But David, the aspiring king, did something quite the opposite. Read on. "And David was greatly distressed; for the people spake of stoning him, because the soul of all the people was grieved, every man for his sons and his daughters: but David encouraged himself in the Lord his God" (1 Samuel 30:6).

The apostle Paul said, "Because of surpassing greatness of the revelations, for this reason, to keep me from exalting myself, there was given me, a thorn in the flesh, a messenger of Satan torment me. To keep me from exalting myself. Concerning this, I implored the Lord three times that it might leave me. And He said to me, "My

Grace is sufficient for you, for power is perfected in weakness..." (2 Corinthians 12:7-9 NASB).

The only strength the warrior has is the still small voice. David encouraged himself in the Lord his God. You must be able to hear the voice of the Lord. When the battle is worse, the only system that strengthens you is the voice of the Lord that you hear from within. It depends on your relationship with the heavenly Father. Without this, it is impossible to win the battle. If you know the end of the fight, you are not troubled.

What You Do for Others Will Save You on That Great Day
A great man of God who was one of the spiritual pioneers in the land slept with the fathers. Before then, while he was still alive, his advice saved me in 2003. The Lord taught me something that I want to share with you. Rev. S. T. A. Tettey, an unyielding man of God, fought so many battles in the Kroboland. His legacy was that of a fighter; he never succumbed until his last breath.

Everything you do in life will save you or break you. In the vision of the night, Rev. S. T. A. Tettey came to me and asked, "What have I done that you can testify about me?"

I answered, "You gave a counsel that saved the church and me."

He said, "Thank you. I need this because I am going to answer some questions tomorrow."

While he was talking, I was curious and looked at his teeth. He was aware, and he covered them with his clerical collar so I couldn't see them and then left. When I woke up, behold, it was a dream, and I began to ponder it, but the Lord gave me understanding. It informs us that when people die, there is a prejudgment. They are busy over there answering questions about how they spent their lives and gifts. It cautions us that when someone comes to us for advice, counseling, or any help, we must be careful to do it according to the will of God. And if we are called to pray, we will account for our intercession ministries.

As I was meditating and asking God what this meant, I received two illuminations. The teeth represented the wisdom of men. As I was striving to see his teeth, that meant I was trying to get an essential knowledge of him, but he knew and he didn't want me to copy him because I could not survive this warfare with such wisdom from him.

The second was the clerical garment. It represents the heavenly wisdom. It depicted the anointing that enhanced his calling. King Solomon observed, "Trust in the Lord with all your heart and do not lean on your understanding. In all your ways acknowledge Him, and He will make your paths straight. Do not be wise in your own eyes; Fear the Lord and turn away from evil ..." (Proverbs 3:5–7).

A Vow to Kill in Three Days
My wife won a soul for Christ, and that launched an attack against her. Here's what happened.

One of the relatives of my wife married a voodoo priest, and a lady came to her with a problem. She then took her to her husband, the voodoo priest. The woman was asked to purchase some items for rituals, and she did. She came back to my wife's relative with the stuff, but suddenly they fell to the floor and broke. So the lady came to my wife to borrow money from her to buy the items again. My wife did not know her, so she asked her why she needed the money. After she had narrated the story, my wife took her to the living room and witnessed to her. She said, "I have no silver and gold, but what I do have I give to you!" (Acts 3:6 ESV). After the conversation, the lady gave her life to Christ instantly, and she thought that my wife's relative would be happy. It turned into a disaster after she reported it to her husband. The voodoo priest became furious and sent a dangerous message to my wife that she would die in three days. My wife, who knew what this battle entailed, went into her room and prayed for God to take care of the situation. Now guess who is no more in the land of the living? The voodoo priest died because he was fighting against the Lord who called us. The battle is the Lord's. Just pray and pray again, and He will answer you.

The Command to Do Spiritual Warfare
You are called to do spiritual warfare. I studied this word in depth, and I realized that Jesus did not call any believer to relax but rather to do spiritual warfare. The Greek word *nikao* means "to overpower," "to overcome," or "to be victorious." The word *overcome* occurs several times in the New Testament. The phrase "who overcomes" occurs nine times in only two books in the New Testament—1 John and Revelation.

Revelation 2:7, 11, 17, 26 says,

To him who overcomes, I will grant to eat of the tree of life, which is in the Paradise of God ... The second death shall not hurt he who overcomes ... To him who overcomes, to him shall I give some of the hidden manna, and I will give him a white stone, and a new name written on the stone which no one knows ... And he who overcomes, and he who keeps My deeds *until the end*, to him I will give authority over the nations ..."

There's no way the warrior can lose the battle because our commander in chief is the Captain of the host of heaven and He has overcome. Don't give up! Fight. "After I looked things over, I stood up and said to the nobles, the officials and the rest of the people, 'Don't be afraid of them. Remember the Lord, who is great and awesome, and fight for your families, your sons and your daughters, your wives and your homes.'(Nehemiah 4:14) I commission you in the name of Jesus Christ, Our Lord. Nikao! Nikao! Nikao! Amen!

ADDITIONAL RESOURCES

Chapter 1
Praying with Power by C. Peter Wagner
Shifting Shadows of Supernatural Power by Julia Loren, Bill Johnson, and Mahesh Chavda
The Seasons of Intercession by Frank Damazio
Why Revival Tarries by Leonard Ravenhill

Chapter 2
Matthew Henry Commentary, Clarke's Commentary, Barnes' Note
Greek Lexicon,
Strongest Strong's Concordance
Dr. Mike Bagwell Bible Study Pages.

Chapter 3
God and the Bible in the U.S. History
By Pastor Steven Andrews

Biographies on Rearch of Rituals
Chapter 4
According to Monica Wilson (1954:241), as cited in Turner ([1969]2009:6), "Rituals reveal values at their deepest level ... Man express in ritual what moves them most, and since the form of expression is conventionalized and obligatory, it is the values of the group that is revealed. I see in the study of rituals is the key to an understanding of the essential constitution of human societies."

Secret Society in Africa—Sande Spirit

Many African rituals come with spiritual initiations. Liberia, Guinea, Sierra Leone, and Ghana have similar traditions. In Liberia, every year, young girls prepare for their introduction into the women's secret society. The list continues—the Ndebu of Zambia (Turner 1967), the Bemba of Zambia (Richars 1982), the Kaguru of Tanzania (Beidelman 1997), and the Gisu of Uganda (La Fontaine 1972). Some of the societies also have initiation ceremonies for girls and boys.

Ministry Information

Action Life Ministries International, Worcester, MA.

To learn more about Samuel T. Padmore and his books and ministries, go to www.actionlifeministriesinternational.org.

If you want him to speak at your church or conference, contact him at pastor@actionlifeministriesinternational.org or providenceorphanage@gmail.com.

New Books Coming Up Soon

1. Tittle: Healing and Restoring Your Family
   Sub-tittle: Conflict Resolution and Relationship Restoration
   By Samuel T. & Providencia Padmore

2. Tittle: How Do You Know God is Calling You?
   Sub-tittle: The Clarity of the Call of God
   By Samuel T. Padmore

3. Tittle: How Do I Become a Person of Value?
   Sub-tittle: The Character of A Great Visionary.
   By Samuel T. Padmore

4. Tittle: Destroying the 7 Strongholds
   Sub-tittle: Capture the Strongman of Depression
   By Samuel T. Padmore

SCRIPTURE REFERENCES

Ephesians 6:10–12
Matthew 6:6, 9–10
Luke 11:1
1 Corinthians 4:20 (NKJV)
Psalm 16:11
2 Corinthians 3:16–18 (KJV)
Mark 11:22–24
Mark 11:25–26
Acts 1:8
Acts1:12–14
Matthew 6:5
Matthew 6:6
Matthew 9:2
Mark 1:35 (NIV)
Jeremiah 9:1
Psalm 91:1
2 Corinthians 3:15–18 (NIV)
Jeremiah 29:13
Deuteronomy 4:29
Psalm 25:14
Jeremiah 33:3
Psalm 27:4, 6 (NIV)
John 15:5
John 4:21–24 (NIV)

Acts 8:31
Hosea 4:6
John 10:16
Jude 1:20 (AMP)
2 Timothy 2:15
Mark 4:9 (NLT)
Revelation 2:29 (NASB)
Genesis 3:8–10 (NIV)
Genesis 6:3
John 4:23–24 (NIV)
1 John 3:8
Matthew 1:23
Revelation 21:3
Ephesians 2:12–18 (NIV)
Romans 5:1–2 (NIV)
Hebrews 10:19–22
2 Corinthians 6:16–18 (NIV)
Timothy 2:5
Ephesians 6:18
Proverbs 22:6
Isaiah 58:12
Mark 11:25 (NIV)
Colossians 1:13
John 1:12, 13 (AMP)
John 14:30 (ASV)
2 Corinthians 4:4 (NIV)
Romans 6:16 (NIV)
Genesis 1:26 (NIV)
John 1:12 (NIV)
Matthew 28:18 (NIV)
1 Peter 3:18–20
Ephesians 6:10
Revelation 12:11
John 4:34 (NIV)

Luke 22:42
John 6:28–29 (NIV)
Psalm 24
1 Corinthians 2:2
Philippians 3:10
Proverbs 14:12, 16:25
2 Corinthians 4:4
Proverbs 3:5–8
1 Samuel 7:15–17, 8:6–9
Job 23:8, 9
Job 23:8,9
Jeremiah 33:3
2 Chronicles 7:14
Ezekiel 22:30
Daniel 10:12–13, 20–2
Hebrews 2:14–18
1 Kings 18:36–39
Jeremiah 1:10
Matthew 17:19–21 (KJV)
Mark 6:22–24
Numbers 31:8, 16
2 Samuel 5:8
James 5:16b–17
2 Corinthians 10:3–4 (NIV)
Genesis 18:17 (NIV)
Numbers 9:20–22
1 Kings 13:24–26
Deuteronomy 11:23–35
Psalm 123:1–4 (NIV)
John 5:17 (NIV)
Number 22:27-31 (ESV)
2 Kings 6:11–12, 15–17
Romans 8:26, 27
2 Corinthians 10:3–4 (NIV)

Acts 2:1–4
Ephesians 6:18 (NIV)
Judges 18:9
Genesis 1:1
Exodus 20:22
Genesis 1:1, 2:1
Revelation 12:9–11 (NIV)
Acts 17:19
Genesis 28:21–22
Genesis 1:26–31 (AMP)
Genesis 2:15–17 (AMP)
Genesis 3:15–19, 22–24
Genesis 3:14
Romans 16:20
2 Corinthians 11:3, 14
Revelation 12:9
Genesis 6:3
Genesis 9:1–17
Genesis 8:22, 9:2
Genesis 13:14–17
Genesis 18:1–13, 15
Genesis 22:1–18
Deuteronomy 7:12
Exodus 20:19, 34:1–9, 15–28
Deuteronomy 5:1–33
Exodus 34:8
Hebrews 9:22
Romans 3:19–24
2 Corinthians 3:7–9
Hebrews 10:1–10
Galatians 3:10–25
1 Chronicles 17:9–15
2 Samuel 7:10–17
Psalm 89:3–4, 34–37

Ezekiel 37:26, 27
Luke 22:19–20
John 6:53–63
Matthew 28:18–20
Psalm 106:34–40
Genesis 12:7–8
Genesis 13:14–18
Genesis 15:7–11, 17–18
Genesis 26:1–6, 24–25
Genesis 28:20–22
Genesis 33:18–20
Genesis 35:1–3, 6, 7, 11–15
Numbers 23:1–8, 23, 24)
1 Kings 18:30–33, 36–39
1 Kings 18:30–33, 36–39
Exodus 27:1–8 (AMP)
Exodus 20:24
Genesis 1:6–10 (AMP)
Ephesians 6:12
2 Corinthians 16:9
Psalm 53:5
Psalms 27:1–3 (KJ21)
Joshua 2:1
Joshua 1:3
Mark 11:24
Isaiah 55:10–11
1 Kings 18:36–37
2 Samuel 24:18–25
Proverbs 4:7
Matthew 12:32
James 5:16b–17
2 Corinthians 10:3–5
James 4:7
Job 41:22, 24, 34

Hosea 4:6

Luke 10:18–19

Ephesians1:3–6

John 1:12

Revelation 1:16

Revelation 1:16

Ephesians 1:16–19

Ephesians 2:4–6

1 Peter 1:5

Luke 10:17

2 Corinthians 3:14–15

2 Corinthians 3:16–18

2 Corinthians 10:6

Ephesians 4:27

Ephesians 6:1–3

Romans 1:19–20

Psalm 66:18

1 John 1:8–9

Mark 11:25

Job 41:22–24, 31

Proverb 16:18

Hosea 12:13

2 Kings: 26–27

Matthew 27:46

Exodus 8:8

Amos 3:7

Acts 12:5–10

Psalm 60:4

Jeremiah 9:1

Matthew 26:38–45

Revelation 8:3–5 (NKJV)

2 Chronicles 7:14 (KJV)

Luke 2:36–38

Acts 4:23, 24

Acts 4:23, 24
Exodus 2:24–25
Daniel 9:2–4
Luke 2:26–38
Jeremiah 29:7
2 Samuel 22:29–30
Psalm 144:1–15
2 Corinthians 12:1-3.
Revelation 2:7, 11, 17, 26

GLOSSARY

altar. According to *Baker's Evangelical Dictionary of Biblical Theology*, an altar is a "structure on which offerings are made to a deity." The Hebrew word for altar is *mizbeah* [ebzim], from a verbal root meaning "to slaughter." Greek renders this word as *thusiasterion* [qusiasthvrion], "a place of sacrifice." In the developed temple ritual, they use the same word for both the altar of holocausts and that of incense. Thus, an altar is a place where they offer sacrifice, even if it is not an event involving slaughter.

covenant. The Greek word *diatheke* is used thirty-three times in the New Testament and is translated "covenant." It's also used interchangeably to denote the term *testament*, which is used thirteen times in the New Testament. Usually, the Greek word διαθηκη (diathéké) (dee-ath-ay'-Kay) is translated "covenant" in the English versions of the Bible. It is a legal term symbolizing a formal and juridical binding declaration of benefits to be given by one party to another, with or without conditions attached. In a nonreligious context, most often, they use it as a "last will." In the Greek version of the Old Testament, διαθηκη (diathéké) was used as the ordinary rendering for the Hebrew word תירב (berith). תירב (berith) is also translated "covenant" in the English versions of the Bible, but, like (diatheke) διαθηκη, it also refers to legal dispositions or pledges that may or may not have the character of an "agreement." Sometimes, a ירב is more like a single or one-sided promise or grant.

darkness. According to *Baker's Evangelical Dictionary*, *darkness* in both the Old Testament (Hebrew *hasak*) and New Testament (Greek *skotos* [skovto]) is an evocative word. If light symbolizes God, then darkness connotes everything that is anti-God, the wicked (Proverbs 2:13–14; 1 Thessalonians 5:4–7).

invasion. An instance of invading a country or region with an armed force; to occupy, capture, seize, annex, take over a kingdom or dominion.

kingdom. A country, state, or territory ruled by a king or queen. The realm, domain, dominion, country, empire, principality, duchy, land, nation, state, province, and territory. The spiritual reign or authority of God or Satan.

keys. Keys represent spiritual authority.

spiritual mapping. Studying and viewing the nations as they exist in the spiritual world and not what we see in the natural.

spiritual gate. The spiritual gate represents the boardroom where decisions are made concerning business, community, city, and nation. Gates are entrances and protection. Spiritually speaking, it is the access through which territorial spirits control a particular geographical location and never allow the gospel to have an effect on the people and the city as well.

Printed in the United States
By Bookmasters